Frost

Interviews with

ROBERT FROST

Edited by Edward Connery Lathem

Holt, Rinehart and Winston

New York   Chicago   San Francisco

In Canada, Holt, Rinehart and Winston of Canada,
Limited

Library of Congress Catalog Card Number: 66–11570

First Edition

85151–0116

Printed in the United States of America

Acknowledgments

Grateful acknowledgment is made to the following agents, authors, magazines, newspapers, and publishers for permission to reprint material from their books, editorials,
interview-articles, and news stories:

The Amherst Student, Amherst College, for interview-articles by Henry Coon and
Markham Ball, which appeared on October 19, 1953, and November 1, 1954.

The Associated Press for interview-articles released by the Associated Press which
were published on November 12, 1939, April 3, 1960, and September 10, 1962.

The Baltimore Sunpapers for an editorial and two interview-articles which appeared in the Sun on February 26 and 27, 1936, and March 27, 1962.

The Boston Globe for interview-articles by Gardner Jackson and Herbert A. Kenny,
and a "Meet the Press" transcript; and as Successors to the Boston Post for an interview done by Carl Wilmore, which appeared in the Post on February 14, 1916.

The Paris Review and Richard Poirier for his interview with Robert Frost, which appeared in the Summer-Fall 1960 issue (No. 24) of *The Paris Review*.

Robert Peterson and King Features Syndicate for his interview with Robert Frost, released on December 10, 1962.

The Philadelphia *Inquirer* (successor to *The Public Ledger*) for the article, "Of Axe-Handles and Guide-Book Poetry," published in the *Ledger* on April 4, 1916.

Rocky Mountain News for the interview by Mary Ruth Barry, published in the *News* on July 17, 1931.

The American Country Life Association and Dr. Benson Y. Landis for his article, "Poetry and Rural Life," which appeared in the June 1931 issue of *Rural America*.

Ad Schulberg for the interview-article by Mark Harris, which appeared in the December 1, 1961, issue of *Life*.

The Scotsman for "A Tour in Britain," which appeared in *The Scotsman* on May 22, 1957.

Joseph E. Seagram & Sons, Inc., for an excerpt from the 1959 Symposium on "The Future of Man."

United Press International for two interview-articles released by United Press International on December 14, 1949, and October 16, 1958.

University of Michigan for an interview-article by Fred Schott, which appeared in *The Michigan Daily* on April 4, 1947, and "Notes from Conversations with Robert Frost" by M. P. Tilly, which appeared in *The Inlander* for February 1918.

The Washington *Post* for an interview-article by Thomas Wolfe, which appeared in *The Post* on May 2, 1961.

The Washington *Evening Star*, for interviews published in *The Evening Star* on May 22, 1958, December 10, 1958, and March 27, 1962.

Contents

Introduction

ROBERT FROST won renown as a poet and public figure. Although the second of these dual elements of his fame was, to be sure, based essentially upon his literary achievement, it existed also as something separate, as a recognition which was, at least in part, independent of that achievement. He was known and widely celebrated not only by those familiar with his poetry, but by countless others as well who had but slight acquaintance with his accomplishments in literature. The public's knowledge of him was derived primarily from three sources: from his published works, his platform appearances, and from the press. Each revealed him in a different fashion, and each, cumulatively, extended his impact and appeal. Of the three, the press, including television, provided (especially in the latter years of his long career) what was undoubtedly the broadest projection of Frost the artist and Frost the man. It was, however, a projection over which he had a decidedly limited command. This was true not merely in the case of articles and stories written about him, but also of press coverage in which he himself was a central participant: in his interviews.

Whatever its virtues may otherwise be, there are inevitably present in any interview factors quite beyond the control of the person being interviewed. The interviewer, for example, exercises a power to stimulate or to stifle discussion and the development of ideas. He constitutes a determinant that is at the very least one of strong influence—and often can be absolute—in shaping the course an interview will take, its mood and tone, its end result. There must be considered, too, the question of how well or how badly what was actually said in an interview is ultimately conveyed by those who report it: their accuracy and comprehensiveness of quotation, the quality of whatever selectivity they exercise, the degree of their success or failure in capturing not only the language spoken but also the atmosphere and spirit that prevailed, and the skill with which necessary background or other supplemental information is provided. These are among the components of any interview which may render the final product either better or worse for their existence but which can never be calculated as simply neutral or passive in nature.

This book consists of a selection of interviews spanning a period of nearly half a century: from 1915, the year Robert Frost returned to America from England, through 1962, just a few weeks before his death. Notwithstanding the fact that they must be recognized as revealing the famous poet at second hand, that they are subject to distortions in a variety of ways, and that their quality with respect to a precise portrayal depends in large measure upon the ability, sensitivity, and care of the persons who have recorded them, these interviews have a special importance. They present Mr. Frost informally, sometimes casually, yet always in the character of a performer—for performance was ever at the heart of what he aspired to as artist and man: the seeking of an attainment, a mastery, combining both substance and form. Within these interviews is found much of significance that is nowhere else preserved. They contain an invaluable documentation centering upon the life and thought of Robert Frost: his activities and concerns, his attitudes and approaches, his views, impressions, and concepts at different times. The best of them, moreover, capture and project something of his personal qualities—his presence and manner—with a directness and vividness that cannot be derived from his works alone nor from the existing recordings of his readings and talks.

All of the interviews that follow have been drawn from printed sources. They are arranged chronologically and divided, by decades, into six sections. Selection has been made with a view to achieving, from among the best of the available material, as wide and balanced a range as possible, regarding both subject matter and period. There exist in published form many other Robert Frost interviews. Some of these, which for varied reasons were not chosen for inclusion in this collection, have been passed over with genuine regret; and some, too, another might well have picked in preference to certain ones here represented. All editorial deletions from the original texts (involving, usually, an avoidance of duplicating matter presented elsewhere within the book) have been indicated by bracketed ellipses. The correction of typographical errors and, in the interest of consistency of treatment throughout the volume, necessary re-styling of punctuation, paragraphing, and similar mechanical features have been done without special indication of incidence.

E. C. L.

Dartmouth College
Hanover, New Hampshire

· I ·

THE TEENS

Robert Frost, New American Poet

*On returning home from England in late February of 1915,
Robert Frost found his literary reputation in the United States
already launched from across the Atlantic. North of Boston
had just been published in New York, and within two months
of his arrival American editions of both it and* A Boy's Will
were in print.

*In May, after having settled himself and his family on a
small farm in Franconia, New Hampshire, RF journeyed to
Boston to give his first professional reading, as Phi Beta Kappa poet at Tufts College in nearby Medford. It was at this
time that he was interviewed by the poet-critic-anthologist
William Stanley Braithwaite. The text of "Robert Frost,
New American Poet" is, as here published, extracted from the
Boston Evening Transcript, where it originally appeared
on May 8, 1915.*

THE success which has immediately come to the poetry of
Robert Frost is unique. It has no exact parallel in the experience of
the art in this country during the present generation. [. . .]

To appreciate Mr. Frost's poetry perfectly one has got to regard
carefully the two backgrounds from which it is projected; fully under the influence of his art these two backgrounds merge into one,
though each has its special distinction. There is the background of
his material, the environment and character which belong to a
special community; and there is the background of art in which the
fidelity of speech is artistically brought into literature. This latter
is a practice that brings up large and important questions of lan-

guage and meaning in relation to life on the one hand and to literature on the other.

Mr. Frost has been through the longest period of experimenta-
tion in mastering the technique of his art of any other American
poet. What he finally arrived at in poetic expression he finds as the
highest accomplishment in the greatest English poets and asserts
that the American poets who have shown unquestionable genius,
especially a man like Edwin Arlington Robinson, have in a large
measure the same quality of speech which is at once both artistic
and the literal tone of human talk. But no poet in either England
or America, except this newly arrived New England poet, has consciously developed and practiced this essential and vital quality of
poetry which he characterizes as sound-posturing.

The poet was in his twentieth year when he realized that the
speech of books and the speech of life were far more fundamentally
different than was supposed. His models up to this period, as with
all youthful poets and writers, had been literary models. But he
found quite by accident that real artistic speech was only to be
copied from life. On his New Hampshire farm he discovered this in
the character of a man with whom he used to drive along the country roads. Having discovered this speech he set about copying it in
poetry, getting the principles down by rigorous observation and
reproduction through the long years which intervened to the publication of his books.

He also discovered that where English poetry was greatest it was
by virtue of this same method in the poet, and, as I shall show, in
his talk with me he illustrated it in Shakespeare, Shelley, Wordsworth, and Emerson. That these poets did not formulate the principles by which they obtained these subtle artistic effects, but accomplished it wholly unconscious of its exact importance, he also
suggested. But with a deliberate recognition of it as a poetic value
in the poets to come, he sees an entirely new development in the
art of verse.

The invitation which brought Mr. Frost to Boston to read the
Phi Beta Kappa poem on Wednesday at Tufts College gave me the
opportunity to get from the poet his views on the principles of
sound-posturing in verse and some reflections on contemporary
poets and poetry in England and America.

: 4 :

Before returning home, it will be interesting to note, the publication of Mr. Frost's books in England awakened a critical sympathy and acceptance, among English writers, of his ideas. His work won over, by its sheer poetic achievement, critics and poets, who had not realized before the possibilities of reproducing the exact tone of meaning in human speech in literary form. Where the poet's work is not fully appreciated in this country is where this principle is not understood. The substance of New England farm life of which his poetry is made has attracted immense interest, but in some quarters the appreciation of this substance is a little modified because the reader has only partially grasped the significance of the form. So it was this I wished the poet to explain in my very first question.

"First," he said, "let me find a name for this principle which will convey to the mind what I mean by this effect which I try to put into my poetry. And secondly, do not let your readers be deceived that this is anything new. Before I give you the details in proof of its importance, in fact of its essential place in the writing of the highest poetry, let me quote these lines from Emerson's 'Monadnoc,' where, in almost a particular manner, he sets forth unmistakably what I mean:

> Now in sordid weeds they sleep,
> In dulness now their secret keep;
> Yet, will you learn our ancient speech,
> These the masters who can teach.
> Fourscore or a hundred words
> All their vocal muse affords;
> But they turn them in a fashion
> Past clerks' or statesmen's art or passion.
> I can spare the college bell,
> And the learned lecture, well;
> Spare the clergy and libraries,
> Institutes and dictionaries,
> For that hearty English root
> Thrives here, unvalued, underfoot.
> Rude poets of the tavern hearth,
> Squandering your unquoted mirth,
> Which keeps the ground and never soars,
> While Jake retorts and Reuben roars;

Scoff of yeoman strong and stark,
Goes like bullet to its mark;
While the solid curse and jeer
Never balk the waiting ear.

"Understand these lines perfectly and you will understand what I mean when I call this principle 'sound-posturing' or, more literally, getting the sound of sense.

"What we do get in life and miss so often in literature is the sentence sounds that underlie the words. Words in themselves do not convey meaning, and to [...prove] this, which may seem entirely unreasonable to any one who does not understand the psychology of sound, let us take the example of two people who are talking on the other side of a closed door, whose voices can be heard but whose words cannot be distinguished. Even though the words do not carry, the sound of them does, and the listener can catch the meaning of the conversation. This is because every meaning has a particular sound-posture; or, to put it in another way, the sense of every meaning has a particular sound which each individual is instinctively familiar with and without at all being conscious of the exact words that are being used is able to understand the thought, idea, or emotion that is being conveyed.

"What I am most interested in emphasizing in the application of this belief to art is the sentence of sound, because to me a sentence is not interesting merely in conveying a meaning of words. It must do something more; it must convey a meaning by sound."

"But," I queried, "do you not come into conflict with metrical sounds to which the laws of poetry conform in creating rhythm?"

"No," the poet replied, "because you must understand this sound of which I speak has principally to do with tone. It is what Mr. Bridges, the Poet Laureate, characterized as speech-rhythm. Meter has to do with beat, and sound-posture has a definite relation as an alternate tone between the beats. The two are one in creation but separate in analysis.

"If we go back far enough we will discover that the sound of sense existed before words, that something in the voice or vocal gesture made primitive man convey a meaning to his fellow before the race developed a more elaborate and concrete symbol of communication in language. I have even read that our American Indians possessed, besides a picture-language, a means of communication (though it was not said how far it was developed) by the sound of sense. And what is this but calling up with the imagination, and recognizing, the images of sound?

"When Wordsworth said, 'Write with your eye on the object,' or (in another sense) it was important to visualize, he really meant something more. That something carries out what I mean by writing with your ear to the voice.

"This is what Wordsworth did himself in all his best poetry, proving that there can be no creative imagination unless there is a summoning up of experience, fresh from life, which has not hitherto been evoked. The power, however, to do this does not last very long in the life of a poet. After ten years Wordsworth had very nearly exhausted his, giving us only flashes of it now and then. As language only really exists in the mouths of men, here again Wordsworth was right in trying to reproduce in his poetry not only the words—and in their limited range, too, actually used in common speech—but their sound.

"To carry this idea a little further it does not seem possible to me that a man can read on the printed page what he has never heard. Nobody today knows how to read Homer and Virgil perfectly, because the people who spoke Homer's Greek and Virgil's Latin are as dead as the sound of their language.

"On the other hand, to further emphasize the impossibility of words rather than sound conveying the sense of meaning, take the matter of translation. Really to understand and catch all that is embodied in a foreign masterpiece it must be read in the original, because while the words may be brought over, the tone cannot be.

"In the matter of poetry," the poet continued, "there is a subtle differentiation between sound and the sound of sense, which ought to be perfectly understood before I can make clear my position.

"For a second let me turn aside and say that the beginning of literary form is in some turn given to the sentence in folk speech. Art is the amplification and sophistication of the proverbial turns of speech.

"All folk speech is musical. In primitive conditions man has not at his aid reactions by which he can quickly and easily convey his ideas and emotions. Consequently, he has to think more deeply to call up the image for the communication of his meaning. It was the actuality he sought; and thinking more deeply, not in the speculative sense of science or scholarship, he carried out Carlyle's assertion that if you 'think deep enough you think musically.'

"Poetry has seized on this sound of speech and carried it to artificial and meaningless lengths. We have it exemplified in Sidney Lanier's musical notation of verse, where all the tones of the human voice in natural speech are entirely eliminated, leaving the sound of sense without root in experience."

A Visit in Franconia

Staff correspondent Carl Wilmore of The Boston Post *provides a record of a visit he made to the Frost farm at Franconia during February 1916. The story, highly imaginative in certain of its aspects, was to prove a source of some embarrassment to its author following its publication in the* Post *on February 14th.*

THIS village is forgotten by the whole world. Buried in the snow, with more snow and more snow, nobody comes here. Once a day an old man in a pung drives over with a few bundles, and leaves them, and drives off again in his old pung; and the thermometer is way below zero, just now, too.

So what in the world can mean a jingling sleigh, with two city folks in it, chasing over the snow out to the Notch, over Mt. Lafayette way?

That's surely what the lone straggler thought when the *Post* reporter came up here. He almost asked the same question of himself. Who wouldn't—with twelve-below weather?

"Follow the road to the first bridge, keep to the right, take the second bridge, and about a mile up there is a little house on the right; that's where Robert Frost lives," the old woman in the deserted general store had directed.

So it was Robert Frost the *Post* reporter was after; Robert Frost, the man who wrote *North of Boston*, the volume of the most original American verse in years, which he had to go to England to get published and which has reached goodness only knows how many editions in America since. And here lived Robert Frost, the least-known man in American letters, and one of the most delightful, lackadaisical, lazy, whimsical, promising makers of verse in contemporaneous literature.

More than this, it struck the reporter strangely to realize that in this poor house, buried here in the snows in the out-of-the-way corner of the mountains, lives the man whom England has recognized before his own America, whom France read before we did, and whom they both hail as the one pre-eminent American poet of today—a sort of modern Poe.

Robert Frost: good name—with twelve below.

And so the city folks drove on through the endless drifts and reached the little house. It looked like a three-room affair, with an ell and a shed behind. Nothing stirred, save a bit of smoke from the chimney.

"This can't be the house," the driver said. "A man like Frost wouldn't live here, would he?"

The reporter also had his doubts. So he piled through the drifts and knocked on the rickety back door—the kitchen door.

Nobody replied. Are they out in the woods? Is everybody gone? Is this a deserted farm? But—the smoke. . . .

The door opened an inch. (People don't throw open doors in twelve-below weather.) A woman peeked out. In an instant the reporter thought: college woman—teacher. Tall, serious face, hair simply brushed back; it was the type.

"Does Mr. Frost live here?" asked the reporter. He had to ask something, though the woman herself had given the answer the moment she appeared.

"Yes, but he's not up."

The reporter made the usual apology for untimely appearance and all the rest of it.

"I'll wake him up and tell him." And the serious-faced woman shut the door and disappeared. The reporter wondered: a farmer and not up at nine in the morning? Mentally he said, "There's a lazy, lazy fellow lives here."

Out to the back, then, to join the driver slapping his sides, while the horses stamped and steamed and shook off the ice that hung all over them from nostrils to tails. The roosters and hens, awakened by the commotion in the midst of this deathly morning mountain mid-winter silence, began to crow and cackle. The horses hugged the sun; the blankets made them forget the twelve-below weather.

The house stood on the road, back some rods. Directly in front was Franconia Notch and above, snow-clad and glittering, rose Mt. Lafayette and the others of his companions, with Mt. Washington off in the distance.

The front door opened and a tall man in a brown suit, collar and necktie and all, said apologetically, "Come in; come in." And all hands went in.

It was nice and warm, with the all-night heat of a country home. "Come in and try to be warm," he said.

If ever they get shy of heating apparatus in the nether regions, they can come and get Robert Frost's stove, and the broiling will be better than ever. The stove reached from floor to ceiling. In fact, the room seemed built to suit the stove. It was the heart of the house.

"I don't usually wear a collar as early as this," said the host as he lolled back in a rocker, "but I wore these things last night to a meeting of a Parent-Teachers' Association and threw them beside the bed. So, I just naturally put them on again this morning."

What a lazy man's explanation! The house seemed still lazily half asleep—his writing table was covered with a myriad of letters which, he sheepishly confessed, he had been too lazy to answer— he admitted he was too lazy, at that early hour of nine a.m., to take coffee before talking to his visitors.

He spoke of the village folk.

"They didn't used to bother me," he smiled, "but last summer a lot of people came here to see us, and they got an idea we were of some account. So, now they've elected me president of the Parent-Teachers' Association."

The reporter remarked about the beauty of the hills (with a silent reservation about having to drive six miles in twelve-degrees-below-zero weather), and through the two small windows of the parlor one could see Mt. Lafayette and the White Notch.

"Yes—we adopted Lafayette long ago. I'm from Massachusetts [and a Californian] by birth, but we have lived in New Hampshire most of our lives, my wife, my four children, and myself."

"Four children, did you say?" gasped the reporter. He hadn't heard any racket, the sure sign of four children.

"Oh, yes; they went to school early this morning. Lesley, my oldest girl, is sixteen; then comes my boy, Carol; then Irma; and then Marjorie, who is nine. Carol does most of the work around the farm."

Carol did the work—what did Papa do? The *Post* reporter intended to find out.

"Who chopped the woodpile that we saw buried in the snow?"

"Oh, I didn't. You know, I like farming, but I'm not much of a success at it. Some day I'll have a big farm where I can do what I please"—he smiled as though he had intended to say "loaf as I please"—"and where I can divide my time between farming and writing.

"I always go to farming when I can. I always make a failure, and then I have to go to teaching. I'm a good teacher, but it doesn't allow me time to write. I must either teach or write: can't do both together. But I have to live, you see?"

"How old are you?"

"I'm forty-three. I suppose I'm just a bit lazy" (again he smiled, knowing that the reporter had guessed it long ago); "so I've had a lazy, scrape-along life, and enjoyed it. I used to hate to write themes in school. I hate academic ways. I fight everything academic. The time we waste in trying to learn academically—the talent we starve with academic teaching!"[. . .]

"And when do you work?" (In a corner stood a homemade writing table made of two short boards nailed together, which, he explained, he had himself made to set on the arms of the Morris chair, so that he could be more at his perfect ease.)

"Oh, I haven't any set times. I write when I feel like it. Sometimes I write nothing for months. Then I'll work a blue streak, and I rave around all day till it's off my mind. I can't do as many writers do, write to keep my hand in. I write only when I can write—when I must write.

"I hear everything I write. All poetry is to me first a matter of sound. I hear my things spoken. I write verse that might be called 'free'—the free-versers have accepted me!—but I believe, after all, that there must be a cadence, a rhythm, to all that is to be poetry at all. I don't mean jingle. I hate jingle; I hate rhyme for itself.

"I want drama, too. Some day I may write a play. But I avoid the sublime, the ecstatic, the flights that three hundred—or is it three thousand?—minor poets of America slop into the magazines month after month. Meaningless twaddle, with a few worn-out tones—You know what I mean by tones? I'll explain presently.—and with all kinds of ridiculous extravagances.

"We don't get tones enough into our poetry. Our schools teach us we must do this, must do that; and we do it. Even England isn't tied to academic teaching as we are. That's why they have some real poets, where we have none. We insist on form and on unity and the rest of old stuff.

"Of course, I know there is a crowd of 'emotionalists' who threw all to the winds except emotion. I think they're perhaps worse than the 'intellectualists,' who are the other extreme. But a happy mixture, that's it.

"When a man's young, he's an emotionalist. When he's old, an intellectualist. Only about fifteen middle years are well-balanced. He should do his big works then.

"But the mediocrities, how they do go on! Take, for instance, the expression 'oh.'

"The American poets use it in practically one tone, that of grandeur: 'Oh Soul!' 'Oh Hills!'—'Oh Anything!' That's the way they go. But think of what 'oh' is really capable: the 'oh' of scorn, the 'oh' of amusement, the 'oh' of surprise, the 'oh' of doubt—and there are many more. But these are disdained by the academic poets.

"America must get away from the schools. Forget the books. I don't mean that one should strive for effects. There are people who write poetry as if they said: 'Let's write a shocker.' Others say: 'Let's write a best seller.' 'Let's write a freak.' So they go on, turning out verses that are bad. Some of the free verse—it is just stupid in its striving after sensation, isn't it? It makes one laugh—not with it, but at it, and at the writer."

"What are you writing now?" asked the reporter, trying to lure him to himself.

He blushed. "Well, my publishers say I'm getting out a new book next fall, but—I don't know. . . . They say I'm going to get out a new one each year. That's how they do it in England.[. . .]"

"Will your new poems be also about the country?"

"I shall always write about the country. I suppose I show a sad side to it too often. It only seems sad to those who love the city. I used to think the mill people, scooting home in the dusk, were sad, till I worked in the mill and heard them singing and laughing and throwing bobbins up at me as I stood up on the ladder fixing the lights.

"I used to know a man once whom I'd drag out to the country with me. He'd lean on a fence a moment, then jump up, sit down on the lawn, jump up again, pick a flower, throw it away. . . . In fact, he was insane to be back in the city—just couldn't stand the country. The very people looked sad to him. That was because he himself was sad. The country isn't really sad. . . .

"To get back. If American poets will only try to use all the tones of life and will drop the eternal sublime and see that all life is a fit subject for poetic treatment, they will do better. We must have new subject matter, new treatment of it, and we must employ the neglected tones and forget the overworked ones."

He talked more: of his English friends, of his American co-versifiers (and he mentioned names right out and said things he didn't want printed); how he had been accused of imitating Theocritus—"and I never even read Theocritus, because I'm too lazy to bother with Greek"; how he makes use of subtle psychological suggestions in such poems as "The Fear" and "Home Burial" and "A Servant to Servants"; how a lady had said of one of his poems, "It is nice; but what would Henry W. Longfellow think of it?"; how he and his family just "smouldered" by way of existence, "not really poor or lacking anything, but constantly on the verge of having something"; how the Franconians looked upon him, and he on them; and how he got along, or rather didn't, with his publishers—and much, much more.

It was time to go. He slopped into a pair of overshoes and saw us to the door. As the *Post* reporter clambered into the sleigh, and the driver grasped the reins, he shook hands with a quiet laugh.

"I'll come to see you when I'm in Boston. I'd like to meet some people, because I want to spread my gospel of getting away from those deadly professors! Good-by!"

As the city folks jingled off over the obliterated road, in that twelve-degrees-below weather, the road didn't seem so long, or the weather so cold, or one's ears so frost-bitten, because of Robert Frost. And this came to the reporter:

Some day, long years from now, will there be a Robert Frost Society, whose object it shall be to preserve, as a memorial, the little old house buried in the mountains, which the world of today passes by, and which was the earlier home of one of America's finest poets?

That reporter Carl Wilmore's account of his Franconia visit was in some of its elements rather too extravagantly colorful was attested to by a taunting communication published in The Boston Post *of February 17th, under the headline "Franconia Comes Back at Post Staff Visitor." This rebuttal was written by Mrs. Etta Howard, who signed herself, with caustic reference to the way she had been characterized in the story, "The Old Woman in the Deserted Store."*

To the Editor of the *Post*:

SIR—Will you kindly inform your staff correspondent Mr. Carl Wilmore that he is only one in this whole world? If he for a moment thinks that two city folks, of which he was one, can come to our beautiful little village of Franconia and then give us and our abode such a slam as came out in *The Boston Post* on Monday last, without causing some little stir, he is very much mistaken.

"Forgotten by the whole world." What a statement! Had there been "anybody home" your reporter would have known better than to have undertaken a five- or six-mile ride in northern New Hampshire on February eleventh with nothing on but a summer overcoat. No wonder his appearance caused Mr. Frost's hens and roosters to cackle and crow. No wonder those two city folks didn't enjoy their ride.

Again, had there been "anybody home" those two city folks would have known by the way their sleigh-runners grated (probably the reason they chose a sleigh was so as to have bells ajingling) that Franconia could not boast of snow enough for even decent sleighing. Here we have been praying for snow for the past four weeks so we could enjoy a good sleigh ride, to say nothing of business lying idle for the want of it, and your reporter reports to the world that we are literally buried in snow and then more snow.

How we pity that poor reporter. No doubt Mr. Frost had to tell him where and what Mt. Lafayette was or he would have imagined it to be an immense snowdrift.

Strange your reporter could have realized our way-below-zero weather and wasn't able to see that we had only a few spoonfuls of snow.

The old man who rides in the old pung will send your poor ignorant reporter the definition of the word pung and also his photograph. Such a nice-looking young man as our stage driver! Do you call forty years, old? If your reporter will be old at forty, he's some old now.

Does he expect to find a crowd in a country store at nine o'clock in the morning? If he had only sent his card ahead, what a scramble there would have been to have gotten to that deserted place so the poor snow-bound country folks could have seen a real smarty chap from the city.

City people are not such a rarity as your reporter seems to think. They are with us the year round. They come to "Pecketts" in special cars just to enjoy our winter sports. There are sixty there at this writing. I defy your reporter or any other city chap to find a better-known, better-kept, and more up-to-date little village in all New England.

We can boast of between forty and fifty private cottages, some very elaborate, owned by people in New York, Chicago, Philadelphia, St. Louis—and, yes, even a few Bostonians spend their vacations here; and some prefer it even in winter rather than waller through the black, muddy slush of your city. There are eight to ten resort hotels in our midst, some ranking among the best in the United States, accommodating from fifty to four hundred people.

We are lighted by electricity, have the best of cement sidewalks, a forty-thousand-dollar library, and an academy unrivaled by any town of its size in New Hampshire, and could your reporter overhear some of our social leaders trying to select a night for some function when there isn't something else going on he might realize that we are very much alive in this corner under the mountains.

: 16 :

Even in winter *The Boston Post* reaches eighty families here daily. Eighty families to learn one sad morning that they were forgotten by the whole world.

By the way, don't forget us so far as not to send *The Boston Post* some day. But I'll tell you confidentially, if that reporter ever happens this way again he had better provide himself with an armor plate or he may never live to send in another report, and he will realize more fully, to quote his own words, what this "deathly mountain mid-winter silence" means.

"THE OLD WOMAN IN THE DESERTED STORE."
Franconia, N. H., Feb. 15.

On the same day that Mrs. Howard's letter appeared in the Post, *Carl Wilmore wrote to RF, observing plaintively: "My little yarn has stirred up such a lot of village ire (I don't say this contemptuously) that I have begun to worry lest you too have felt resentment, not so much because of my pictorial isolation of Franconia, as because of my describing you as (I hesitate) — lazy."*

In a second letter, on February 29th, the newspaperman — obviously writing now in response to a message from the poet himself—closed the matter gingerly by declaring that if RF's Franconia friends prove really to be troubled, ". . .please blame it all on me. Say I misquoted. . . ." And then, among other points, he added defensively: ". . .perhaps I did put it into your mouth that you were lazy. But nobody takes such things seriously. Anyway, down deep in your heart you know it's true."

Of Axe-Handles
and Guide-Book Poetry

*Among RF's engagements in the spring of 1916 were appear-
ances that took him to Philadelphia, where he gave this interview, published in* The Public Ledger *on April 4th.*

*The newspaper's allusions to his New Hampshire farm as
located on Sugar Hill (a fashionable resort area, at that time
a part of the adjacent town of Lisbon) are incorrect. Actually,
the Frosts were situated on a country road a mile or so south
of the Franconia village.*

*The poem "The Axe-Helve," referred to as something RF
was then "shaping up," was first printed a year and a half
later, in* The Atlantic Monthly *for September 1917.*

RULE Number One for poets who hope some day to dupli-
cate the success Robert Frost, poet of the granite-hilled farms of
the White Mountains, has achieved in his *North of Boston* is:
"Never larrup an emotion. Set yourself against the moon. Resist
the moon. If the moon's going to do anything to you, it's up to
the moon."

Mr. Frost has wind-blown cheeks and clear blue eyes. He's a
Yankee of Yankees and glad of it, even though eminent critics of
the stamp of Edward Garnett haven't hesitated to rank him with
Theocritus and Wordsworth as a delineator of pastoral life in
such of his poignant poems as "The Death of the Hired Man" and
"Home Burial."

Fresh from his farm on Sugar Hill, Franconia, New Hampshire, where Mt. Lafayette towers and the Old Man of the Mountains frowns, Mr. Frost is paying his first visit to Philadelphia. Quite recently he's been skiing over rugged country, tapping maple trees, and shaping up new poems.

Mr. Frost lolled back in a comfortable chair at the Art Club yesterday and talked of one of these new poems—not because he's writing it, for he's very shy in speaking of his work, but because it illustrates his grip on humanity the world over. It's a poem that concerns an axe-handle.

"The thing you hate in poetry is segregated stuff—like love, the moon, and murder," he said.

He lighted a cigarette, commenting that he had learned cigarette smoking in England, where one of his cronies was Rupert Brooke, most promising of young English poets, who lost his life at the front.

"Love, the moon, and murder have poetry in them by common consent. But it's in other places. It's in the axe-handle of a French Canadian woodchopper, and it's in 'poultry-stricken ground' (quoting John Masefield).

"You know the Canadian woodchoppers whittle their axe-handles, following the curve of the grain, and they're strong and beautiful. Art should follow lines in nature, like the grain of an axe-handle. False art puts curves on things that haven't any curves.

"We think the word 'provincial' is a shameful word here in America. But it is [the] Englishman's pride. You can't be universal without being provincial, can you? It's like trying to embrace the wind."

It wasn't so very many months ago that Mr. Frost "arrived." He is a man of about forty-five years and has a wife and four children living in his little farmhouse on Sugar Hill. Near him are the White Mountain homes of Prof. Cornelius Weygandt of the University of Pennsylvania and Justice Robert von Moschzisker.

The poet is staying here with Dr. Weygandt. He was entertained at luncheon at the Art Club yesterday by the Justice. He spoke last night in Germantown and reads at four o'clock this afternoon before the Arts Association of the University.

The recognition that has come to him as a successful and

powerful poet is perhaps best indicated by the fact that he has been selected as this year's Phi Beta Kappa poet at Harvard. The magazines are clamoring for his work, and the colleges and universities want him as much—even more, since he is an American— as they wanted John Masefield or Alfred Noyes.

Mr. Frost is simplicity itself, a strong man, a direct man—a man who believes, as he says, that America needs poets who "get tight-up to things." He detests what he calls "guide-book poetry." He admits that he is a poor farmer. He believes, strange as it may sound, that Puritanism "hasn't yet had its day, and it might be fun to set it up as an artistic doctrine."

Speaking of Puritanism, Mr. Frost has no use for "easy criers and weepers."

"Which is the more terrible," he asks, "a man or a woman weeping? The men, of course. That's Puritanism."

He intends to be "more of a farmer" than he is, but never a "kid-glove or gentleman farmer."

"My country," he says, "is a milk and sugar country. We get what runs from the trees and what runs from the cows. You can't do much real farming, for we have frost every month in the year. You know, the White Mountain farmers say they have nine months of winter and three months of late-in-the-fall!" He laughed as he recalled his struggles with the granite soil.

If anything more than a reading of Mr. Frost's poem "Home Burial" (in which a rugged father buries his child in the yard of his farmhouse) is needed to convince everyone that he's a Yankee to the backbone, he will admit that his ancestors found New Hampshire back in 1630.

"One of them was an Indian fighter, and a cunning one," he says. "He invited the Indians to a barbecue. They stacked their arms, and he promptly killed them. Unfortunately for that ancestor, he didn't kill all of them. A few who were left came back after him on a Sunday morning after he'd finished praying, and got even."[. . .]

Mr. Frost had a very bad grudge against "guide-book poetry" yesterday. It was so bad that he gave a couple of very bad examples of it, dictating them with a Yankee twang, softened somewhat into a drawl by his life in England.

"This is ridiculous, of course," he said, "but it's guide-book poetry—certainly vers libre; you know the White Mountains goes in for vers libre!—and it shows what's the matter with American poets who lay poetry on things. I don't remember who wrote it!

> One of the most deplorable facts about the White Mountains
> Is the lack of legends.
> Imagination, therefore, must be requisitioned
> To supply the story
> That gave a name to this beautiful spot."

He chuckled. Then:

"The point I'm making lies in that line, 'Imagination . . . must be requisitioned.' The curse of our poetry is that we lay it on things. Pocketsful of poetic adjectives like pocketsful of peanuts carried into a park for the gray squirrels! You can take it as gospel, that's not what we want.

"But people say to me: 'The facts themselves aren't enough. You've got to do something to them, haven't you? They can't be poetical unless a poet handles them.'

"To that I have a very simple answer. It's this: Anything you do to the facts falsifies them, but anything the facts do to you— yes, even against your will; yes, resist them with all your strength —transforms them into poetry."

Which, as any one who reads him or talks with him will soon discover, is the secret of Robert Frost's success. He is a Puritan who has fought the soil for sustenance and has fought the world for recognition as a poet. He has won success because he has fought his own emotions, digging into them and behind them, the better to strike the universal note that makes poetry out of axe-handles.

Notes from Conversations

Morris P. Tilley, a member of the English Department at the University of Michigan, became acquainted with RF in the White Mountains during the summers of 1915 and 1916. In letters written at that time he recorded not only his impressions of the poet but also much that was said in the course of their talks together.

Drawing upon these letters and acting at the request of the editor of The Inlander, *an undergraduate publication at Michigan, Professor Tilley prepared for the magazine's February 1918 issue "Notes from Conversations with Robert Frost," from which the following text is excerpted.*

ROBERT FROST is a real poet. He has had the determination to struggle for twenty years towards that end.[. . .]

"It was instinct that kept me going in the direction I took, all the time. A sort of feeling told me that I was doing the right thing. I cannot explain it. I had made up my mind not to have my poetry recognized. So, of course, the day my poetry was accepted in England was one of the happiest days in my life."

Frost is a delightful personality, frank, straightforward, and honest. I have been charmed with his candor. He is without pretense of any kind.[. . .] His personal view of everything is most pronounced. "I am very personal," he said to me once; and it is true. There is no restraint about him at all. He is rather like nature in his abundant outgiving, which is no effort to him, but obviously a joy.

His strength is easily felt. As one of his critics has said of him, he is a "robust philosopher."

"I do not like S——," he said, referring to an acquaintance we avoided in common, "because he sees but one side, the bad side. I do not object to expressing an unfavorable opinion, and to the point, when there is need for it, but I insist that we see the other side also."[. . .]

I turned the conversation to his poetry and said that I should like to see him try his hand at drama. He finds himself interested in drama but not in the conventional kind of poetic drama that holds the stage today. Speaking of effective dramatic composition, I referred to Pope's statement that in one of the weakest of Shakespeare's plays, *Love's Labour's Lost*, the speeches are so characteristic that if the names of the speakers had not been left us, we should still be able to assign each line to the proper character. This interested Frost and he dwelt on it.

"I have three characters speaking in one poem, and I was not satisfied with what they said until I got them to speak so true to their characters that no mistake could be made as to who was speaking. I would never put the names of the speakers in front of what they said. They would have to tell that by the truth to their character of what they said. It would be interesting to try to write a play with ten characters and not have any names before what they said."

Teaching English was a favorite theme of conversation with Frost. He had taught this subject at Pinkerton Academy.

"I did not have a textbook in my English teaching. Sometimes I was in good condition, and at others I could not do a thing. I never kept on reading a book that made the class listless. If I saw the class uninterested I always closed the book and passed the rest of the hour some other way. I learned to watch for the 'fidgets' on the part of the students, and when I saw them in evidence I recognized them as a danger signal. They were given the children to protect themselves with. I was taken from teaching English and transferred to the State Normal School to teach psychology."

Both at Dartmouth and at Harvard Frost was a student for a short while. The regular routine of college life was irksome to him, so that he did not stay at either place[. . .].

"I could not then live in a college or university atmosphere, because of the restraint. I could not do things because they had to be done. I suppose I have been guided in my life so far by instinct to protect what I was or wanted to be. The most pronounced instance where my life was influenced by this instinct was when I gave up my work at Harvard. I lost friends by leaving Harvard. I did not regret leaving, however, for I could not stay. I could not have explained then even to myself why I did not stay. I just had to go."[. . .]

In his poetry Frost avoids poetic diction. He uses only words of his own, always striving to be natural and sincere. His blank verse is nearly the normal blank verse, with only a few changes of his own. He has not been devoted at any younger period to the influence of any great writer. He believes that conversation with friends has given him the moments of highest joy, greater than that of books. The words "close" and "near" were of much meaning to him in the days of his formative period. He felt that he wanted to get the qualities of intimate conversation into his poetry.

Next to this influence, Wordsworth (who to him is a very great poet), Turgenief, in his *Sportsman's Sketches*, and the *Odyssey* have influenced him most. He has much pleasure in Milton, too. His "Lycidas" he greatly admires. He endeavors to be simple and straightforward in his work, to strip a theme bare of all but the essentials. He is going to talk in St. Johnsbury soon on "Sound in Poetry," about which he has interesting theories. He thinks that the creative power of the voice is all important in poetry. Theocritus, to whose writings critics say that he is indebted for some of his ideas of style, he has not read.

In his earlier student days he worked much in the classics. Speaking of the *Odyssey* he applauded the strength and restraint that he finds in the poem. He dwelt on the value of restraint in poetry and how one had to avoid doing in poetry many unwise things.

"All must be rigorously rejected that is not perfectly true and sincere. In the *Odyssey* the swim of Ulysses from the raft has powerfully possessed my imagination. It is one of the things that has gripped me. I spent three years studying Greek and six or seven years studying Latin." (Significant testimony, in view of the unpopularity of the classics and the growing popularity of vocational studies, which he deplores.)[. . .]

Today Frost spoke about the trials of a poet in arriving at the goal where he wins some success.

"I never took the foolish attitude that I was not judged rightly and that the people didn't know what they were talking about. That is a mistake. It might be the poetry was not good enough, in which case all I had to do was make it better. It might be that it was not to the personal taste of the reader, in which case I had only to go on writing to my own taste. There is no other way to attain to poetic success than by stern emotional control and absolute adherence to sincere endeavor. Slopping over isn't poetry."

Speaking of his theory of poetry Frost laid especial stress upon the importance of conversational tones in poetry.

"There is the visual appeal of poetry. We all recognize so-called poetic words that visualize pictures for us. As this is the appeal to the eye, so there is a more important appeal to the ear. The music of poetry is not like the music of an instrument, however. It is something different. Music in poetry is obtained by catching the conversational tones which are the special property of vital utterances. There is the sense the words convey, and there is also an emotional quality, an interpretative quality, in the tone in which the words are uttered. To gather these, because they are significant and vital and carry through the ear an appeal of sincerity, is a main effort in poetry.[. . .] Conversational tones are numerous in dramatic poetry. As a result, the dramatic is the most intense of all kinds of poetry. It is the most surcharged with significance."

Frost cannot write unless he can hear in him the voices carrying on the conversation that he records. These visitations of style, as Stevenson calls them, are not at his command. His poem "The Death of the Hired Man" he wrote ten years ago in two hours, without changing a word, at a time when his nature was in equipoise. At other times he can't write at all. He has to wait until he has the inspiration very clearly, although he does not employ the word "inspiration" when speaking of his poetic mood.

In talking about poetry he does not employ the conventional words that one usually hears in such discussions. He objects to the expression "creative imagination."

"One critic says that I make my imagination too concrete. As if imagination could be made too concrete! Poetic diction is all wrong. Words must be the ordinary words that we hear about us, to which the imagination must give an iridescence. Then only are words really poetic.

"Words that are the product of another poet's imagination cannot be passed off again. They have done their work. One of my abominations is the word 'immemorial,' which every poet for years has pulled in whenever he has had need of a long word. They can't get away with it. One poet made an effort to use in his poetry Shakespeare's word 'incarnadine.' And again no one has been able, although many have tried, to employ with success Keats' 'alien' in the beautiful line, 'She stood in tears amid the alien corn.' All this using of poetic diction is wrong. I use only the words I find in conversation, making them poetic as best I can with what power I command."

"Swinburne's line is the humming kind of meter. Swinburne writes conventional poetry without real feeling. He piles on the epithets that appeal to the eye. But there is something more in good poetry. That is the appeal to the ear. This he did not make. As the picture is drawn for the eye, so the conversational tones of the words have a special message to the ear. Everything worth saying has its own particular way, its own inevitable way, of being said.

"There is a tone of surprise or of embarrassment or of wisdom or of horror or of hope. My effort is to catch the high emotions of the race that have these marks on them for the ear. There are hundreds of these expressions that when we hear them we recognize. It is the character that the voice lends to the meaning that tells the whole tale to the ear of the listener. The poetry that has this quality is what I should like to write."

· II ·

THE TWENTIES

A Visit in South Shaftsbury

In 1920, after two and a half years as a member of the Amherst College faculty, RF resigned his teaching position and later in the same year bought, at South Shaftsbury, the first of the several Vermont farms he was to acquire during succeeding decades.

On April 11, 1921, the Boston Traveler *published this interview, based on a visit to South Shaftsbury by its staff reporter Paul Waitt.*

I'M atop of a crumbling stone wall by the side of a sunbathed road. A song sparrow is sweetly present above me in a maple tree. Surely the bulging red buds on every twig-tip must burst into leaf within the week. There is a white house—a little one—diagonally across the road from where I sit. A man is taking off the storm doors. In the farmyard, close by the gaping black door of the adjacent weather-stained barn, a woman in blue and white gingham is looking off toward the Green Mountain range to the east, all veiled in opal haze. Far off to the west a sorrel horse, free as the sweet morning air, gallops madly up the meadow slope—apparently from sheer joy that the spring has truly come again. On every side these meadows stretch clear to the dim foothills, and bright green is wooing sombre brown everywhere. There is a hill ahead, and my stone wall marks the way—up, up to the top where trees sway in the warm, puffy breeze.

Presently I shall move on up that hill, because up behind those trees, near the pale blue cloudless sky, there is an old stone house.

I can not see it, but I know it is there. They told me so down at the village grocery as I came along.

He lives there—the man whom I am going to see. It is spring-time and I can think of no other man upon whom I would rather call than he at this particular season of the year. His name is Robert Frost. England hails him as America's greatest poet, quite the equal of their best, the superb John Masefield. As an American I can think of no poet greater than Robert Frost.

A patriarch of these rolling Vermont hills in brown overalls just passed me by, and it was he who said "Good morning!" first. He was headed toward the village.

"Do you know where Mr. Frost lives?" I had said, knowing well that he did. And he had answered quickly, as he waved his sun-brown hand back over his shoulder, "Up the hill in the old stone house behind the trees."

I wonder if this poet wears a collar and necktie? I'll find out soon enough. My, but it's a long, steep hill! But what a day!

Had Wallace Nutting been walking along that country highway which leads from the village of South Shaftsbury to Bennington, Vermont, the other morning, he would have paused on the hilltop about a mile on from the general store to unsling his magic camera. Because here among the trees—maple, horse-chestnut, elm, and apple—was a Nutting picture.

Pictorially, as I first saw it, it might have been a scene of a hundred and fifty years ago. Sturdy folk of yesterday had built that quaint old house: gray block stone two-thirds of the way up, with dark-red clapboards continuing on above to the long, sweeping roof. Dutch curtains, patterned in dark brown, swished and rippled just within the open windows. On the wide doorsill of the massive colonial doorway, comfortably resting against one side, sat a silver-haired gentlewoman in buff and white, her fingers and needle danc-ing in and around a strip of crochet work which overlapped her wrist and fell into her lap. A tall, thin young man in blue overalls, whom I shortly learned was the son of the family, thumped a big, flat rock down into the brown earth path he was making new for the spring. He padded fresh green sod around it and then wet it down with generous sploshes of water from a pail. There was a green iron pump immediately to his left, with a shining dipper upside down on the snout. A few weeks more and the pump will be in the shade of maple leaves.

The left of the picture seemed a perfect balance for the rest: deep ruts in rapidly greening sod, which led downward between venerable walls of stone, by an apple orchard on one side and a weathergrayed barn on the other, apparently meeting, at last, the open sky.

Far down the road toward Bennington a single house gleamed white in the sun. It was the only house to be seen. Phoebes sang from the ridgepole of a second barn directly across the street, but all else was rolling meadow and stone wall—a glorious rural world fenced in by misty mountain heights to the north, south, east, and west.

What a world of contentment and peace! And the eyes of the doorstep figure—full, rich, brown eyes—reflected it all. So did the eyes of Lesley Frost, who had appeared, half timidly, in the doorway behind her mother. She was twenty-one and wore a brand new pair of oxblood oxfords with sensible heels.

"He" would be back presently. He had just walked down the road "a piece" with a young student poet from Amherst who had been spending a few days with them.

In that first moment of meeting Mrs. Frost, in which she had invited me into the "cool of the house," I well knew that her talk would not be of the local church social or about the man on the farm below who had been kicked by his horse last Thursday afternoon. She had been a bit disappointed in Sinclair Lewis's *Main Street*, because, after all, "there must have been some fine people and worthwhile things in Gopher Prairie." Oh, it was a charming chat we had in that simple, spacious living room waiting for "him" to return.

"I think he's coming, Mother," suddenly came to us through the window.

I arose and went to meet him, and I noticed his suspenders first as the sunlight brought the straps into high relief against his dark gray flannel shirt. He wore no hat. I do not quite remember how it all occurred, but from the moment that I joined him I seemed to be walking along the road by the side of an old friend and just talking naturally of many things.

One of his literary friends prominent in New England letters had told me some time ago that Frost was "one of the most lovable men in the world." I could not help thinking of this remark as I gazed into the remarkable face of the man by my side and listened to his talk. It is a large face with mobile features—strong features that radiate peace, contentment, and the perfectly balanced solidarity of the inner man. My mother would have said that his was a good face.

His movements were most deliberate and his grayish hair was plain "mussed up." He wore a very old pair of bluish-gray, striped trousers, mended a bit on the inner side of the bottoms. A wisp of worn leather flipped and flapped from the bottom of one shoe, near the toe, as he walked along. The occasional smile which illumined his whole face when it came was the smile of genuine pleasure or amusement. No, he didn't look like the popular conception of a poet at all. But he surely did look as if he could write beautiful poetry. His voice bore the same mold as his appearance—deep, kindly, warm, slow, at times almost a drawl.

In a word, even on such short acquaintance, I didn't have to wonder what kind of a man he was. I already knew.

We paused under the maple tree by the pump, he taking the straight-backed chair which leaned against the bark and I the more comfortable arm chair which faced him. He had insisted that such should be the order.

"Did you ever stop to think this weather talk we have so much of and which drives some people to desperation is, after all, a kind of amateur nature poetry?" he continued, one leg slung over the other and his hair against the rough bark.

"Most folks are poets. If they were not, some of us would have no one to read what we write. Perhaps a few of us specialize just a little more, that is all. There is an old idea that poetry is only in special things. Many people think that.

"But it is in everything. Perhaps it seems as if there were more poetry in this particular season of the year than in other seasons, but it is in all of them. Yet. . . ." (He began to break a stick which he held in his big hands into small pieces and then to throw the fragments out in front of him as he talked.) "Yet," he went on, "I guess it is easier to write poetry on spring and autumn than on the other two seasons. I know it is much harder for me to find summer poetry."

He was the picture of ease and self-possession up there against that tree.

"A little spring poem, you want, to fit the season? You know, I somehow have always written more about just that period when the backbone of winter breaks and the thaw starts. Somehow that part of spring seems to appeal to me more. No, I will not say that it appeals to me more, but I just seem to have written about it more.

"Let me see. Perhaps 'Blue-Butterfly Day' might interest you. Yes, it is for just about now. You have seen those thousands of little blue butterflies that come in the muddy season of the spring, haven't you?"

He tilted his head and thought for a moment. "Let me see," he said, "it goes like this:

> It is blue-butterfly day here in spring,
> And with these sky-flakes down in flurry on flurry
> There is more unmixed color on the wing
> Than flowers will show for days unless they hurry.
>
> But these are flowers that fly and all but sing:
> And now from having ridden out desire
> They lie closed over in the wind and cling
> Where wheels have freshly sliced the April mire."

It seemed like a beautiful song there on the breeze-swept hillside under the maple tree. His whole quiet being seemed to leap into life as he recited. Then, as he finished, he became the solid, easygoing man once more.

"Occasionally a man comes along," he went on, "who says, you can't tell me there is any poetry in the process of scratching a pig's back! But I don't know. The farmer on the Sunday holiday is apt to stray out just to scratch the back of his pig or to salt the cattle. It is a little ceremony—a kind of a poetic ceremony—tender-like.

"You know after a severe winter the farmer will go out to his trees and proceed to pick off a few blackened buds, and there is a little poetry in that, more or less—a practical thing, to be sure, but another little ceremony into which enters the element of poetry.

"Milking the cow is old-fashioned nowadays, but we can all recall the charming old milking songs. Things have just shifted a bit, that is all. Of course there are very few subjects which are wholly poetical."

I was not "interviewing" Robert Frost, the greatest of all American poets. We were just chatting, that is all—just rambling along; yet I wanted to know his conception of purely poetical subjects.

He has a peculiar little way of saying, "Well, now, what are they?" Or, "Just how would we arrive at so and so?" and similar things—questions to himself—but his mind works clearly and sharply underneath these questions, and the well-formulated answer comes immediately.

"Well, now, what are they?" he was saying. "The moon and running water surely are purely poetical subjects. Yet it is very hard to do anything with the moon—so much has been done with it. I am apt to like a poet who writes about unusual things. It seems to me to be the best proof of a real poet. Moons and running brooks have been written about over and over again. Anyone can borrow them out of a book.

"Then again, it is easy to write about certain traits of character: generosity and heroism, for instance. These subjects have been written on innumerable times. However, there are shades of character which are harder to see, and when a man notices these, to my way of thinking, he is a real poet."

"After all," I said, "we have been getting a great preponderance of nature poetry—is that what you call it?"

"Yes," he answered, as he leaned over and grasped a handful of dried grass. "Real nature poetry has been coming in large doses. Up to a hundred years ago we did not have any. The Greeks or the Romans didn't write it. That doesn't mean that it was not in the race or speech, but it was not in books. We have had so much of it during the last century that there is almost a revulsion against it at the present time.

"Only the other day Katharine Lee Bates and I were judging some poetry of this kind—description touched with emotion—and we both came to the conclusion that in such poetry there is too much of but one thing. And that one thing was not enough to make a poem. It seemed to us something else was necessary. There must be a human foreground to supplement this background of nature. There are beautiful stage settings in the theater, but few people would go to see them if there were no actors or actresses. I am convinced that we must put people in the foreground."

Certainly there was the subject for a poem out on the front door path. Son Carol's face was still awince, following the falling of one of the big stones upon his toe. I wondered if Mr. Frost had noticed it. No, I'm sure that he had not.

"But one must not scoff at nature poetry," went on the poet. "The writers are serving a kind of an apprenticeship, and it is not a conscious one. However, I feel that eventually they will get the human foreground in. We have had nature poetry now for a hundred years. Now we must have the human foreground with it." (The last with conviction.)

It was time for dinner. Mrs. Frost had announced this from the window. So we went in.

I could write at length on that event. It was all so homelike and charming. The spring air made me eat my steak with ravenous relish, but it was the bread pudding which followed that touched the spot.

"We have to have it often to use up the pieces," said Mrs. Frost with a gentle smile.

Here for the first time I met Irma, seventeen. Marjorie was away at school, at Bennington.

Laughter sat with us at that table. I shall never forget it. After dinner we went outdoors again.

"Come on," he said.

He led the way around the house, by the maple tree, down to the grass-rutted path, and up toward the barn. Along the way, between the stone walls, we passed the orchard and the barn, talking of many things. Still on went the pretty lane. And as we traversed it I learned, among other things, that he was forty-five and that success had not come to this remarkable man until he was thirty-eight, but seven short years before. I learned that too much of the city disconcerted his train of thought, and hence his simple life among the hills.

Presently we came to a new world at the end of the lane, and the miles of rollicking meadow and field stretching off to the mountains in every direction seemed to belong to just us two. There was not even a house to be seen. He led the way to a little elevation which commanded an unobstructed view of the whole valley sweep. It was evidently a dreaming spot of his, because two rocks and boards before us made perfect lookout seats.

"Sit down," he said. And down I sat. He sat down, too, and straightway buried his hand into the dark brown soil. He talks best with a handful of something—something which he can sift or break or throw.

For an hour or more we rambled along our verbal road—and the world before us came in for its share of attention. I could see him watching things, things close and far off, at intervals. I know he saw the score or more of blackbirds that scolded in the elm tree top some way below us. Twice hawks flew over the valley, slowly but powerfully; and though we talked, we both watched them until, like specks, they became lost in the mountain haze.

Not once through that charming afternoon, and we were there on the meadow elevation for more than four hours, did Mr. Frost make an obvious remark or say a single thing for effect. He reminded me of the country all about—rugged and real. When he told me of himself it was all so naturally and simply done. And the recital was romantic and intensely dramatic in its very simplicity.

I had always been under the impression he was Massachusetts-born. He was born in San Francisco but bred in the old Bay State.

"Yes, my father was a California editor in charge of both the San Francisco *Bulletin* and *Post*," he was saying. "But I was brought up in Lawrence, Massachusetts, and was graduated from the Lawrence high school. My wife was graduated from that school also. Yes, I worked in the mills there to help out after Father died.

"None of my relatives wanted me to write. Grandfather wanted me to be a lawyer. My mother was very fond of poetry, and, while she never said so, I always felt that underneath she wanted me to write. So I entered college. While my marks were always good, I somehow felt that I was wasting time, and so I left college. Later I tried it again, but eventually had the same feeling, and I left again. My grandfather was disgusted. I was never going to amount to much. Most folks felt that way about me. Thus I drifted along.[. . .]

"I told that boy from Amherst this morning not to get the conquer-the-world-next-year-or-quit idea into his head. I told him that it was nice if the magazines let him in, but if they did not, why, not to worry about it. The poet must plan wide. He must be willing to wash dishes if necessary or to do other things, and then do what he can with his writing as he can. It took me twenty years. I taught school on the side. I have done many things to make both ends meet. We have seen hard times financially—very hard times. But now I am getting all I need for our living, a comfortable one, through my poems.

"I have always felt that sometime I would write a novel and do big things for the family. Every time I started one I found myself writing poetry at the end of the first chapter. I just had to, that is all.

"We are patient people, my wife and I. We had to be. Affairs were not looking very well when one day Mrs. Frost went to Grandfather and asked him to buy me a little farm. Grandfather had no use for me whatever, but he bought the place on the ground that I had to die somewhere and it might as well be on some out-of-the-way farm.

"It was a little two-thousand-dollar affair up in Derry, New Hampshire. I had to teach in the academy to make both ends meet, and then they did not meet. There came a time when our bread and butter was a serious affair. Then came that novel idea back again.

"I said to Mrs. Frost, 'Let us go find some little cottage in England where I can write this novel.' So we sold the farm—part of it was mortgaged—and with very little money the six of us started for England in 1912. We found a cute little place in Beaconsfield with a little high-hedged yard. I always meant to write that novel, honestly, but I always found myself writing poetry. I kept it in a stack, and every once in a while I would weed it out or add more to it.

"One day the question come over me: What have I here, and is it good for anything? I got down on the floor and sorted out a series that had to do with my younger days from eighteen to twenty. I put them together with a preface and called them *A Boy's Will*. Then I went down to London to see a man whom I hardly knew—the man who had told me where I could get my little cottage—and see if he could tell me of some publisher who might buy my verse. He was an ex-policeman. I had no letters of introduction when I went to England.

"I asked him if he knew of some small respectable publisher who might buy my poems and not kick me out of the door. He said that no one published poems and that I would myself have to pay to have them printed. I never wanted to do that. Somehow I never liked the idea.

"In the conversation this man named David Nutt. Then and there I went over to Nutt's establishment, left the poems, and in two days he wrote me to come in to sign a contract. So you see it was a very accidental beginning.

"This book got me a little start, and I was invited about some. Then in 1914 my success came with my book *North of Boston*. It was named at the end of the year among the four best in England, along with those of Masefield and Wilfrid Gibson.

"But you know great success with a book of this kind over there doesn't mean much in a financial way. I had my reputation but not much money to back it up, so in 1915 back we came to America.

"I'll never forget it. We arrived in New York on George Washington's birthday. I had hardly landed when I picked up a new paper, which I had never seen before, called *The New Republic*. My name stared up at me from the front page. There were two columns in it about me. It was written by Miss Amy Lowell of Brookline, who did not know me then. I also learned that a couple of weeks earlier they had published a poem of mine called 'The Death of the Hired Man.'

"Then I went up to a little farm in Franconia, New Hampshire, and from then on—this was in 1915—telegrams began to come, and they have continued to come ever since. From that time living has not been a problem.

"Yes, there is lots of luck in it. Both my wife and I liked the long, quiet, sustained adventure of it all. Mrs. Frost went with me in the same spirit. I never allowed the spirit of I-must-get-a-reputation-or-die to take hold of me. The reward lies really in the end when people like what you write."

A damp had crept into the air. We might have been sitting on the edge of the future with the western sky aflame before us. But we had been talking of the past. The frogs far off down in the valley had long since tuned up. The shadows were creeping farther and farther up through the increasing haze at the base of the far away yet near mountains.

"Hoo-Hoo!"

It came shrill behind us. It was Lesley calling us to supper.

We went back to the house to another meal of cheer, and when the table was cleared he read me from his poems for an hour or more in the light of the oil lamp, with mother and the children sitting silently farther back in the dim shadows of the big colonial room.

Small wonder that Robert Frost can write poems in a home like this! And one of the poems he read was this:

A Prayer in Spring

Oh, give us pleasure in the flowers today;
And give us not to think so far away
As the uncertain harvest; keep us here
All simply in the springing of the year.

Oh, give us pleasure in the orchard white,
Like nothing else by day, like ghosts by night;
And make us happy in the happy bees,
The swarm dilating round the perfect trees.

And make us happy in the darting bird
That suddenly above the bees is heard,
The meteor that thrusts in with needle bill,
And off a blossom in mid air stands still.

For this is love and nothing else is love,
The which it is reserved for God above
To sanctify to what far ends He will,
But which it only needs that we fulfill.

An Unauthorized Interview
and an Unsent Letter

A newspaper item that roused RF's indignation and anger appeared in the New York Tribune *on January 14, 1923, written by Burton Rascoe.*

Rascoe, then literary editor of the Tribune, *not only published parts of what the poet had considered to be a private conversation, but, moreover, he garbled RF's comments in reporting them.*

The offending passage is here extracted from Rascoe's entry for "Saturday, January 6" in his feature column "A Bookman's Day Book."

WENT to Lawton Mackall's house-warming in the new offices of *Snappy Stories* and *Popular Radio* and found there Robert Frost, Carl Van Doren, Harry Kemp, Christopher Morley, Kendall Banning, Robert McBride, Pierre Loving, Milton Raison, Hugo Reisenberg, Adolphe Roberts, and a host of others.

Thomas Facett gave a very funny imitation of a village choir, and Chris Morley kidded Mackall about his magazine very amusingly and then read some pieces he said were imitations of "The Waste Land" and other modern poems. If what he read bears the slightest resemblance to "The Waste Land," then I'm the Prophet Jeremiah and all his lamentations.

Kemp is a hulking fellow with a red face, a surly mouth, and eyes which wear a look of surprise.

Robert Frost in voice and demeanor reminds me much of Sherwood Anderson. He has the same deliberate and ingenuous way of speaking; he is earnest, earthy, humorous, without put-on, very real, likable, genuine. I admire him very much as a person. I regret that I find almost nothing to interest me in his poems. They are deft, they are competent, they are of the soil; but they are not distinctive.

Frost and I left the party together and went to Grand Central Station, where we talked for half an hour about Ezra Pound, T. S. Eliot, Conrad Aiken, and Amy Lowell. He astonished me somewhat by telling me that Prof. John Livingston Lowes, author of *Convention and Revolt in Poetry* (an excellent treatise, insofar as it touches poets established by time), snaps his fingers in dismissal of T. S. Eliot, and that in doing so at a recent encounter at Miss Amy Lowell's house he had incurred the wrath of William Rose Benét.

Frost himself has little sympathy with Eliot's work, but then he wouldn't naturally; his own æsthetic problem is radically different from that of Eliot's.

"I don't like obscurity in poetry," he told me, voicing the familiar complaint. "I don't think a thing ought to be obvious before it is said, but it ought to be obvious when it is said. I like to read Eliot because it is fun seeing the way he does things, but I am always glad it is his way and not mine."

I take it to be self-evident that those who talk of Eliot's "obscurity" are using the word as a defense through an inability to derive any emotional response from it. But why should one defend himself, especially upon such unreasonable grounds? There is no law requiring one to read Eliot and like his work. "That is poetry . . . ," says Saintsbury. "That is poetry to a man which produces on him such poetical effects as he is capable of receiving." And adds Professor Lowes, "That is poetry to a critic which produces on him such poetical effects as he is capable of perceiving."

Obscurity is a term to be used only in connection with prose, the medium of exact ideas. One of the primary differences between poetry and prose is that prose denotes and poetry connotes. A poem may be as obscure as Shakespeare's "The Phœnix and the Turtle" or as explicit as his Hundred and Thirty-eighth Sonnet without affecting its poetic content whatever.

"I have heard that Joyce wrote *Ulysses* as a joke," said Frost to me, repeating what I have heard a dozen times from the credulous about both *Ulysses* and "The Waste Land."

Dismissing for a moment the absurdity of the notion that a penniless man in ill health would spend four years writing a half-million-word novel without hope of adequate remuneration merely as a joke, whether he did or not would have nothing whatever to do with its artistic significance and importance. The first principle of æsthetic judgment is that the critic be concerned with the achievement, not with the motives prompting it. Sincerity, as we ordinarily understand the term, has nothing whatever to do with art. "The truest poetry," says Shakespeare, "is the most feigning"; and Verlaine's "Art Poétique" no less than the essays by Coleridge, Dryden, and Poe testify to the irrelevancy of "sincerity." All the sincerity in the world does not make Mr. Harold Bell Wright's *When a Man's a Man* a work of art. There is evidence to support the belief that Shakespeare never wrote a "sincere" play in his life.

Six days from the publication of the above text found RF writing from South Shaftsbury to his friend Louis Untermeyer in New York, enclosing a blistering missive to Rascoe that he had just drafted. "Elinor thinks perhaps I ought not," he explained, "to send a letter like this. You judge for us. If you don't think I'll live to be sorry just put it into another envelope and send it along to Burton. . . . I ought," he added, "to let one at Burton. If you'd like the fun of seeing me punch him I'll come down and punch."

Three days later, and now in a rather less petulant mood, RF acknowledged Untermeyer's prompt response: "You and Jean think such wrath ill becomes me. I'm over it now anyway. We won't send the letter to Burton the rat. My grounds for wanting to let him have both fists in succession in the middle of the face are chiefly that he stated me so much worse than I know how to state myself. That is the greatest outrage of small town or big town—misquotation. It flourishes worst, it seems, among these smart cosmopolites. But never mind."

The unsent letter, preserved over the years by Untermeyer, was finally published in 1963 in The Letters of Robert Frost to Louis Untermeyer *and is here quoted from that source.*

YOU LITTLE RASCOL: Save yourself trouble by presenting my side of the argument for me, would you? (My attention has just been called to what you have been doing in the *Tribune*.) Interview me without letting me know I was being interviewed, would you?

I saw you resented not having anything to say for yourself the other day, but it never entered my head that you would run right off and take it out on me in print.

I don't believe you did the right thing in using my merest casual talk to make an article of. I shall have to institute inquiries among my newspaper friends to find out. If you did the right thing, well and good; I shall have no more to say. But if you didn't, I shall have a lot to say.

I'm sure you made a platitudinous mess of my talk—and not just wilfully to be smart. I saw the blood was ringing in your ears and you weren't likely to hear me straight if you heard me at all. I don't blame you for that. You were excited at meeting me for the first time.

You seem to think I talked about obscurity, when, to be exact, I didn't once use the word. I never use it. My mistake with the likes of you was not using it to exclude it. It always helps a schoolboy, I find from old experience, if, in telling him what it is I want him to apprehend, I tell him also what it isn't.

The thing I wanted you to apprehend was obscuration as Sir Thomas Browne hath it. Let me try again with you, proceeding this time by example, as is probably safest.

Suppose I say: Of all the newspaper men I ever met, you most nearly resemble a reporter I once talked with casually on the street just after I had paid ten dollars in court for having punched a mutual friend. I talked to him exactly as I talked to you, without the least suspicion that I was being interviewed. He must have taken sides with the mutual friend, for he ran right off to his office and published everything I had said as nearly as he chose to reproduce it.

There you have what I call obscuration. "I say no harm and I mean no harm," as the poet hath it; but the stupider you are the more meaning you will see where none is intended. The really intelligent will refuse to listen to such old-wives' indirection.

Or again, suppose I say: Just because you have won to a position where you can get even with people is no reason why you shouldn't perform face forward like a skunk, now is it? I only ask for information.

Or to "lay off" you personally for the moment, suppose I say: I learn that someone is bringing out an Anthology of the Best Lines of Modern Poetry. He proposes to run the lines more or less loosely together in a narrative and make them so much his own that anyone using them again will have to enclose them in double quotes, thus:

" 'What sayest thou, old barrelful of lies?' "

" 'Not worth a breakfast in the cheapest country under the cope' "

" 'Shall I go on, or have I said enough?' "

These three lines are from Chaucer, Shakespeare, and Milton respectively. Please verify.

Or suppose I say: Good sense is plebeian, but scarcely more plebeian than any sense at all. Both will be spurned in aristocratic circles this summer.

I thought you made very poor play with what I said about the obvious. The greatly obvious is that which I see the minute it is pointed out and only wonder I didn't see before it was pointed out. But there is a minor kind of obviousness I find very engaging. You illustrate it, when, after what passed between us, you hasten to say you like me but don't like my books. You will illustrate it again if, after reading this, you come out and say you like neither me nor my books, or you like my books but not me. Disregard that last: I mustn't be too subtle for you. But aren't you a trifle too obvious here for your own purpose? I am told on every hand that you want to be clever. Obviousness of this kind is almost the antithesis of cleverness. You should have defended your hero's work on one Sunday, and saved your attack on mine for another. You take all the sting out of your criticism by being so obvious in the sense of easy to see through. It won't do me the good you sincerely hoped it would.

You are probably right in thinking that much literature has been written to make fun of the reader. This my letter may have been. Do you remember what Webster said or implied about the farmer who hanged himself in a year of plenty because he was denied transportation for his grain?—or what Nemphrekepta said to Anubis?

: 44 :

When my reports are in on your conduct, I may be down to see you again.

I shall be tempted to print this letter some time, I am afraid. I hate to waste it on one reader. Should you decide to print it take no liberties with it. Be sure you print it whole.

Ever yours,
ROBERT FROST

"We seem to lack
the courage to be ourselves."

Printed in The New York Times Book Review *of October 21,
1923, under the title "Robert Frost Relieves His Mind," this
interview by Rose C. Feld appeared as RF was preparing to
return to the faculty of Amherst College. He had spent the
two preceding academic years at the University of Michigan.
Early 1923 had seen the publication of his* Selected Poems,
and that volume was followed in November by New Hampshire, *RF's first Pulitzer Prize book.*

HAVE you ever seen a sensitive child enter a dark room, fearful of the enveloping blackness, yet more than half ashamed of the
fear? That is the way Robert Frost, poet, approached the interview
arranged for him with the writer. He didn't want to come, he was
half afraid of coming, and he was ashamed of the fear of meeting
questions.

He was met at his publisher's office at the request of his friends
there. "Come and get him, please," they said. "He is a shy person
—a gentle and a sensitive person—and the idea of knocking at your
doors, saying, 'Here I am, come to be interviewed,' will make him
run and hide." The writer came and got him.

All the way down Fifth Avenue for ten or fifteen blocks he smiled
often and talked rapidly to show that he was at ease and confident.
But he was not. One could see the child telling itself not to be afraid.

Arrived at the house, he took the chair offered him and sat down rigidly. Still he smiled.

"Go ahead," he said. "Ask me the questions. Let's get at it."

"There are no questions—no specific questions. Suppose you just ramble on about American poetry, about poets, about men of the past and men of the present, about where we are drifting or where we are marching. Just talk."

He looked nonplused. The rigid smile gave way to one of relief and relaxation.

"You mean to say that you're not going to fire machine-gun questions at me and expect me to answer with skyrocketing repartee. Well, I wish I'd known. Well."

The brown hand opened up on the arms of the chair and the graying head leaned back. Robert Frost began to talk. He talked of some of the poets of the past, and in his quiet, gentle manner exploded the first bombshell. He exploded many others.

"One of the real American poets of yesterday," he said, "was Longfellow. No, I am not being sarcastic. I mean it. It is the fashion nowadays to make fun of him. I come across this pose and attitude with people I meet socially, with men and women I meet in the classrooms of colleges where I teach. They laugh at his gentleness, at his lack of worldliness, at his detachment from the world and the meaning thereof.

"When and where has it been written that a poet must be a club-swinging warrior, a teller of barroom tales, a participant of unspeakable experiences? That, today, apparently is the stamp of poetic integrity. I hear people speak of men who are writing today, and their eyes light up with a deep glow of satisfaction when they can mention some putrid bit of gossip about them. 'He writes such lovely things,' they say, and in the next breath add, half worshipfully, 'He lives such a terrible life.'

"I can't see it. I can't see that a man must needs have his feet plowing through unhealthy mud in order to appreciate more fully the glowing splendor of the clouds. I can't see that a man must fill his soul with sick and miserable experiences, self-imposed and self-inflicted, and greatly enjoyed, before he can sit down and write a lyric of strange and compelling beauty. Inspiration doesn't lie in the mud; it lies in the clean and wholesome life of the ordinary man.

: 47 :

"Maybe I am wrong. Maybe there is something wrong with me. Maybe I haven't the power to feel, to appreciate and live the extremes of dank living and beautiful inspiration.

"Men have told me, and perhaps they are right, that I have no 'straddle.' That is the term they use: I have no straddle. That means that I cannot spread out far enough to live in filth and write in the treetops. I can't. Perhaps it is because I am so ordinary. I like the middle way, as I like to talk to the man who walks the middle way with me.

"I have given thought to this business of straddling, and there's always seemed to me to be something wrong with it, something tricky. I see a man riding two horses, one foot on the back of one horse, one foot on the other. One horse pulls one way, the other a second. His straddle is wide, Heaven help him, but it seems to me that before long it's going to hurt him. It isn't the natural way, the normal way, the powerful way to ride. It's a trick."

"What is it you teach at Amherst and how?" the writer asked while Mr. Frost was speaking about his students.

"Well, I can't say that you can call it teaching. I don't teach. I don't know how. I talk and I have the boys talk. This year I'm going to have two courses, one in literature and one in philosophy. That's funny. I don't know that I know much about either. That's the reason perhaps that we get along so well.

"In the course in literature we're going to read a book a week. They're not going to be the major authors, the classics of literature, either. They're going to be the minor writers—people that aren't so well known.

"Why do I [do] that? For a reason that I think rather good. Those boys will, in the course of their education, get the first-rank people whether I give it to them or not. That's what education very largely means today—knowing the names that sound the loudest. That's what business means; that's what success means. Well, I'd like to get out of that rut for a while. I'd like to get the boys acquainted with some of the fellows who didn't blow their trumpets so loudly but who nevertheless sounded a beautiful note.

"We're not going to read the works in class; we couldn't do all of that. The boys will do their reading at home. They'll read in class the things that appeal to them most: an incident, a bit of dramatic action. I'll let them read what they wish. And then we'll have some fun in their telling me why they made their choice; why a thing called to them.

"I don't want to analyze authors. I want to enjoy them, to know them. I want the boys in the classes to enjoy their books because of what's in them.

"Here again, perhaps, I am old-fashioned. Youth, I believe, should not analyze its enjoyments. It should live. It doesn't matter what they think Hazlitt thought or tried to do in his works; what matters is the work, the story, the series of incidents. Criticism is the province of age, not of youth. They'll get to that soon enough. Let them build up a friendship with the writing world first. One can't compare until one knows.

"I hope it will work out all right. I don't know. I haven't done just this thing before. I don't like teaching the same thing year after year. You get stale doing that.

"Philosophy—that's another subject that I'm going to teach. Philosophy of what? Of life; of people about you, of course.

"What's my philosophy? That's hard to say. I was brought up a Swedenborgian. I am not a Swedenborgian now. But there's a good deal of it that's left with me. I am a mystic. I believe in symbols. I believe in change and in changing symbols. Yet that doesn't take me away from the kindly contact of human beings. No, it brings me closer to them.

"It's hard to explain this thing; it's hard to talk about it. I don't expect to talk much about it to the boys at college. But I want them to feel that a philosophy of life is something that is not formal, that means delving in books and superimposing on themselves. No, a philosophy of life is an attitude to life.

"Plato doubtless thought that he was discovering something new when he wrote his treatise. He didn't. He gave written expression to an attitude toward life that he had probably found in some of his friends. It wasn't worked out like a problem in mathematics. It grew in men. Men are the important factors to remember. They are the soil which brings forth the fruit.

"One cannot say that the real American poetry is the poetry of the soil. One cannot say it is the poetry of the city. One cannot say it is the poetry of the native as one cannot say it is the poetry of the alien. Tell me what America is and I'll tell you what its poetry is. It seems to me we worry too much about this business. Where there is life there is poetry, and just as much as our life is different from English life, so is our poetry different.

"The alien who comes here for something different, something ideal, something that is not England and not France and not Germany and finds it, knows this to be America. When he becomes articulate and raises his voice in an outburst of song, he is singing an American lyric. He is an American. His poetry is American. He could not have sung that same song in the place from where he hails; he could not have sung it in any other country to which he might have emigrated. Be grateful for the individual note he contributes and adopt it for your own as he has adopted the country.

"America means certain things to the people who come here. It means the Declaration of Independence, it means Washington, it means Lincoln, it means Emerson—never forget Emerson—it means the English language, which is not the language that is spoken in England or her provinces. Just as soon as the alien gets all that— and it may take two or three generations—he is as much an American as is the man who can boast of nine generations of American forebears. He gets the tone of America, and as soon as there is tone there is poetry.

"People do me the honor to say that I am truly a poet of America. They point to my New England background, to the fact that my paternal ancestor came here some time in the sixteen hundreds. So much is true, but what they either do not know or do not say is that my mother was an immigrant. She came to these shores from Edinburgh in an old vessel that docked at Philadelphia. But she felt the spirit of America and became part of it before she even set her foot off the boat.

"She used to tell about it when I was a child. She was sitting on the deck of the boat waiting for orders to come ashore. Near her some workmen were loading Delaware peaches on to the ship. One of them picked out one of them and dropped it into her lap.

" 'Here, take that,' he said. The way he said it and the spirit in which he gave it left an indelible impression on her mind.

" 'It was a bonny peach,' she used to say, 'and I didn't eat it. I kept it to show my friends.'

"Looking back would I say that she was less the American than my father? No. America meant something live and real and virile to her. He took it for granted. He was a Fourth-of-July American, by which I mean that he rarely failed to celebrate in the way considered proper and appropriate. She, however, was a year-around American.

"I had an aunt in New England who used to talk long and loud about the foreigners who were taking over this country. Across the way from her house stood a French Catholic church which the new people of the village had put up. Every Sunday my aunt would stand at her window, behind the curtain, and watch the steady stream of men and women pouring into church. Her mouth would twist in the way that seems peculiar to dried-up New Englanders, and she would say, 'My soul!' Just that: 'My soul!'

"All the disapproval and indignation and disgust were concentrated in these two words. She never could see why I laughed at her, but it did strike me very funny for her to be calling upon her soul for help when this mass of industrious people were going to church to save theirs.

"New England is constantly going through periods of change. In my own state (in Vermont, I mean) there have been three distinct changes of population. First came the Irish, then the French, and now the Poles.

"There are those among us who raise their hands in horror at this, but what does it matter? All these people are becoming, have become, Americans.

"If soil is sacred, then I would say that they are more godly in their attitude to it. The Pole today in New England gets much more out of his plot of ground than does his Yankee neighbor. He knows how to cultivate it so that each inch produces, so that each grain is alive. Today the Pole may not be aware of the beauty of the old Colonial house he buys and may in some cases desecrate it, but three generations from now, two generations, his children will be proud of it and may even boast of Yankee heritage. It has been done before; it will be done in the future.

"And if there are poets among these children, as surely there will be, theirs will be the poetry of America. They will be part of the soil of America as their cousins may be part of the city life of America.

: 51 :

"I am [im]patient with this jealousy of the old for the young. It is change, this constant flow of new blood, which will make America eternally young, which will make her poets sing the songs of a young country—virile songs, strong songs, individual songs. The old cannot keep them back.

"I was amused years ago by the form this jealousy of tradition will take. One of the most brilliant pupils in the class at college was the son of a Polish farmer. Everybody admitted his mental superiority. But the old New Englanders would not swallow the pill as given. They sugar-coated, by backstairs gossip, which insisted that the real father of the boy must have been a Yankee.

"We are supposed to be a broad-minded country, yet in this respect we are so very narrow. Nobody worries about foreign strains in English or French literature and politics. Nobody thinks that England has been tainted by Disraeli or Zangwill or Lord Reading. They are taken as Englishmen; their works are important as English works. The same is true of French writers of foreign strain. We seem to lack the courage to be ourselves.

"I guess that's it. We're still a bit afraid. America, for instance, was afraid to accept Walt Whitman when he first sang the songs of democracy. His influence on American poetry began to be felt only after the French had hailed him as a great writer, a literary revolutionist. Our own poet had to be imported from France before we were sure of his strength.

"Today almost every man who writes poetry confesses his debt to Whitman. Many have gone very much further than Whitman would have traveled with them. They are the people who believe in wide straddling.

"I, myself, as I said before, don't like it for myself. I do not write free verse; I write blank verse. I must have the pulse beat of rhythm, I like to hear it beating under the things I write.

"That doesn't mean I do not like to read a bit of free verse occasionally. I do. It sometimes succeeds in painting a picture that is very clear and startling. It's good as something created momentarily for its sudden startling effect; it hasn't the qualities, however, of something lastingly beautiful.

"And sometimes my objection to it is that it's a pose. It's not honest. When a man sets out consciously to tear up forms and rhythms and measures, then he is not interested in giving you poetry. He just wants to perform; he wants to show you his tricks. He will get an effect; nobody will deny that, but it is not a harmonious effect.

"Sometimes it strikes me that the free-verse people got their idea from incorrect proof sheets. I have had stuff come from the printers with lines half left out or positions changed about. I read the poems as they stood, distorted and half finished, and I confess I get a rather pleasant sensation from them. They make a sort of nightmarish half-sense."

As he rose to go, he said, "I am an ordinary man, I guess. That's what's the trouble with me. I like my school and I like my farm and I like people. Just ordinary, you see."

A Visit in Amherst

RF's initial period as a member of the faculty at Ann Arbor had consisted of two successive one-year appointments, first as Poet in Residence and then as Fellow in the Creative Arts. Late in 1924, however, it was announced that he would return to the University with permanent status, as Fellow in Letters.

Gardner Jackson was the recorder of this interview, given at Amherst and published in The Boston Sunday Globe *on November 23, 1924.*

ROBERT FROST, the poet, has won a long fight. He has forced the American system of education to make a place for him on his own terms—terms so contrary to those usually extracted from the teacher by that system that his success is all the more remarkable.

Mr. Frost has little use for conventional educational methods in this country. He never has had. Ever since he entered Dartmouth in 189[...2], "prepared," as he says, "to pass the examination, but not prepared to find it so unintellectual," he has gently but firmly refused to conform.

When Mr. Frost takes up his residence at Ann Arbor next fall as permanent Fellow in Letters at the University of Michigan, he will be officially freed from all obligation to conform to any of the rules of that educational community. Naturally, he is pleased. No regular classes to meet, no routine duties, social or academic; nothing but the spur of his own spirit to prod him. He is simply going to live in that college community and do what he pleases.

"I go primarily for my own work," he agrees, "but I wouldn't go if I wasn't interested in education. I look upon myself as a stake where the engineers are staking out the line for the next advance in education."

He is a firm believer in the "take-it-or-leave-it" theory of education. The compulsion that lies behind the present lecture-quiz-examination-marks system is all wrong to him, and absurdly futile. And that applies to primary and secondary schools, as well as colleges. Too much of the system is taken up with "busy-work"— work prescribed because so many hours must be filled according to schedule and not because either teacher or student is having fun in the work.

His remarks were given in the soft tone of voice so characteristic of him. For the ninth time since we commenced to chat he ran his long fingers through his gray hair and rumpled it into a new disarray. He was slouched down, with legs outstretched, in an easy chair occupying a corner of the small, comparatively undecorated, and somewhat disordered study of his Amherst home.

He wore a soft white shirt without a necktie. (I hesitate to include that detail, knowing his scorn of people's concern in the external appearances of dress and such matters.) His deep-set blue eyes were merry, and chuckles bubbled in his conversation as he recalled the pained looks that have greeted his irregularity in educational communities.

"Some people think," he said, "that the chief aim of education is to find out what a man is fitted for. Quizzing shows that in its crudest form. Of course, that is not education's chief aim. You never quiz in good society.

"Lecturing is a step better, but it's not much good. Controversy or debate is examining in a natural way—is finding each other out —and is considerably better than the other two ways. But communion of minds is the best way; it is an ever-going self-revelation."

"The research laboratory, studio apprenticeship, and the salon of good minds" are the three devices for the perfect education, Mr. Frost feels. At Ann Arbor he will employ all three devices. In fact, he has done so all his teaching life.

He figured largely, incidentally, in stirring Amherst College to see the wisdom of bringing to Amherst a painter of national repute.

This painter's studio is open to Amherst students. They come and watch him at work when they will.

How may men bring about the better form of education?

Mr. Frost says, "Have courage and a little willingness to venture and be defeated." He has put that advice into practice.

He has been frowned upon in academic circles. What claim to teaching ability can be made by a man who frequently doesn't show up for his classes, who allows his students in the classroom to write letters, play cards, or whisper while he's reading poetry? And yet out of each class you'll find a certain group who swear by Mr. Frost as they've never sworn by any teacher before.

And he has quietly climbed from academy faculty to normal-school faculty to college faculty, without having so much as an A.B. degree and without so much as conforming regularly to the academic dictates for one single semester. Now he's free, as he says, "to teach only when I have something I want to tell them."

But to turn away from Robert Frost, the teacher, for a minute (though what man is not always a teacher in the sense Mr. Frost means, if he has an active and open mind?). Mr. Frost's life has been no soft one. He and his family have known want. Supporting a wife, three girls, and a boy on a New England farm, even when the income was increased by teaching at a neighboring academy, isn't conducive to an expansive frame of mind. Yet it was under just such circumstances that Robert Frost produced some of his best poems.[. . .]

He recalls with considerable mirth the amazement and discomfiture his easy-going teaching methods caused among his fellow teachers at Derry.

Especially he remembers the day the superintendent of schools called at the school and caught him "having some fun with the class."

"I didn't know what to do," he said. "The superintendent was reputed to be a hard master. But he came in and sat down, and I just went right on having fun with the class. And he didn't mind at all.

"He afterward told me he didn't care what I did so long as I knew what I wanted to do. But with most teachers it's a case of having to tell them what to do, he said, and I guess he's right.

"You saw what Stuart P. Sherman said the other day: that people don't want to be told what to think and what to do. They're like sheep. Most teachers are that way."[. . .]

At the beginning of this article it was stated that Mr. Frost has won a long fight and has forced the American system of education to accept him on his own terms. Perhaps that statement is not quite accurate. Mr. Frost is not a fighter in the sense that he goes out and wildly criticizes anything. He is rather a passive fighter who refuses to be other than himself under any circumstances. He will not alter his habits of life or thought because the system tells him to or because it is fashionable to.

When asked if the materialism of this age does not appall him, he replied, "Yes, of course it is materialistic, but the only way to counteract it is to create spiritual things. Don't worry yourself about the materialism too much. Create and stir other people to create!"

This philosophy has moved Mr. Frost throughout his life. He has been severely criticized, not only in academic circles, for his apparent indifference to the practical affairs of life. But he stood firmly by his vision.[. . .]

His poems accumulate year by year. He keeps them in a little pile without any special protection. They are written on any old piece of paper that happens to be at hand. Every now and then he sits by the fire or the wastebasket with them and weeds out those he thinks unworthy.

"In the pile I have there," he said, pointing to a nearby bookshelf, "are some I wrote twenty years or more ago. One or two of those in my last book, *New Hampshire*, were written that long ago.

"How do I go about it? Well, an idea flashes into my mind anywhere. If I'm where I can sit right down and work it out, I do. If I'm not, I tuck it away and keep my mind averted from it. Sometimes days and weeks intervene before I get a chance to work it out. But I don't think about it in the meantime. You ruin a thing if you think too much about it."

He takes no notes. He just remembers.

He is not pessimistic about American poetry. He finds the younger generation widely interested. He abhors the fancy and exotic in poetry or in any phase of life. He is the apostle of "heartiness." He is a Puritan in his tastes.

His classes at Amherst are large, but his home is the real scene of his teaching. Students visit him continually, as they did and will do at Ann Arbor. These home visits are not taken up solely with poetry or writing. The discussion ranges over all subjects.

He shows particular interest in the diffident undergraduates who, for one reason or another, are considered queer by their classmates. He is, as he says poetry should be, "a rallying point for poets on the sly."

He defines poetry as "a way of grappling with life" and says that there are many more poets than write poetry. A scientist friend, for instance, he regards as a true poet.

His informality, his candor, and his humor combine to make him a highly attractive person, but one must have a robust disregard for the conventional views of life if a conversation with him is not to prove upsetting. He values only the life of the intellect and spirit, so naturally in these times he disturbs some people.

As he stood on the step of his Amherst home bidding his guests farewell, the moon shone full upon him. His gray hair was tousled in the most grotesque manner, his hands were extended in a curious, generous gesture, and his voice carried across the yard a gentle invitation to come again.

It was a picture not soon forgotten. It typifies one of the friendliest spirits in the land, a spirit that refuses to attack, but refuses to conform, one that sees the creative impulse as the hope of the world.

On Poetic Drama

"Robert Frost on Poetic Drama" appeared in The Christian Science Monitor *for July 14, 1925, and was based on an interview done at RF's farm in South Shaftsbury.*

POETIC drama," mused Robert Frost with contemplative interest, as he sat just beyond the pale gold blot cast by the oil lamp in the pleasant old parlor of his farmhouse in South Shaftsbury, Vermont.

"Poetic drama. Yes, of course. Interesting subject. People should discuss it more. I wrote a play once. I'm always on the verge of drama I expect. . . . Something happened before my play was produced. Things often happen before plays we confidently expect the world is waiting for can be produced."

The deep, soft voice murmured against the silken wind swishing in piles of hay east of the house. It was for the listener to learn that one may talk with Robert Frost (of whom Miss Amy Lowell said, "He is New England.") and ultimately hear what he has to say upon a subject, but that there can be no haste—that he will talk but that also he will think before he talks and be hurried by no clock or circumstance.

The slow, melodious voice droned on in the quiet, a voice that must be one strong factor in the poet's success as college professor.

"One must think out such a thing as the poetic drama slowly. Let me see. . . . The ingredients. . . .

"Shakespeare, most of all, I think. There are the speaking passages and the rhetorical passages to choose from. When I think of successful poetic drama I think of the speaking passages. They are the best of Shakespeare to me—lean, sharp sentences, with the give and take, the thread of thought and action quick, not lost in a maze of metaphor or adjective."

Mr. Frost considered whether there was any subject he himself would prefer to use in making an original poetic drama—considered obediently, acting upon suggestion, although his manner spoke subtly of dislike for the limitation which proceeds from specifying merely one or two in the wealth of subjects the world holds. As he considered he twirled a bright steel knitting needle into the hole he was gradually deepening in the wood arm of his chair. Occasionally he smiled a little as the lamplight reached and made the steel flash in his fingers.

"No. . . . Let me see. . . . No, I don't believe I'd limit the field, any more than I would limit the field for poetry. I don't know what subject poetry might not be written about, and I don't know what a poetic drama mightn't be written about.

"People seem mightily interested just now in Mr. Coolidge and the White House. I shouldn't object to anyone's tackling that as the subject for a poetic drama. . . ."

Under the shock of tangled gray hair the poet's eyes were alert, watchful, may have been holding back a smile. It was impossible to tell whether he was serious or not. The voice rumbled on, and if there had been a smile it was gone.

"If I have any preference it is for the idyllic. I am weary of the heavy-laden problem plays with their almost political sorrows. Some of the war plays have been beautifully done, but their mode should change, I think, to pleasanter things, things closer to the idyllic.

"I am thinking of a play that it would be nice to do. . . . Yes, I see it take shape. . . . A little. . . . Not much. . . . The chief character would be a house. . . . The play would turn on the reaction of people to the state in which they found the house. . . . I should have to find some way to make a defined set and relationship between the people, but I see that little house, scene after scene, with its intimate meaning the dominant note.

"Yes, yes, I must think some more about that presently. I wonder. . . . One dreams of those things, of manipulating unexpected stuffs into idyllic drama, doesn't one?

"If you took Shakespeare to build on, you would have to face the question of whether to base upon the speaking passages or the rhetorical passages or on both. There has been a danger that modern poetic drama might base itself entirely upon the rhetorical passages, the long speeches; but to my mind that way sacrifices opportunity for effect, leads to small audiences or to none, which is certainly not what the author would desire.

"The little theater is an excellent medium at hand for those who would develop the poetic drama as a more frequent mode of expression in the theater. But the little theater now needs, I think, to concern itself with deeper impressions.

"Bulk ought not to count, ought it? A small, perfect jewel is supposed to be quite as beautiful as a larger jewel. Yet, somehow, I feel as if the theater had reached a point in its development where I should dislike to be caught doing a one-act play, as if it were too trivial a play form, lazy man's way.

"I won't have it, in poetry, that bulk counts. People say to me, 'Now settle down and do a long work, since you have shown the public that you can produce beautiful short poetry.' And their implication tells me that making two verses or a short poem does not satisfy their concept of what an accomplished poet should be able to do. Bulk they want, as evidence of a man's power.

"It's modern, the craving for quantity, isn't it! Nevertheless I feel as if a full evening, in the theater, were the thing. Yet I have been charmed by certain curtain raisers.

"I think it should be possible to print a good poetic drama first as prose and then, in precisely the same order of words, as verse. Good verse must, in my opinion, be good prose as well.

"There seems to be a sort of prejudice against poetic drama. Flummery, I've heard it called, and that makes writers loath to undertake writing it.

"I think Mrs. Marks had the divine spark. She wrote poetic drama beautifully and graciously. She had a concept of what it should be. She found Shakespeare the obvious, logical pattern. Yet she did what others who would seek her medium must do, she did not select the wrong atoms from him.

"The height of poetry is in dramatic give-and-take. Drama is the capstone of poetry. In the lyric the dramatic give-and-take is within

: 61 :

oneself, and not between two people. Granting, then, that the height of poetry is drama, then some of the time I feel that we ought to have both brought together and set upon the stage, in order that they may declare themselves in their essential forms."

"There will always be
something left to know...."

The Detroit News published this interview, done at Ann Arbor by Allen Shoenfield, on October 11, 1925, under the headline "Science Can't Dishearten Poets, Says Robert Frost."

Although it was intended that RF's new association with the University of Michigan would be a continuing one, he resigned the post after only a year and returned once more to Amherst.

HAS the scalpel of science within recent years probed so deeply into the mysteries of the air, the earth, and the waters beneath that all the phenomena of nature, stimulating the imagination of man from time immemorial, are at last reduced to "laws" and formulae? Is the unknown now so knowable that the poetic genius must seek in vain for the free play of his fancy?

Robert Frost, reckoned among the great of the world's living poets, who has returned to Ann Arbor to assume his unique position as Fellow in Letters on the University of Michigan faculty, would answer both questions with an emphatic negative.

Recently acquired knowledge, he declared in a chat following his arrival and marked with all his boyish enthusiasm, so far from clipping the wings of Pegasus has but spurred on the poet's classic steed to loftier flights. What if cold science has reduced the Jovian thunderbolt to a charge of electricity tearing earthward from the skies? What if the Homeric legend of a Cyclops is found based on the discovery by an ancient and ingenuous race of a mastodon's skull and the great blank socket of the one-eyed giant merely the trunk-cavity of the prehistoric beast? "Still, science offers just compensation," says Dr. Frost.

"Think of the great abysses opened up by our study of the atom. Think of the strange and unaccountable actions of the hurrying winds experienced by our travelers of the skies. Think of the marvels of marine life lately brought to us by the explorers of the distant oceans, each more wonderfully wrought than ever mermaid or water sprite of which the poets dreamed.

"Life has lost none of its mystery and its romance. The more we know of it, the less we know. Fear has always been a great stimulus to man's imagination. But fear is not the only stimulus. If science has expelled much of our fear, still there is left a thousand things from which to shape our dreams.

"Keats mourned that the rainbow, which as a boy had been for him a magic thing, had lost its glory because the physicists had found it resulted merely from the refraction of the sunlight by the raindrops. Yet knowledge of its causation could not spoil the rainbow for me. I am so sure that it is not given to man to be omniscient. There will always be something left to know, something left to excite the imagination of the poet and those attuned to the great world in which they live.

"Only in a certain type of small scientific mind can there be found cocksureness, a conviction that a solution to the riddle of the universe is just around the corner. There was, for example, Jacques Loeb, the French biologist, who felt he had within his grasp the secret of vitality. Give him but ten years and he would have it fast.

"He had the ten and ten more, and in ten more he was dead. Perhaps he knows more of the mystery of life now than ever he did before his passing.

"I have heard it cried that America has become a standardized nation and that Americans have long ago ceased to seek expression for their individuality. I do not believe it.

"It may be true that our breakfast food is made in one city, that our clothes are of the same cut and fashion and made by three or four clothiers, that we live in virtually the same sort of houses, possess the same general type of furniture, seek the same sort of amusements, drive the same makes of motor car, utter the same conversational idioms, and, it is said, think the same thoughts. I say this may be true and it may not. But even if it were, I am not fearful of uniformity, even though it led to external monotony. For this monotony can not go beyond externals. The ultimate things are too spiritual for that.

"Look at the sea. Where in all the world is there anything more monotonous—sky, water, wind, and a few boats perhaps? Yet, consider the literature that has come from the ocean, its mass, its kind, and its infinite variety. The very monotony of the sea has driven man in upon himself. Finding no variation in nature, he sought and found it in himself. That is why all our science, all our so-called civilization—our standardization, if you will—need never give the poet pause.

"Monotony? Have we not always had the same stars and the same sky above us, changing only in its shades of blue and gray and purple black? And who shall say that such themes are exhausted? Have we not always had love and passion, war and peace, summer and winter and spring and fall with us? And are these things unable longer to impel us to spiritual variations?"

The poet has only good-natured pity for the shortsightedness of those near-literati who bemoan the passing of "the good old days" and believe the nation committed to hopeless Babbitry because of its flivvers, radios, phonographs, motion-picture theaters, railroads, breakfast foods, ready-made clothes, telephones, newspapers.

"Why," he said with a laugh, "all these things are merely mixing machines. The nation owes to them its preservation.

"For one thing, you cannot have a fairly homogeneous people without presupposing some sort of uniformity. For another, you cannot have a people as far-flung as this, practising efficient self-government, without providing them first with rapid means of communication.

"In the days of the stagecoach some very well-grounded fears were entertained for the continued existence of the Republic. Since then our territory has expanded from ocean to ocean, and were it not that the people of California and Texas are as closely in touch with their representatives at Washington as are the citizens of New York and Florida, we might have good reason to fear for the worst."

Dr. Frost has spent his first days in Ann Arbor renewing old friendships made in 1921 and 1922 while holder of the University Fellowship in the Creative Arts. With Mrs. Frost he has engaged a charming house on the edge of town and, pending its complete furnishing, is living with Joseph A. Bursley, Dean of Students. During the present semester he plans to give a few open readings and to gather together a group with which to form a seminar in writing, starting next semester.

"This will have to be limited to about a dozen upperclassmen, I suppose," he said. "But I shall only want those people who would be writing anyway. There will be no assignments. I am just going to sit and listen to what they have written and talk things over with them.

"Please don't call this a course in 'creative' writing. I hate that word. Writing's writing and that's all there is to it."

Education by Presence

Written by Janet Mabie, this interview was in its original form entitled "Robert Frost Interprets His Teaching Method," and it was first published December 24, 1925, in The Christian Science Monitor.

WHEN Robert Frost read at the Institute of Modern Literature at Bowdoin College earlier in the year he suggested, in passing, a new method of instruction, employed by him at Amherst, which he would like to see in more general use in the colleges and which he has taken with him to his new post at the University of Michigan. "Education by presence," he called it, pausing then only to emphasize the obvious effects upon university students of the mere presence among them (upon the campus) of leading scholars in major lines, even if those leaders never took textbook in hand to conduct ordinary courses of classroom instruction.

Robert Frost is a poet. (He is several other things besides, but first of all he is a poet—although it is true that for some time more people knew him as school teacher, rather than poet.) It is not common for poets to have radical ideas upon a subject which has become, on the whole, as standardized as college instruction. Perhaps it is because Mr. Frost is primarily what he is that there is a poetic twist to the method he would like to see used for teaching college students.

Twenty years ago Mr. Frost was a poet. Over a considerable portion of the intervening years he was one of the few people who knew this, he says. Now, although he does not say it, a great many people know it.

In the long years before recognition warranted his choosing the field of poetry above school teaching, Mr. Frost was doubtless busy with considering this plan for education which he has now been willing to discuss with a representative of *The Christian Science Monitor*. Mr. Frost had ample experience with teaching in one way and another. He would not be arbitrary concerning the greater usefulness of the one he is now engaged in; neither is he hesitant about pointing out some advantages he feels it has for his purposes —possibly for the purposes of other teachers as well.

"The most impressive thing in a college career," said Mr. Frost, "is often having over one someone who means something, isn't it? It is hard to tell how teachers act upon a student, but part of their impress must be the effect of their reputations outside the college. Students get most from professors who have marked wide horizons.

"If a teacher is evidently a power outside, as well as inside, the college, one of whom you can hear along other highways, then that teacher is of deep potential value to the students. If the student suddenly finds that the teacher he has perchance listened to with indifferent attention, or not at all, is known all over the country for something not too bad, suddenly his communications take on luster.

"The business of the teacher is, I presume, to challenge the student's purpose. 'This is life, your career is ahead of you,' he must say. 'Now what are you going to do about it? Something large or small? Will you dabble or will you make it a real one?'

"I do not mean the challenge should be made in words. That, I should think, is nearly fruitless. It must soon begin to sound to the students like rote. Besides, a man can't, you know, be forever standing about on a campus crying out at the students, 'What are you going to do about it?' No, what I mean is that his life must say that; his own work must say that.

"My greatest inspiration, when I was a student, was a man whose classes I never attended. The book that influenced me most was *Piers the Plowman*, yet I never read it. When I realized how much the book had influenced me I felt I should read it. But after considering it I decided against reading it, fearing it might not be what I had thought when I started out to do what I have since done— what the book, unread, inspired me to do.

"Everybody knows that there is such a thing as education by

presence and has benefited more or less by it. You take my own case, for instance. I never have set up to be a particularly good teacher in regular catch-as-catch-can, catch-them-off-their-guard-three-days-in-the-week classroom work. I refuse to quiz day after day, to follow boys up with questions I myself can answer. I refuse to stand up and lecture a steady stream for fear of the consequences to my character.

"Three days in the week, thirty-five weeks in the year is at least three times as much as I have it in me to lecture on any subject anyway. It is at least three times as often as I have the nerve to face the same audience in a week, and three times as often as I have the patience when I know the audience has been doing nothing to help itself in the intervals between my lectures.

"No, I am an indifferent teacher as teachers go, and it is hard to understand why I am wanted around colleges unless there is some force it is thought I can exert by merely belonging to them. It must be that what I stand for does my work.

"I am right in the middle of certain books; that is to say, I have written four of them and expect to write about four more. Well, these books, as much the unwritten as the written, are what I am to the college. If teaching is, as I say, asking rather than answering questions, my books do most of mine with very little help from me. Or so I like to think.

"What I am saying is that there are and always have been three ways of teaching, namely, by formal contact in the classroom, by informal contact, socially as it were, and by virtually no contact at all. And I am putting the last first in importance—the teaching by no contact at all.

"I have always thought a man's chief strength came from being able to say (after St. Paul and Kipling) 'Of no mean city am I'—of no mean college am I—speaking intellectually. It must mean something to the student to be aware of the distinguished research scholars around him. For my part I am helped by the thought of the artists who are my fellow citizens. It is encouraging to belong in the same circle with people who see life large.

"The teacher who has student contacts which are but informal—extra-class, say—fills a spacious place in the student's needs. Perfect informality of contact is in offering oneself as someone the student may like to show his work to. Men have come to me with paintings, because they felt my sympathy with anything they might do, even though it was frequently intrinsically something I knew little about. The college, I think, could be partly built, in the upper tier, of teachers who offered themselves or were offered thus.

"By 'upper tier' I mean a few of the teachers could be offered wholly this way and all of the teachers more or less. Every teacher should have his time arranged to permit freer informal contacts with students. Art, the various sciences, research, lend themselves to this treatment.

"You could perfectly well build an institution on informal contacts. I'd give every teacher who wanted it—who could be happy in it; who wouldn't despise it—a chance at this informal teaching. Some I'd give more; some I'd give less. Some I'd give—isn't there a phrase, 'nothing else but'?

"Half the time I don't know whether students are in my classes or not; on the other hand, I can stay with a student all night if I can get where he lives, among his realities. Courses should be a means of introduction, to give students a claim on me, so that they may come to me at any time, outside of class periods. If the student does not want to press his claim, well, for him I must give an examination. But he has already lowered his estimation. The student who does not press his claim has to that extent been found wanting. I favor the student who will convert my claim on him into his claim on me.

"I am for a wide-open educational system for the free-born. The slaves are another question. I will not refuse to treat them as slaves wherever found. 'Those who will, may,' would be my first motto; but my close second, 'Those who won't, must.' That is to say, I shouldn't disdain to provide for the slaves, if slaves they insisted on being. I shouldn't anyway unless I were too busy with the free-born.

"One mark of the free-born, however, is that he doesn't take much of your time. All he asks of his teacher is the happiness of being left to his own initiative, which is more of a tax on the teacher's egotism than on the teacher's time. Give me the high-spirited kind that hate an order to do what they were about to do of their own accord.

"It is amusing the way your best-laid plans go wrong in dealing with a class or audience. An examination often turns into an examination of the teacher's ability to ask questions clearly.

"I recently was compelled to give an examination, since such must be. In my classroom at the appointed time I said, 'Do something appropriate to this course which will please and interest me.' (It was a course in literature. There had been a wide choice of books.) I left the room.

"I thought probably three or four would get up and go home, thinking I already knew them well enough, that I already had their grades ready anyhow to hand in at the office. I thought others would come to me, a little later, and take it out in talk. I placed a limit upon them of four bluebooks, and you know perfectly well no one ever wrote four bluebooks in Amherst College; but I hoped some poor boy might write four in order to convince himself he was doing everything he should.

"I went away, upstairs. Presently one after the other, 'the whole kit and caboodle,' came ambling upstairs and waited their turns to say something pleasant to me in parting. That's the way they understood the word 'please' in my leading question. You never can tell what you have said or done till you have seen it reflected in other people's minds.

"We haven't talked of formal classroom teaching. There, I suppose, it is the essence of symposiums I'm after. Heaps of ideas and the subject matter of books purely incidental. Rooms full of students who want to talk and talk and talk and spill out ideas, to suggest things to me I never thought of. It is like the heaping up of all the children's hands, all the family's hands, on the parental knee in the game we used to play by the fireside."

· III ·

THE THIRTIES

Poetry and Rural Life

The following interview by Benson Y. Landis originally appeared, under this same title, in the June 1931 issue of the periodical Rural America.

It was during that June also the announcement was made of RF's second Pulitzer Prize, awarded for his Collected Poems, *which had been published in November of 1930.*

I RECEIVED my inspiration to seek an interview with Robert Frost from George Russell. AE had suggested in many of his addresses on his tour of America that we should enlist the poets in our efforts to build a worthy country life in America. He had said, "It ought not to be hard to interest a man like Robert Frost."

I had seen Robert Frost fill a good-sized auditorium in New York City when he read his own poetry. I had seen a large class, of which any professor would be proud, hang on his words when he lectured on poetry: for example, on such subjects as "Where Poetry Comes In," "Where Poetry Gets Off," or "Poetry in the Schools."

When Mr. Frost consented to see me I went without a set of questions, but relied upon the moods of the occasion. He was much interested in AE's idea that the poets might help to rebuild the countryside. He told me much of his own philosophy and autobiography. He told me in no uncertain terms his ideas of the values of rural life.

"Poetry is more often of the country than of the city," insisted Mr. Frost. "Poetry is very, very rural—rustic. It stands as a reminder of rural life—as a resource, as a recourse. It might be taken as a symbol of a man, taking its rise from individuality and seclusion—written first for the person that writes and then going out into its social appeal and use. Just so the race lives best to itself—first to itself, storing strength in the more individual life of the country, of the farm—then going to market and socializing in the industrial city.

"I should expect life to be back and forward—now more individual on the farm, now more social in the city—striving to get the balance.

"We are now at a moment when we are getting too far out into the social-industrial and are at the point of drawing back—drawing in to renew ourselves. The country life we are going back to I can't describe in advance, but I am pretty sure it will not be the country life we came out of years ago. Farming, what survives of it, has demeaned itself in an attempt to imitate industrialism. It has lost its self-respect. It has wished itself something other than what it is. That is the only unpardonable sin: to wish you were something you are not, something other people are. It is so in the arts and in everything else.

"I think a person has to be withdrawn into himself to gather inspiration so that he is somebody when he comes out again among folks—when he 'comes to market' with himself. He learns that he's got to be almost wastefully alone.

"The farmer has industrialized to his own hurt. He has made himself too social right on the farm. He has entered into the competitive outside life. The strength of his position is that he's got so many things that he doesn't need to go outside for. The country's advantage is that it gives many pleasures and supplies many needs for nothing. The tendency of our day is to throw away all of these things and count them worthless.

"Many of our country people don't value anything unless they buy it in the town—where townspeople buy it. Country people go to the movies instead of looking around them. Some want to put into district schools manual-training and agricultural courses which are more elementary than the training of a child on the farm. It is ridiculous.

"The farm is a base of operations—a stronghold. You can withdraw into yourself there.

" 'Fill your cellar and fill your larder' so that you can go into the siege of winter with zest. Go to the cellar stairs; look at the preparations for winter. Smell the apples. Have a good cellar. That is a part of the good life.

"A person is always being pulled out of himself socially, and it is always in the person, and up to the person, to take corrective measures. He should know when to say, 'I am too much out of myself—too overt.'

"The tendency for preservation of his individuality draws him back, and I would guess that the loss of a people is in its industrialization. They are inclined to draw away from their base which is in the country.

"I don't know whether we can 'take thought' to make us turn back. The thing will almost take care of itself. But we won't go back the way we came. We may have a richer farm life when we go back to it."

I referred to AE's leadership in organizing co-operatives and in other social action.

"AE has done wonderful things with the co-operatives in Ireland. But I am not much interested in movements. I am not a person of that kind. I am not enterprising enough. I am too irregular. I keep bad hours. I do not try to reform. I have no quarrel with life, and I myself do not try to 'run' life. I simply express confidence that the kind of thing I naturally like is always going to be the important thing in life."

I persisted in questioning about co-operatives. I wanted to know if Mr. Frost thought that the farm people he met were becoming more co-operative. He gave me the gist of his ideas as to why people should co-operate.

"You co-operate in order that you may be a better individual. You associate yourself with your fellows in order that you may be the stronger yourself. The individual and the social—I know those two things are always getting something out of each other. But I am mostly interested in solitude and in the preservation of the individual. I want to see people sufficiently drawn into themselves.

"Most of the iceberg is under the water. Most of oneself should be within oneself. A man must do that in order to be somebody when he comes out to market with other folks. He should be a large-proportioned individual before he becomes social. If a man is wastefully alone, he should be better company when he comes out."

I asked Mr. Frost of his impressions of modern city life.

"Whenever I am in the city I hear people say they want to go to the country—to the open places. People are sick of each other. They have no reserves; the beat, beat of their many contacts wears them down. There are too many late nights.

"Furthermore, the city is no place for children. There is too little of that feeling of the old time for children. The country is the place for children.

"As to the meaning of what is happening in Russia? I don't know. I feel that what is happening is against me—against my ideas. They seem to be industrializing the work on the land."

I also learned of Mr. Frost's affection for the small district school. He had taught the district school from time to time. He thought there were great values in having many little schools if only we were wise enough to put good teachers into them. What if there were only a few boys and girls—might there not be more opportunities for learning?

"I am not a 'back-to-the-lander.' I am not interested in the Thoreau business. Only a few can do what Thoreau did. We must use the modern tools at our disposal.

"I think we can get an analogy for our ways of living from the American Pullman car. There we are mostly alone, but there is opportunity to step out and be a little with people.

"I am for the artist, who is more alone than he looks. I am not for the reformer, who is always active but usually has nothing to give. The real thing that you do is a lonely thing. And remember the paradox that you become more social in order that you may become more of an individual."

Two Interviews in Denver

RF journeyed to Colorado in the summer of 1931, principally in order to visit his daughter Marjorie, then recovering from tuberculosis at a sanitorium in Boulder. His engagements on this trip included, in addition to a period at the University of Colorado, a public appearance in Denver. Arrangements for the latter were made by a professional agent who angered the poet both by his manner and by his handling of certain of the details. "I let him have me interviewed for his publicity twice on arrival," wrote RF to a friend indignantly, "once in the station and once in a newspaper office, a place where in all my years of reading to people I have never gone for anything."

These brief interviews are here reprinted, substantially in full, from the two Denver papers in which they were published on July 17th.

By Mary Ruth Barry, *Rocky Mountain News*:

ROBERT FROST, white-haired poet of pastoral New England, arrived here yesterday to spend a few weeks in Colorado. He will appear at three forty-five p.m. Monday in a recital of his own works, with comment on American poetry of today, at the University Civic Theater.[. . .]

"I always read my own verse in classes and lectures," said the candid Frost. "Why bother with the other fellow's. I know my own so much better."

This outstanding American poet [. . .] suggests in his rough-hewn face and figure the austerity of a Vermont landscape. Yet he is not at all stern. His reticent manner melts quickly when he starts to talk. Wit, satire, sympathy, and a warm humanity animate his keen gray eyes and awkward gestures.

"A poet's mind need not be ordered," he explained. "It is not like the scientific mind. The urge to express myself in poetry was with me in earliest youth. My mind has always been filled with a jumble of things. The art is in the communication of them.

"That is where the extreme modernists are defeating themselves. They do not care whether their communication is intelligible to others. It suffices that it has significance only to its creator. They desire, also, to play always on the insane fringe of things. Their interest is only in the abnormal. In painting and music, too, the same theory is now in vogue.

"Fashions in poetry change almost like fashions in clothing. Not so long ago the more advanced used Browning as a cudgel to beat Tennyson with. Now they have thrown away the stick. Browning loses his prestige in the poetry world. A short time back Carl Sandburg was a revolutionist in poetry. Now he is one of the old-timers to these ultra-moderns.

"Perhaps this insane fringe will accomplish something after all, however. Future generations, looking back, may say that there is where they deflected the line of art a bit. Their work reflects the philosophy of this generation, probably."[. . .]

By L. A. Chapin, *The Denver Post*:

Robert Frost [. . .] arrived in Denver Thursday, still following the road less traveled by, the road he took when he abandoned farming for verse. After a brief stop here he continued to Boulder, where at the University of Colorado summer school he will undertake "to disabuse students of the idea that they should try to write poetry."

"What I mean," Frost hastened to add, "is that they shouldn't write poetry if they can help it. In fact, they shouldn't do anything if they can help it.

"People should learn to take advantage of their natural laziness. The idea that humans are born full of natural ambition is all wrong. As a matter of fact, everyone is born lazy."

It seemed to be Frost's way of saying that poetry is not the result of conscious effort, but, rather, of impressions and emotions gained in leisure hours, yet irresistible in their demand for expression. Or perhaps he meant something else. You do not feel sure you are keeping up with the poet's agile mind when he is talking to you.

"I heard a good one the other day," he continued. "The question which was asked was, 'Are poets born or made?' The answer is that, 'Most people can't bear poets.'

"I must remember to send that one to Louis Untermeyer. He is quite a punster, but I can never remember them when he is around."

Robust, with disheveled gray hair and dressed comfortably in a baggy gray suit, Frost has the appearance of a kindly, small-town doctor, instead of America's most-eminent poet[. . .].

A glance around the busy office of *The Denver Post*, where he was being interviewed, seemed to remind him of the world of rushing events through which he wends a peaceful way.

"Happenings are what is important in any age, don't you think?" he said. "Poets and such never amount to anything—at least not until long after they are gone. It takes years for the small voice of poetry to be heard. Why, even Shakespeare didn't amount to anything in his own time."

Latest Poem By Robert Frost
Versifies New Deal Is Lost

The above headlines appeared over an interview in the Febru-
ary 26, 1936, Baltimore Sun, *together with the following*
rhymed sub-heading: "New England Poet Strums His Lyre,
And Says The Nation's Plight Is Dire As Projects Swerve
'Twixt Pan And Fire."

RF's political remarks, and the text of the newly published
poem he had quoted, attracted no small amount of notice, in-
cluding editorial comment in The Sun *and* The New York
Times. *The stir created by his* Sun *interview also drew from*
RF at least one letter of explanation.

Both of the editorials and the letter (as included in Law-
rance Thompson's edition Selected Letters of Robert Frost)
are here appended to the interview itself.

The last step taken found your heft
Decidedly upon the left.
One more would throw you on the right.
Another still—you see your plight.

ROBERT FROST has descended from the poetical Parnas-
sus to the political arena. But the figurative lyre he strummed in the
New England hills—strummed until he has become one of America's best-known poets and won two Pulitzer Prizes—is being
lugged along to confuse and refute Administration lions.

Pausing yesterday before catching a train out of Baltimore after a brief visit here, the versifier, whose home is in Vermont, asserted he was anti-Roosevelt. He declared he once had held high hopes for Henry Wallace but had lost them. He bitterly condemned an alleged Administration policy of regarding farmers as possessors of what he called submarginal minds. And, with something of a flourish, he produced a new poem, "To a Thinker."

The verse, he indicated, was written about the President. Mr. Frost smiled sardonically.

"I'm going to stay a Democrat if I have to push everyone else out of the party but Carter Glass," he said. "I'm a pursuitist, not an escapist. And I'd rather cast an idea by implication than cast a ballot."

The complete text of "To a Thinker" read:

> The last step taken found your heft
> Decidedly upon the left.
> One more would throw you on the right.
> Another still—you see your plight.
> You call this thinking, but it's walking.
> Not even that, it's only rocking,
> Or weaving like a stabled horse:
> From force to matter and back to force,
> From form to content and back to form,
> From norm to crazy and back to norm,
> From bound to free and back to bound,
> From sound to sense and back to sound.
> So back and forth. It almost scares
> A man the way things come in pairs.
> Just now you're off democracy
> (With a polite regret to be),
> And leaning on dictatorship;
> But if you will accept the tip,
> In less than no time, tongue and pen,
> You'll be a democrat again.
> A reasoner and good as such,
> Don't let it bother you too much
> If it makes you look helpless please
> And a temptation to the tease.
> Suppose you've no direction in you,
> I don't see but you must continue
> To use the gift you do possess,

And sway with reason more or less.
I own I really never warmed
To the reformer or reformed.
And yet conversion has its place
Not halfway down the scale of grace.
So if you find you must repent
From side to side in argument,
At least don't use your mind too hard,
But trust my instinct—I'm a bard.

"Seriously though," said Mr. Frost, "I'm not horribly anti-Roosevelt. Henry Mencken bears down on the President pretty hard. Roosevelt is making his mistakes, just as we did. But I'm very much a country man, and I don't like to see city against country. And I can't stand coercion."

The New England poet doubts whether his venture into political verse will have great influence. The late Rudyard Kipling, he asserted, was very successful in influencing men and events through poetry; but Mr. Frost indicated he was dubious about the possibility of a repetition of Mr. Kipling's success by an American poet.

Turning to other topics Mr. Frost, who is a Professor of English at Amherst College, declared American literature was in an exceedingly healthy condition.

"Thirty years ago, to my own personal knowledge, American literature was seldom spoken of in colleges," he said. "Now students are hearing it treated with respect, and that means a lot."

In what he termed the "peace and quietude of farms"—and the New Englander has probably written as much verse about farm and countryside as any other American poet—Mr. Frost believes men can find a solution for unrest.

"I have always thought that if I were a king, and if there were a row of buttons in front of me to press, I'd press the one which would strengthen farming," he said. "Farming has languished. It's the kind of life you'd hate to see a country lose. They've lost it too much in England now."

The poet, white hair gleaming above ruddy face, looked dreamily into space. But he was not thinking of mending walls—the theme of one of his most famous poems—nor of a New England countryside under snow. He had turned again to politics.

"Two lines from one of my earlier verses really sum up my whole viewpoint," he asserted. "The poem ran:

I never dared be radical when young
For fear it would make me conservative when old."

Editorial from the Baltimore *Sun*, February 27, 1936:

RECRUIT LEGISLATOR

"Poets" Shelley wrote in "A Defence of Poetry," "are the hierophants of an unapprehended inspiration; the mirrors of the gigantic shadows which futurity casts upon the present. . . ." And in a shorter and even more famous sentence, "Poets are the unacknowledged legislators of the World." Many doubtless have recalled his words with satisfaction at times when they sat in darkness and sang to cheer their own solitude.

Recent years, however, have found the poets using Shelley's dictum for more than solace; construing it in a very literal sense, and thinking of their legislative powers in terms of laws of Congress and Parliament. Certainly they are no longer content to see their legislative proposals pass "unacknowledged." They have been eager enough to declare their political position in their work. And it would be difficult plausibly to argue that by so doing they outran Shelley's meaning, for he was, in part, very much the propagandist poet. Anyway, the reader has no right to object to a writer's concern with politics so long as those "gigantic shadows of futurity" do not utterly obscure the bright mirror of his verse.

The latest poet to turn legislator, it seems, is Mr. Robert Frost, whose "To a Thinker" was quoted in *The Sun* of yesterday. But Mr. Frost's enrollment in the ranks of the lawmakers is unusual in two ways. His verses and his comments upon them make it clear that he has not joined the camp of the poetical Left—easily the larger at present time. And he says with great modesty that he doubts that his poem will have much influence. This uncertainty about the effect of the raising of his voice is one with his eagerness to point out that he is not really "horribly anti-Roosevelt."

Probably really moving poetry, whether it be of the "anti-Jacobin" kind or the somewhat subtler sort that comes now from the younger English poets, can be written only out of strong feeling, never out of a wish to be fair all around, to say just so much and no more and then to temper and explain what has been said. Surely Kipling, whose success Mr. Frost aptly recalls, never wrote in any such spirit. No, it is doubtful that Mr. Frost is a lawmaker after all, however he ranks as poet. But, of course, he will not concede that much. The last line of his "To a Thinker" tells us unqualifiedly that he feels he is in the right as a legislator even if the fact goes unacknowledged.

Editorial from *The New York Times*,
February 28, 1936:

POET IN POLITICS

Waiting for a train in Baltimore Mr. Robert Frost was caught by a reporter of its *Sun*. Conforming to the custom of the place, he talked politics. He even produced a political poem. His first venture in a field new to him, so far as we know, is called "To a Thinker." Mr. Roosevelt is the addressee. Even at the risk of taking liberties with copyright, the first few lines must be borrowed to whet the curiosity of the great army of Frostians:

> The last step taken found your heft
> Decidedly upon the left.
> One more would throw you on the right.
> Another still—you see your plight.
> You call this thinking, but it's walking.

It must be admitted that walkers habitually use the left foot and the right. Mr. Frost admires [. . . birches] because they bend to the left and right. If he walks much in Vermont, he must have to take a good many sharp turns. If he implies that Mr. Roosevelt's thought is pedestrian, the implication is a compliment. A statesman who has his feet on the ground can't very well have his head in the clouds. So the poet contradicts himself when, inspired perhaps by the Liberty League oracle, he tells the President:

> Just now you're off democracy
> (With a polite regret to be),
> And leaning on dictatorship.

But he'll be a Democrat again if he'll take Mr. Frost's tip. For
Mr. Roosevelt, the walker who doesn't think, is a "reasoner and
good as such." Mr. Frost is playful and benign. Not for him the
absurd vehemence of Coventry Patmore, straying into politics, or
the bitterness of William Watson. He winds up with a jest:

> So if you find you must repent
> From side to side in argument,
> At least don't use your mind too hard,
> But trust my instinct—I'm a bard.

In his political prose Mr. Frost jabs the Administration for looking on farmers as possessors of "submarginal minds." But he's a
Vermonter by adoption. "I'm going to stay a Democrat if I have to
push everyone else out of the party but Carter Glass." So "Yankees
are what they always were"; and Mr. Frost, like Brown who made
the Willy-Nilly Slide, is a "politician at odd seasons."

Letter to Henry Goddard Leach of *The Forum*:

[*Originally called "To a Thinker," the poem had first been
printed, with the extended title "To a Thinker in Office," in*
The Saturday Review of Literature *for January 11, 1936,
six weeks before RF's Baltimore interview; and it was soon to
appear in RF's book* A Further Range. *The following letter
responds to a request that* The Forum *be permitted to
publish it.*]

15 March 1936   Cambridge

DEAR MR LEACH

Here is the offending poem. It is already in book form and about
to be published. It first appeared in The Saturday Review. I am
sorry you are too late. I should have liked you to have it in The
Forum. You will see that it was only by restriction of meaning that
it was narrowed down to fit the President. Changing the title from

: 87 :

"To a Thinker" to "To a Thinker in Office" helped do the business. As a matter of fact it was written three years ago and was aimed at the heads of our easy despairers of the republic and of parliamentary forms of government. I encounter too many such and my indignation mounts till it overflows in rhyme. I doubt if my native delicacy would have permitted me to use the figure of walking and rocking in connection with a person of the President's personal infirmities. But I am willing to let it go as aimed at him. He must deserve it or people wouldn't be so quick to see him in it.

Sometime soon I'll hope to have something for you—political or unpolitical. Thank you for the kindness of both your letters.

Sincerely yours

ROBERT FROST

"I say let the sheep and the goats run together...."

This text appeared in the Burlington, Vermont, Free Press and Times *on August 19, 1936, where its main heading read, "Poet Would Give Young Folks More Time to Find Themselves."*

The article, which reveals, in part, something of the climate of the depression years, resulted from an interview done, according to its dateline, at South Shaftsbury on August 18th.

T HEY say 'you can't make a silk purse out of a sow's ear,'" said Robert Frost, "but who knows whether you can or not?"

Mr. Frost was talking about public education, a subject upon which he is considered an authority of unusual astuteness, for that insight which has made him a poet of international reputation has given him also a keen understanding of the problems of youth. That his reputation in this field is recognized is evident from the fact that so many colleges have found or made a place for him on their faculty, believing that even if their students got nothing else from him, the mere contact would be of lasting benefit to them.[. . .]

"The interesting thing about education in the United States," he said, "is that hitherto we have generally made it possible for most anyone to go as far in any direction as he seemed willing and capable. More recently, however, there seems to be evident a tendency to cut down on education—to curtail appropriations, close down schools, and cut down teaching staffs—and to say to students, 'Get just what you need and call it quits.'

"This tendency has alarmed a good many people, for they see in it a dangerous implication. However, I am not alarmed, especially for us in New England. The tradition of having a good, general education available for anyone who wants to get it is too strongly rooted among the New Englanders. I believe we'll go on thinking that everybody should get as much education as possible for a long time yet.

"Economic conditions may cause us to cut down somewhat on our educational program, but as soon as conditions become better you will find us back where we were. We will begin asking ourselves, 'Have we reached a point of being glutted in education, and are we going on a diet?' And I think the answer will be, 'No.' We are too used to having education around where young people can get at it."

Advocating the extension of general education and the postponement of specialization until later years, Mr. Frost said, "I'd like to see more young folks continue with their general education up to the age of eighteen or twenty and not begin to concentrate on specific fields too early in life. We ought to give a boy or girl at least eighteen or twenty years to learn all he can about the world he is living in and to find himself out.

"Sometimes a person's real character is slow in blossoming. Until I was fourteen I had never read a book. I thought, and those who knew me thought, I was more mechanically minded than anything else. But after I had read my first book a new world opened up for me, and after that I devoured as many of them as I could lay my hands on. By the time I was fifteen I was already beginning to write verses.

"That's why I didn't like to see the attempts some educators are making to separate the sheep from the goats at too early a stage. They say 'you can't make a silk purse out of a sow's ear,' but who knows whether you can or not. I say let the sheep and the goats run together for a good long while and eventually they will separate themselves.

"It is true that some people seem to have a word-gift and nothing else, but it won't hurt them to get as much general education over as wide a field as possible. I myself, for instance, have a great itch to do wood-carving, but I know that I will never be able to do any wood cuts, because I never learned how to draw. Now if I had learned just a little bit about drawing in public school, I know I would get a great deal of satisfaction out of making wood cuts.

"Yes, I say let the sheep and the goats run together. You've got to leave something to accident and not try to regiment young people so much.

"Some college presidents are threatening not to give the goats a chance. They want to give a student a standardized test and if he doesn't measure up to their standardized marks, out he goes. But it seems to me that any teacher that takes any sort of standardized system of marking too seriously is a fool. As you associate with people as teacher and fellow-student you get to know their qualities, some of which may have nothing to do with books and cannot be measured by marks.

"No, we don't want to be too rigorous and trust our judgments too much. Most young people don't even know themselves, so how can anyone else know them? I say, let them run around loose in the pasture for a while."

An Annotated Interview

In 1940 the International Mark Twain Society published A Chat with Robert Frost *by Cyril Clemens, President of the Society. It was based on a conversation with RF which was identified as having taken place at St. Louis in March of 1937.*

The text pages of the little booklet are here reproduced from a copy now in the Barrett Collection at the University of Virginia Library. Identifying this as the "First fully annotated copy," RF in December 1944 penned marginal notes of comment and correction on nearly every printed page.

His observation at the opening of the account reads: "Due allowance must be made in all this for the interviewers imagination, sense of form and will to make me as presentable as possible. There are certainly startling vestiges of me all through it." At the close of the text, however, he has added: "But on the whole I have to hand it to Cyril for his friendly way of supplying me with language."

A Chat with Robert Frost

When Robert Frost reached St. Louis in March, 1937, to receive the Mark Twain Medal, the writer had the pleasure of an informal talk with him on literary matters now for the first time set down from notes taken at the time.

Sixty-two years old at the time, Frost gave one the impression of being hale and hearty· His head was topped with a shock of white hair and his blue eyes had a peculiar. bright, uplifted look. They were truly poetic eyes, but otherwise he looked just like a farmer; indeed, he took pride in being just that. He talked freely in a husky, but not unpleasant, New England voice.

"Are you in the habit of taking any notes when you read," I asked as we seated ourselves.

"I have always had an aversion to annotating books as I read," remarked Frost. "What you can't remember probably isn't worth remembering. It is what clings to people that makes them what they are. Two people who have lived together all their lives are different because they have chosen to remember different things."

"Not long ago," he continued, "a man asked me what I thought was the worst thing about the United States and what I thought was the best thing. He was asking a lot of people that and writing a book about their answers. I didn't answer him because I couldn't

7

think of anything bright at the time. But afterwards it occurred to me the worst thing about not only the United States but the world, is its lack of faith in disinterestedness. We try to see a personal or ulterior motive in everything· The highest faith there is, is faith in disinterestedness."

After a while Frost continued:

"In my boyhood I read the radical works of Edward Bellamy and Henry George but I have never been a radical. I wrote a two line poem once. It was,

" 'I never dared be radical when young
   For fear I might be conservative
       when old.'

"I can stand a great deal of change in politics. But what I care about isn't settled by elections. I was brought up a Cleveland Democrat and in an off-hand, playful way I've remained that."

Frost was soon talking of philosophy,

"Unlike the Humanists who would perform a sort of latter day renaissance of classical thought in order to start mankind again on the classical pattern, I believe we can accomplish the same thing without reference to the past. I believe mankind continues in a sort of circle duplicating not only the thought but the social experience of bygone generations—all without conscious imitation of antecedents.

"I sometimes have the whimsical desire to see all civilization obliterated in order to stand, timeless at some cosmic vantage point and watch the slow, painful process of rebuilding.

"I would look down and see here a priest appear, and there a father, and there a mother and there a child, and so on until the whole works came back

8

again. The thing is that with certain shadings the thoughts and institutions of men reappear· We don't need to go back to the Greeks and Romans to think like they did. We can do it if we will just let ourselves loose."

"As I said before my poems come from nowhere. Things I had been through and hadn't noticed at the time later come to me when I write," he explained. "In forty-five years, I have produced but six books. The only time I ever wrote on an assigned subject was when I worked on a newspaper.

"Occasionally I am a bit ashamed when a technical name of a flower gets in one of my poems because I feel a poet should not include in his writing anything that the average reader will not easily understand."

Asked if he read the criticisms of his works, Frost replied,

"I sometimes do, but recently when one critic described me as 'non-intellectual,' I didn't read the rest of the criticism. I would very much dislike being a critic or a 'poetry taster' because such work would drive me crazy. Nonetheless I believe I do read more of my contemporaries' work than do most other poets."

"Did you read Edgar Lee Masters' recent biography of Vachel Lindsay?"

"Not yet," answered the poet, "but I have been meaning to, for I am an admirer of Vachel's work—so thoroughly and completely American. What, for instance, could be more native than 'Adventures While Preaching the Gospel of Beauty' or 'A Handy Guide for Beggars'? It always grieves me to reflect that his writings brought him such small financial returns. In this land of plenty and abundance he prac-

9

tically lived in want. I managed to se-
cure a number of lecture engagements
for him, but my efforts were only a
drop in the bucket."

"The very year of his tragic death,"
I said, " a professional reciter appear-
ing before a St. Louis woman's club
received the incredible sum of five hundred dollars for recitals of Lindsay's
poetry. While the poet counted himself
lucky if he could obtain fifty or a hundred dollars for a reading from his own
work! How do you account for it?"

"Well, for one thing, Lindsay possessed a strong aversion to anything
that smacked of self-advertising, and
he hated the mere thought of 'forcing'
himself before the public. I understand
that his friends kept urging him to let
a lecture bureau handle his engagements, but apparently without success.
There may have been in the back of his
head, the idea that such affiliation
would tend to commercialize his recitals. But if he had taken the step,
doubtless all his financial troubles
would have ended."

Upon my mentioning that I was concluding a biography of Father Prout,
Frost seemed interested,

"Isn't that the nom de plume of
Francis Sylvester Mahony who wrote
the graceful "Bells of Shandon"?—one
of the things I know by heart. I was
also fond of some Irish humorous verse
entitled, 'The Night Before Larry was
Stretched.' Do you know the doggerel?"

"Indeed I do. I'll recite the first
stanza right off,

" 'The night before Larry was stretched,
The boys they all paid him a visit;
A bit in their sacks, too, they
    fetched—
They sweated their duds till they riz it;
For Larry was always the lad,
When a friend was condemned to the
    squeezer,
But he'd pawn all the togs that he had,
Just to help the poor boy to a
    sneezer,
And moisten his gob 'fore he died.' "

"Yes, that's it and a rollicking piece, too," smiled Frost. "Who's the author?"

"I am pretty sure Mahony is, for the piece appears in the 'Reliques of Father Prout' — a wholly delightful book for dipping into whenever one feels a bit gloomy. Prout can always be relied upon to evoke a smile or a laugh from his reader. If my forthcoming biography makes him better known to American readers my pains shall be well repaid."

Frost then remarked that it was to be regretted that each generation allows its trashy, ephemeral writings to crowd out the worthwhile literature. The former attracts attention just long enough to distract the reader and then literary weeds wither away when the harm has been done; and the genuine stuff comes back slowly—if at all."

Soon we were talking about Mark Twain. Like most Americans, Frost's boyhood was made the happier by the *I knew him best in short things, his joke pieces.* reading and re-reading of "Huckleberry Finn," "Tom Sawyer" and the other immortal Twain works. What impressed Frost most were the "little touches of nature description that appear here and there so unobtrusively,

11

yet so effectively. You recall the time Tom awoke by the pirate-camp fire,

" 'It was the cool gray dawn, and there was a delicious sense of repose and peace in the deep pervading calm and silence of the woods. Not a leaf stirred; not a sound obtruded upon great Nature's meditation. Beaded dewdrops stood upon the leaves and grasses. A white layer of ashes covered the fire and a thin breath of smoke rose straight into the air.' "

"What is your favorite work, Mr. Frost?"

"I never care to pick favorites, especially as regards authors that I highly esteem, but I like a shorter piece he has done as well as anything, 'The Jumping Frog of Calaveras County,' than which nothing American in prose or verse is more lyric to my ear. The story is a great parable in education and a poem in cadence. Mark Twain and Emerson have been the two greatest literary influences thus far exerted to make Americans what they are."

Frost had such a passage as the following in his mind when he spoke of the lyricism of "The Jumping Frog,"

"But as soon as the money was up on him, he was a different dog; his under-jaw'd begin to stick out like the fo--castle of a steamboat, and his teeth would uncover, and shine savage like the furnaces. And a dog might tackle him, and bully-rag him, and bite him, and throw him over his shoulder two or three times, and Andrew Jackson—which was the name of the Pup—Andrew Jackson would never let on but what he was satisfied, and hadn't expected nothing else—and the bets being doubled and doubled on the other side all the time, till the money was all

12

up; and then all of a sudden he would grab that other dog jest by the j'int of his hind leg and freeze to it—not chaw, you understand, but only jest grip and hang on till they throwed up the sponge, if it was a year."

When I mentioned that the late A. E. Housman had once told me that the Ode to Stephen Dowling Botts in "Huckleberry Finn" was one of the pieces he knew by heart, Frost commented,

"Strangely enough just a few weeks ago I was reciting that poem aloud to myself—which I must have memorized when I first read the book as a lad in Lawrence, Massachusetts. How the quaint lines linger with one,

"They got him out and emptied him;
Alas, it was too late;
His spirit was gone for to sport aloft
In the realms of the good and great·"

"I have lately been reading Thomas Love Peacock's 'Gryll Grange' which always acts upon me as a tonic. Do you get much time for novels?"

"No, never have I read many novels, and of late extremely few. I suppose it is because I am too lazy to cover anybody's life—even in a fictionized form. I'm largely living my own. I only wish the summers were longer and I would set them an example of laziness that would stand till the next Olympics!"

"When do you do most of your work, Mr. Frost?"

"I have spells. They come in flocks and I like a little break in between."

Hearing of my suggestion to propose him to succeed the recently deceased John Drinkwater as Chairman of the

13

Mark Twain Society's Poetry Committee, Frost declared,

"It will never do for you to make me chairman of your poetry committee. I make it an absolute rule to hold no responsible offices in connection with the arts. I am sorry to have to turn down your kind suggestion so pre-emptorily, but poetry to me is writing and reading—not offices and positions in societies. You have to take poetry in your way, I have to take it in mine."

Our delightful "gossip" had now to come to an end, for time was passing, which — according to old Artemus Ward—is a habit time has, but let me assure all that in real life, Robert Frost fully measures up to his books—which cannot be said for every author.

But on the whole I have hand. it to bynd for his friendly way of supplying me with language. R.F.

14

A Visit on Beacon Hill

Having in the previous year resigned, following Mrs. Frost's death, from another period on the Amherst College faculty, RF in 1939 accepted appointment as Ralph Waldo Emerson Fellow in Poetry at Harvard.

Interviewed in his Boston apartment at 88 Mount Vernon Street by Associated Press representative Francis E. Carey, the poet's remarks, as here reported, relate not only to certain of his thoughts on pedagogy and life, but reflect, also, signs of the war then getting underway in Europe.

The text is reproduced from the Springfield, Massachusetts, Sunday Union and Republican *of November 12, 1939.*

R OBERT FROST, the famed poet-farmer who was allergic to colleges in his youth, is back at one of his part-time alma maters as a lecturer—all keyed up about helping to make colleges become "factories for turning out human self-starters."

Self-styled "holder of numerous honorary degrees but no honest ones," the Pulitzer Prize-winning muse of New England farms, stone walls, and people already has started at Harvard the closest thing to a formal class he has had in the last twelve years of lecturing at institutions which have been "so patient with my educational heresies."[. . .]

He will give marks, of a sort, but they will be secondary. Frost says he'll do most of the talking, but if mere talking won't stir up some enterprise among his hearers, "I'll just keep silent, or even lie down on the desk, until it is realized that what I want is self-starters, not followers of a set routine."

One night a week, in a little counsel room at Harvard's Adams House with a group of forty undergrads and graduate students, will be Frost's stint. Between times, he will visit his Vermont farm or travel about the country giving lectures—perhaps, doing a little private horse-trading on the side.

"In the West," he smiled as he slouched down in his easy chair in his Beacon Hill apartment, "I shall try to steal a Morgan horse and bring the stock back to Vermont where it belongs."

No rustic house "by the side of the road" is the hill-top citadel for Frost's present musings. From the window of his smartly furnished apartment he can look down on historic Louisburg Square with its cobbled streets and ancient lamps under which, at Christmastime, strolling carollers fill the crisp air with their singing.

To Frost, who says, "A poem begins with a lump in the throat," the Hill has not yet led to verse, but it has been "the nearest thing to a Vermont mountain" he has found for his daily walks. He also has been shopping around for a tennis partner, but, so far, there's been no luck.

When he's at home the poet dons a pair of low blue sneakers, white duck trousers, and a sack coat worn over an open-collar white shirt. A shock of unruly white hair tops off a wise, weathered face; and when he talks it is with a quiet, humorous voice.

Compared, through the years, to everything from puck-in-a-sack-suit to a Yankee hired man, Frost can change his conversation from talk alive with epigram to the homey, earthy speech of some of his New England poems.

"The world," he mused, "is swaying to the left and to the right. It is a drunken world, going home we know not where, but the important thing to realize is that it is not swaying too far to the left or too far to the right."

He is recognized today as one of America's foremost poets, but there were times when he worked as a mill hand, a country schoolteacher, a shoemaker, and a writer of poems which "did not bring enough money to buy salt with."

And yet—"My life has been all holidays, whether it has been work or play. The secret? I say it is this: Never allow yourself to become a 'case' if you can help it; and never froth at the mouth about things.

"That's the trouble with too many people. They froth at the mouth because they're reading the same newspaper too much. They get all scared about what they think Germany's going to do. They get all worried about 'Reds' in the country. They get all frothed up about what's going to become of democracy. And all the time they forget that there are limitations to all things, that there always is a balance to everything."

Once he expressed it another way in verse:

> Let the downpour roil and toil!
> The worst it can do to me
> Is carry some garden soil
> A little nearer the sea.

The Harvard catalogue lists Frost's course simply as "Poetry," so he thinks he'll have a lot of leeway.

"I can talk politics under that heading," he grinned. "I'll tell the boys the world speaks to them and they have to answer back. I'll tell them always to have something to say or they will be on their way to become 'cases.' Say something to Hitler, to Chamberlain, or to the drama; but say something—something with a kick in it."

He is settling in a world-famed university, convinced that "the things most like the arts in a college are the college sports."

"It's live or die in a football game," he said, "and that's the way it should be with writing. One should not write just for the practice of writing as is done in classroom routine. One should write only when he has something to say, and then it should be live or die, as in the football game."

It was because "I only wanted to write when I could write for keeps" that he ran away from Dartmouth when he was seventeen. And that's why he "walked the streets of Cambridge night after night" when later he was a student at Harvard. That's why he has preached through the years against "routine and curriculum."

And today:

> They would not find me changed from him they knew—
> Only more sure of all I thought was true.

·IV·

THE FORTIES

Of Baseball Shoes, Poverty,
War, Simplification, et cetera

"Frost Owes Success to Not Swallowing Nails" is the headline
*under which this interview by Henry Lee was originally print-
ed in the February 4, 1941,* New York World-Telegram.
*Mention is here made of the painful consequences suffered
by RF from having accepted an assignment to write a poem
for Harvard's tercentennial celebration in 1936, as well as
to his preparation of a new book of poetry* (A Witness Tree)
*and a volume of prose (a project never completed by RF).
Published a year later, in the spring of 1942,* A Witness
Tree *earned RF's fourth Pulitzer Prize (an honor shared by
no other writer)—*A Further Range *having won the third,
six years before.*

T HE last person who interviewed Robert Frost was a lady reporter in Florida.

"She looked down at my feet," Mr. Frost said today in the office
of his publishers, Henry Holt and Company, 257 Fourth Avenue,
"and said, 'Why, Mr. Frost, you've got baseball shoes on.' "[. . .]

"After she said that," he explained cheerfully, "I knew that no
matter what I said the shoes would be the story. So I said, 'Yes,
baseball shoes, but without any cleats on them.' "

Today he was most cautiously dressed: a gray, academic-looking
suit, a blue-figured tie that was lost under the ample collars of his
white shirt, conventional walking shoes. He is rugged and elderly,
with the leathery face of an outdoors man, his white hair cut square

in the Elihu Root style. His manner is so simple that he might be a retired small-town businessman, even a farmer, which he is; almost anything but a poet.

"People ask me what most influenced my life," he said in somewhat pained fashion, "what book or what event I owe the most to.

"Well, when I was twelve I worked in a little shoeshop, and all summer I carried nails in my mouth. I owe everything to the fact that I neither swallowed nor inhaled. But my grandchildren— they're not the man I was; they'd swallow the nails.

"Now don't make me out a hero or say who's nicer to the proletariat, me or someone else.

"A woman said to me once, 'You've written so nicely about the poor.' And I said, 'If I did that, it was when I was so poor myself that I was looking up to them.' It's neither the rich nor the poor that I was writing about. Just about people like us."

Unlike more tropical souls among the poets who have shrivelled under the cold water of Hitlerian realism, Mr. Frost falls back on New England's heritage of chronic adversity. He has the Yankee's vinegary caution and serene balance—caution of England and her ways, though he admits owing much to English recognition— balance in an almost fatalistic assumption that if war must come, it must come. In fact, to a woman who moaned of dire, impending things he had the perfect answer.

" 'I wish they would come with less talk and more bloodshed,' I told her. She was horrified."

And he said, "I have an admiration for England, but I would let them keep my admiration by winning their own war."

With an economy of word and directness of thought, he talked of characters he has known.

"He's an old-time humorist," he said of one, "and he has ceased to be funny."

Then there was the New England banker whom he knew—

"He entertained me by driving me around in a car and showing me all the empty properties the bank owned."

And the people who always counter, "Ah, but aren't you oversimplifying?"—

"Every act is a great simplification," he said earnestly. "The act of electing the President of the United States is a simplification.

Twenty-two million people are eliminated, and twenty-five million people count.

"All heroes are ruthless simplifiers who don't stick at trifles. There are three or four in the world right now. And we only hope that our hero will out-simplify the other heroes."

At the moment he is annoyed and somewhat flustered by people who are trying to marshal poetry for national defense. To him poetry is emotion in reminiscence, and he can't evoke or analyze feelings for a special occasion. Once, recently, when he consented to write a commemorative ode he fled to a farm in Vermont, got the shingles from worry, and had to give it up.

"I won't come out and tell them in words of one syllable," he said. "It's sort of cheapening. What I am isn't gotten up for democracy. Either I have written it or I never will write it.

"Of course, I think: Who am I to say I must do a thing well? Better I should do a great thing badly.

"But I just got stuck; I always fail. I tried, like an honest and modest—please give me credit for the modesty—man, and I got the shingles on my face. People say the shingles are from worry. I can't write on assignment."

Everything he has ever written, he said, comes from the people and things he knew in a little circle that runs from Derry[, New Hampshire,] down to Lawrence, Massachusetts. He says he deprecates sectionalism, except in humor, but unconsciously he compares all other land to New England.

He talked, enviously, of Iowa's "rich land—different than ours—and the fatted cattle they have." Of Florida, where he is starting a modest orange grove near Cocoanut Grove, which has "funny land." And he told the story of a Westerner who watched a Vermonter hoeing his thin soil and commiserated with him on the difficulty of making a living there:

"Well, we make a living, and a little more than a living," said the Vermonter, "and what more than a living we make—we invest that in Western farm mortgages."

"But in the words of the old song," he added hastily, " 'any little state that's a nice little state is the state for me.' "

He said, in proof, that he now lives in Ripton, Vermont (not New Hampshire), where he has two farms.

Right now he is preparing another book of poems and a book of prose which will come out this spring containing, among the few prefaces and speeches he has saved, a curious essay entitled "How You Can't Know How Bad the Times Are."

"Every generation remakes the past in its own image," he explained. "The Victorians, for example, rewrote the history of Rome. You can just know your own life—and you like to stay around to see certain outcomes."

Because of this curiosity he would like to explore politics a little deeper—as a Congressman, he says, though he thinks the times and methods of politicians are "bullying."

"You'd better not say I will run from Vermont," he said reflectively. "Vermont hasn't heard about it yet."

As Reported on Campus

The years of World War II and its immediate aftermath were ones of activity for RF: teaching, writing, and traveling to far-scattered places to talk and "say" his poems.

In 1943, he resigned his post at Harvard to become George Ticknor Fellow in the Humanities at Dartmouth. Then, in 1949, he accepted appointment as Amherst's Simpson Lecturer in Literature, an association he was to continue through the remaining years of his life.

In his travels—"barding around," he called it—RF was a familiar visitor to colleges and universities all across the country. His countless interviews done for undergraduate publications are here represented by a selection of seven, ranging over the period 1944–1954.

The Harvard Service News, May 16, 1944:

"WAR has not taken the minds of the people off literature," declared Robert Frost, famous New England poet, who is now in Cambridge to give his third reading of the season for service men on May nineteenth. Having just completed a tour of America, during which he gave a series of these readings, Frost found that despite the preoccupation with war news, the people still were highly interested in all forms of the arts.

A two-fold problem exists, Frost pointed out. One is how much attention war should give poetry, and the other is how much attention poetry should give war. The seventy-year-old poet mentioned

General Wavell's latest anthology of verse, *Other Men's Flowers*, which contained only a minimum of war poetry.

At Vanderbilt, Frost found a strong literary movement in progress. "The Agrarians," a group which included John Crowe Ransom, Allen Tate, Robert Penn Warren, and William Y. Elliott, had become increasingly important and influential, much in the tradition of the old literary groups at Harvard and Yale.

Clarifying the meaning of "Mending Wall," Frost denied that he had any [. . .] allegory in mind other than the impossibility of drawing sharp lines and making exact distinctions between good and bad or between almost any two abstractions. There is no rigid separation between right and wrong. "Mending Wall" simply contrasts two types of people. One says, "Something there is that doesn't love a wall." And the other replies, "Good fences make good neighbors."

Though political implications can be read into almost all of his poetry, Frost denies that he had them in mind while writing the verses. He believes that after a man has written a poem others often give it a new and false meaning; he calls this "the play of wit."[. . .]

Frost's consideration that equality is both an ideal and an illusion has influenced his philosophy of "Let me be the one to do what is done." It is better to be the helper than the helped, he feels. Despite the present Administration's attempts to do everything for the individual, Frost still supports portions of it, because of a personal friendship with many of the leaders, including Vice-President Wallace.

Maintaining that the present Administration is more interested in promoting the arts than any previous one has been, the poet declared that most of the programs have been successful. He believes that most of these state-sponsored programs are mere dilettantism and do not tend to produce great artists.

Developing his idea of equality, Frost rejects the idea of socialized medicine as breeding class distinctions. Although socialized medicine will lead to greater security among the poor, Frost believes it will cause those who can afford it to seek their own private doctors and, consequently, will widen the gap between the privileged and underprivileged classes.

As to the Communistic experiment in Russia, the poet asserted that they have already been forced to recognize the advantages of advancement and promotion.

"Although I knew complete equality could never be achieved," stated Frost, "I'm glad they tried it."

"I judge a man by his anecdotes," commented Frost. "If he always attaches a famous name to them, like the 'last time I saw the Duke of So-and-so,' then I don't like him nearly as much as the man whose anecdotes are about the common people and common, everyday things."

This attitude of sympathy with the country folk and the simple people who make up the bulk of our population has remained with Frost despite his great success. Unlike other authors, who wouldn't be seen with anyone but a well-known man, Frost still enjoys chatting with an old-time friend.[. . .]

By Fred Schott,
The Michigan Daily, April 4, 1947:

The students who were able to talk to Robert Frost yesterday were no less pleased than he was.

"It's the nicest kind of a thing, to be able to talk with the young people here," he said in an interview yesterday.

Although somewhat surprised by the throng of students now in school, he said that he liked a big school.

"It's a good place to lose yourself in, if you want to."

He said he was interested in how the student veterans came out of the war.

"I hope they aren't mad at the world," he said. "Especially the writers. I think maybe some of the most bitter books about the war got written by those who saw the least meaning in it."

Always happy to talk poetry with students, Frost says he doesn't like to be called a teacher.

"I don't give marks or anything," he said. "I have a room in the library at Dartmouth, and I have just a few students come and see me. I'm not so much interested in their writing as I am in their thinking."

He said he sometimes sends students rummaging through secondhand bookstores looking for odd bits of "Americana."

"Once someone discovered a very old little book written by a farmer who had witnessed the beginning of the Revolutionary War. It was an authentic and curious little thing, full of bad spelling and all that."

His real interest, he said, is in this "Americana."

"Some people have called me a nature poet, because of the background, but I'm not a nature poet. There's always something else in my poetry."

He did remember one nature poem, however, that he wrote when he lived in Ann Arbor.

"I lived out on Pontiac Road then," he said. "One night I sat alone by my open fireplace and wrote 'Spring Pools.' It was a very pleasant experience, and I remember it clearly, although I don't remember the writing of many of my other poems."

Then, speaking of poetry in general, Frost said that sheer emotion doesn't explain it.

"All this rolling around on the floor and kicking and screaming isn't poetry. It must be controlled: emotion must be harnessed to a wit-mill and turned out carefully."[. . .]

By James H. Wheatley,
The Dartmouth, April 18, 1950:

Sitting in the living room of the home of a friend in Hanover yesterday, Robert Frost answered a variety of questions on a variety of subjects.

"There's something of a fashion today of deliberate obfuscation in poetry," he said in reply to a query on the bewildering complexity of modern poetry. "And there are always readers who like to be literary snobs and think that they're understanding something that nobody else does."

But the famous American poet doesn't think that poetry should be too simple.

"There's no fun in telling something that's apparent from the start. You want to keep 'em with you until the last paragraph, and let them see it unfold."

How about people who want to know just what he means in a certain poem?

"I tell 'em that if I wanted them to know what I was saying I would have told them. There's a certain reserve in all of us. Didn't Shakespeare say it, 'I refuse to have the heart plucked out of my mystery'?"

A discussion of literary revivals inevitably led to F. Scott Fitzgerald.

"At the time he died, no one had read him for five years. Then a couple of friends got people to reading him again. The same thing happened with John Donne about thirty-five years ago. Those things just happen."

What about poets as critics?

With the exception of such professional editors as T. S. Eliot, Mr. Frost felt that "these fellas waste their time having opinions. I just don't criticize."

Mr. Frost did not believe that trends in poetry followed current trends in prose or even that there was any particular trend in poetry today.

"We're striking out in a lot of new directions, and there's so much experimenting going on. It's the same in every kind of art," he said.

Robert Frost felt that every poet is "having fun with his poetry." Only in the case of some modern authors, the "fun" takes a radically different form. As for himself:

"I just take poetry easy."

By Richard Watt,
The Dartmouth, November 28, 1951:

"Projects?" Robert Frost answered, sinking farther into his chair, all of him looking relaxed except his mind. "Oh, I'm always having those, and then dropping them. My writing never comes out of them. Tonight's talk was something like a project, I suppose."

He meant, as always, that a poem has to have surprise, "something you didn't know you knew." But that didn't dismiss the Great Issues lecture he had just given; he'd been surprised by a few of the things he'd said. And the audience was the other half.

But the toughest part of the talk was the chance of having some people there who only had to come—their project.

"I'm always skeptical about education. But I'm always around, always interested. Take most of my young friends, writing more in a year than I do in twenty years. Papers, projects! And reading more than I've done in a lifetime."

Which sounded a little like his story of the student who'd "studied ten civilizations before Christmas."

"I'd like to see more free agents, people who don't act like they're majoring in something. I admire people who neglect their studies for dancing or sports. And especially those who neglect them to study, of course.

"Maybe they have to decide to take a lower mark, but usually it isn't even conscious. At best, they don't have any choice. Of course the pressure of the institution counts for something: to learn to pay the price for what you care for. Education may be to learn to take boredom and injustice—and to learn to read.

"That's what I tell high-school seniors: that college is a second chance to learn to read. If they know already, maybe they oughtn't to take any chances on forgetting. But the pressure's there, the burden of responsibility."

"That's one of the ideas that came out with all this birthday stuff about me in the papers. I was misquoted all over the country. I told a reporter maybe everyone should have twenty acres, to teach more responsibility.

"He got it all wrong. People started writing from all over, taking it for a new 'right.' And someone tried proving to me that there aren't twenty good acres of land for everyone, not enough to go around.

"That isn't what I meant. Twenty acres of forest, or desert even: to go hunting in or go be a saint in—and pay taxes on, whatever the rate. Lots of possibilities. Might make people think of staying home instead of starting wars. You can't tell."

By Patsy McKenna and Alan Gussow,
The Middlebury Campus, May 15, 1952:

"A poem is a little voyage of discovery."

Robert Frost said it in the car as we drove him up to Ripton Saturday morning. He had spent the winter away from his summer home, but the rugged profile under the weather-beaten brown hat showed little emotion. He was talking about poetry.

"If there isn't any surprise for the poet in writing it," he said, "there won't be any for the reader. A poem should have a quality of dawning."

A fat brown-and-white rabbit thumped by the car and kept us company through the town of Ripton.

"A domesticated rabbit," observed Frost in the middle of commenting on man's unfortunate willingness to depend on psychiatry.

"You've got to go it alone," he said. "Men should learn to contain their own poison."

We were almost to the Breadloaf School when Frost said, "That's my road." It was a dead end.

"It used to go up over the hill," he said, "but it's closed up now so there aren't so many people going by."

Off in one corner of the field three men were chopping wood in the sun. Mr. Dragon, the caretaker, met Mr. Frost midway of the front lawn. A starved 'coon, trapped under the barn all winter, was the problem of the moment, and we all went over to see it. Brown and mangy, it lay curled in a sunny corner of the field. Mr. Frost and the caretaker, though worried about the corn the coon would eat when it got well, let it lie.

Over by the unpainted lower house a few peony sprouts defied the last tang of winter air. Frost laid his coat, hat, and a bag of sandwiches on the ground and walked up to the house. He almost ran up the last little hill, and we had to hurry to keep up with him.

The house still smelled of winter. Chintz drapes covered the furniture, and a copy of Einstein's *Theory of Relativity* lay on the table.

"Yes," he said of a Healy water color hanging in the corner, "that's the place down where the road turns off."

He took us on a tour of the house, proudly pointing out a new den and bedroom he had designed and added on last year.

Out in the sunshine again, the three of us climbed the hill to the log cabin where Frost spends most of his time.

"I must see how my trees have wintered," he said, and paused to examine a row of young fruit trees. "A mouse's been at this one," he said, and then went on to see whether any of the other saplings had been "girdled."

At the upper end of the orchard was his "nursery," a collection of rusty tin cans holding a few baby plants. Frost was pleased to find that most of them had survived the winter.

Our next stop was the cabin. Trailing him past the graying wood-pile and around the corner of the house, we followed him into the small living room. A shrivelled white weasel lay dead on the floor, and Frost said, pointing to the rat poison beside it, "He died of the same thing the Russian royal family died of: internal bleeding."

We headed back down the hill again, Frost talking all the while:

On T. S. Eliot's latest play—"Cocktailian Episcopalia." On Eliot himself—"He fell for the idea that this was the worst of all ages." On voting for President—"The best thing about it is showing Stalin how many of us there are." On politics—"My first experience was working with my father for the election of Grover Cleveland. The Mugwumps made the difference then. Now we call them independent voters."

He talked about everything.

One of the virtues of organized religion, he thought, is that it admits the existence of both good and evil. Emerson "said some beautiful things," but he didn't give enough credit to evil.

Even the question of fraternities didn't escape Frost's curiosity. He wanted to know about Middlebury, and told us that he had been a Theta Delt at Dartmouth. Someone found out about it once and sent a delegation of brothers to greet him before a lecture.

"When they found out I wasn't coming to the house," he said, "they didn't even stay for the lecture."

One of our last stops before we left him was beside a budding lilac bush.

"I'm going to miss them this year; they'll all be gone by when I get back," he said.

This visit to Ripton was, he told us, only an interlude in the midst of a spring lecture tour.

By Henry Coon,
The Amherst Student, October 19, 1953:

"What is man but all his connections? He's just a tiny invisible knot so that he can't discern it himself: the knot where all his connections meet."—Robert Frost.

Perhaps the most striking feeling that one gets from speaking with Robert Frost is the conviction that here is a man who has formed a philosophy of life on a down-to-earth basis. The freshness of speech with which he expresses his ideas and attitudes serves to further this opinion. It consists of simple words and metaphor drawn from a busy and acute observation.

Mr. Frost is a curious admixture of farmer and intellectual.

"I've always farmed ever since I was a baby in San Francisco, in the backyard," he says, and adds that, "What really saved me was going farming eight years," referring to his return to the country after two years of study at Harvard.

But those who regard Mr. Frost as country poet will be surprised to hear of his scholarly interests. Since boyhood he has had a keen interest in reading, and his enrollment at Harvard was prompted by a desire to explore Latin and Greek and to study philosophy under such men as William James and George Santayana.

But in his poetry Mr. Frost avoids usage of classical allusion and employs subjects and imagery drawn from his own experience and observation, usually of the countryside. He is distressed by the people who "press that [his poetry] for more than was ever put into it" and points out the shifts he makes between specific and general, the "sway back and forth between concrete and abstract."

Of himself he claims, "I'm a lazy writer. I don't write much; I lived a lot more than I've written."

On poetry in general, Mr. Frost says, "I think that you come to poetry from Mother Goose up—rhymes, meters, wit, insight, cleverness."

The range of poetry is illustrated by the different scope of meaning which Mother Goose holds for child and adult.

He describes reading poetry as an attempt to "get the feel of ease, the grace . . . to take the mental stance of the author. . . . What's going on there? Am I missing any tricks?"

Mr. Frost is deeply interested in the problems of education. He states that "the beauty of college is to do a lot of things, of hard things, which you can't do again," thus taking a friendly attitude toward liberal education; though, he adds, "I like it better when I'm on top than when I'm on the bottom, like you boys."

"The literature courses are for those who aren't going to be writers, who're going to be readers. The writers should take history, science, philosophy."

As a man who has devoted a great deal of his life to contemplation, Mr. Frost likes to speak of the experience of thought. He refers to the conception of ideas as "events" in one's life, and of the process of learning he states that "what [ideas] I cling to is less important that what clings to me."

"My great interest in Americans is having more things [ideas] occur to them."

Mr. Frost refers to original ideas as "mental luck."

"When you're old you wonder if you are going to have any [any] longer; when you're young you doubt that your ideas are any good. . . . But you can't just stay around learning all the time. You should go ahead on insufficient information."

By Markham Ball,
The Amherst Student, November 1, 1954:

"I never look back," said Robert Frost, "I run on ahead of myself."

The poet was describing his speechmaking at a recent congress of writers in São Paulo, Brazil. It also seemed, to this reporter, an apt description of Robert Frost's way of life.

We were asking Mr. Frost [. . .] how a man acknowledged one of the world's foremost writers spends his time. Our interest was not impersonal, for Robert Frost has become a part of Amherst tradition. A teacher for eighteen years, he has kept his ties with the college close by spending part of each year in Amherst and speaking annually in chapel and in fraternities.

Mr. Frost began by attempting a description of his profession, a problem, he admitted, which he has often had to face before "on my income-tax return."

"I have gone in," he said, "as teacher or farmer. Lately I've decided to say 'retired.' Next time I think it would be amusing to say 'resigned'—and then, in parentheses, 'to everything.' "

"In England," Mr. Frost continued, "you get knighted, and then you can call yourself a poet. Here, that's too close to self-praise. You have to let others say it."

And as he talked, the blue eyes under the gray, shaggy brows seemed to laugh at this presumption.

The most-recent landmark in the activities of Robert Frost was his function as representative of the United States at conferences which commemorated the four-hundredth anniversary of the University of São Paulo this summer. Again, he refused to take his part seriously. There were, he related, conferences of doctors, lawyers, writers, and intellectuals.

"I was supposed to go with the writers, but due to some little delay and accident, I got among the intellectuals."

"They spent most of their time worrying about us [the United States]—not hating us so much as worrying. They worry about our materialism, think we lead them astray with our movies, automobiles, our chewing gum, and Coca-Cola."

In his speeches, he said, "I reassured them. If they don't trust us, they shouldn't buy our things. They shouldn't be so willing to be seduced."

Mr. Frost seemed a little dubious about worrying over international good will.

"I'm a nationalist," he said, "and I expect other people to be."

Summing up his venture into the realm of international goodwill, Robert Frost termed it all "very pleasant." His speeches did not increase anyone's worry.

"If I say an offensive thing, I say it so they don't know it."

When asked of his future plans, he said, "I never plan—no planned economy for me."

He will spend the fall in Amherst, with speaking trips to Washington, Cincinnati, and New York. In Washington he will address the Pan-American Union on his South American trip. He anticipated this as a novel experience—"diplomats and that kind of thing." In the spring he will speak in chapel and some fraternity houses.

"I'm like the boll weevil," said the New England poet, "I don't have any home. I spend most of my time at my farm in Ripton, Vermont." Cambridge, Massachusetts, and Amherst are his other customary residences.

Mr. Frost refused to consider his farm in the domain of gentleman farming.

"They're the ones who spend money and have Angus cattle." Instead, he uses his farm to "putter around on."

"I write anywhere, never had a desk. When I go anywhere, I look for a board. You can see where that came from." (And he indicated his current writing surface, previously a shelf in his closet at the Lord Jeffery Inn.)

At any time, in any place, even "standing on my head," Robert Frost can write the poetry that has made him internationally famous—and the object of some pride in Amherst. Even though he will not take himself seriously, there are others eager to do so.

A Medal and Two Interviews

The 1940's were marked by the publication of several new books by RF. In addition to A Witness Tree (*1942*), *there was* A Masque of Reason, *in 1945, and both* Steeple Bush *and* A Masque of Mercy *appeared in 1947. The period also saw the issuance of three different collected editions of his poetry.*

RF was in New York to receive from the Limited Editions Club special honors for his Complete Poems 1949 *when he granted the following interviews.*

By Harvey Breit,
The New York Times Book Review,
November 27, 1949:

THE other day a select literary audience gathered to pay tribute to America's leading poet, Robert Frost. This reporter saw Mr. Frost before the ceremonies. He found the seventy-four-year-old poet in good form—a gracious, alert, somewhat shy man, whose powerfully sculptured head was made gentle by the softness of his deepset eyes. Mr. Frost talked—without colloquialisms or pretensions—in a slow, engaging, and impersonal manner that somehow created an extraordinary effect of a man's intactness and incorruptibility.

Someone once said about Rilke that he carried his own atmosphere with him. It was so that morning with Robert Frost, and this reporter settled into Mr. Frost's enveloping atmosphere of quiet and contemplation and gentleness with an alarming—and a very real—alacrity.

There was no universe—to use Mr. Eliot—"to roll up into a ball to ask an overwhelming question." There were many questions, small ones, perhaps, about poets and poetry.

"I don't go delivering opinions about other poets," said Mr. Frost in his deep poet's voice. "I have my opinions, of course; opinions that are the result of a slow growth. There's always tentativeness, isn't there? It's the same as with the bomb. You don't go around screaming about it. The next day you may have a new opinion."

What did Mr. Frost have to say to the young poet today?

"One thing I care about," Mr. Frost said evenly, "and I wish young people could care about it, is taking poetry as the first form of understanding. Say it: my *favorite* form of understanding. If poetry isn't understanding all, the whole world, then it isn't worth anything.

"Young poets forget that poetry must include the mind as well as the emotions. Too many poets delude themselves by thinking the mind is dangerous and must be left out. Well, the mind is dangerous and must be left in.

"If a writer were to say he planned a long poem dealing with Darwin and evolution, we would be tempted to say it's going to be terrible. And yet you remember Lucretius. He admired Epicurus as I admired, let's say, Darwin. And he wrote a great poem. It's in and out: sometimes it's poetry, sometimes intelligent doggerel, sometimes quaint. But a great poem. Yes, the poet can use the mind—in fear and trembling. But he must use it."[. . .]

"I am not a regionalist. I am a realmist. I write about realms of democracy and realms of the spirit. The land is always in my bones.

"Someone once asked me if I was for democracy or against it, and I could only say that I am so much of it that I didn't know. I have a touchiness about the subject of democracy, of America. It amounts to a touchiness. I know how much difficulty there is about democracy, and how much fun it is too."

Of all modern poets, perhaps only Yeats and Frost had managed in their best work a simplicity out of complexity—which led Mr. Frost's reporter to the question of obscurity in modern verse.

"You know," Mr. Frost said, "if the obscurity was really a new thought, if it was really that. . . . But if it was a slackness, a not thinking through and getting to the right phrase, I couldn't be bothered with it. The test is when you've worried a poem out. Then you should know whether you've got anything really new; we won't say original, but we can say a fresh thought.

"For instance, follow what you get out of a man like Matthew Arnold, who was confident and authoritative in his prose and a lost soul in his poetry. You get that lostness in phrase after phrase in his poetry. (It's by phrases that you know a man.) Arnold has explained the academic world to me."

Mr. Frost leaned back and declaimed:

"A plain 'Where ignorant armies clash by night.' There is in the line the idea that the world is meaningless, is corrupt and impure. Arnold says—I don't remember exactly—

> Let the long contention cease
> Geese are swans, and swans are geese.

It's the despair from sitting out instead of sitting in.

"Arnold is asking too much. We all who are literary feel a little of that. But there is difference and harshness and difficulty, and that's all right. You have to be blinded by something. There has to be a blinding light. Love has to be blinding to make things right."

Mr. Frost's interlocutor recalled an aphorism of Pascal: "The heart has reasons which the reason knows nothing of." Mr. Frost nodded.

"Yes," he said, "Pascal's is a great kind of mind that has to be in poetry. If those things that Pascal knew are not in poetry, then you're just fastidiating along, wantoning along."

What about the gold medal? What was it for?

"The gold medal," Mr. Frost said with both amusement and defiance, "means all of me, my *Complete Poems*: six hundred pages written in the last sixty years. That's all of me."

By John K. Hutchens,
New York Herald Tribune Book Review,
December 4, 1949:

The day after he received the Limited Editions Club's fifth gold medal for the book (*Complete Poems*) deemed "most likely to attain the stature of a classic," Robert Frost—seventy-four, hale, hearty, kind, and salty—received an interviewer and said, among other things:

"I've had the same publisher for thirty-five years (Henry Holt and Company), and those fellows there who have been my editors —Alfred Harcourt, Lincoln MacVeagh, Herschel Brickell, Richard Thornton, Denver Lindley, William Sloane—they've all been friends of poetry; they've been my kind of man.[. . .]

" 'What do you write poems for?' people ask me. I say, 'I write them to see if I can make them sound different from each other.' The clew to the difference between them is content. This scorn of content—it's queer. If you try only to put words together that were never put together before, it's too limiting.

". . . Just about every emotion is legitimate in poetry except *botheration*. The time comes when you refuse to be *bothered* any more.

". . . Yes, people do read things into my poems. That's all right. A good story has analogues. One's grateful to see his poems turn up in strange uses. That's one reason you write them.

". . . I read my fellow poets, newspapers, old books like Gibbon's *Decline and Fall*, an occasional novel, and short stories. I like the short story form—the way a good short story strikes a bell in the first sentence and you can hear it still ringing in the last.

"The promising young poets, the hopefuls? I'd name Richard Wilbur, Peter Viereck, Karl Shapiro, Elizabeth Bishop, Robert Lowell, John Ciardi.

". . . I don't go around thinking words like 'welfare state.' Too vague. I have all sort of friends—rich, poor, jaunty riffraff. To all intents and purposes I was riffraff myself in the years when Holt and Company wasn't taking care of me. I believe in a man's inalienable right to go to hell in his own way."

"I'm just a natural gambler."

This interview-story by columnist Inez Robb was done at New York City and issued by International News Service for publication on December 14, 1949.

MAYBE it was an impertinent question, but I wanted to know the answer. And certainly the man sitting across from me was the ultimate authority. So I took a chance. I asked the greatest living American poet, "Can a man today earn a living at poetry?"

"No!" said Robert Frost, seventy-four, four times winner of the Pulitzer Prize for poetry and recipient of more honors, medals, degrees, and fellowships than he can shake a rhyme at.

"No," said Mr. Frost again, with the light, tolerant chuckle that bubbles through his conversation. "When you're very young, you think you can. Then you write poetry because you have a weakness for it, like a weakness for wine, women, and song.

"Then you gradually find out that you can do it [make a living via poetry] if you do it by hook or crook. I've stayed at poetry by doing odds and ends."

The odds and ends have been a lifetime of farming the stern New England soil, of teaching and lecturing, particularly at Amherst College, to which he has been attached since 1916.

"Amherst has been my great friend," he continued. "I'm not very useful any more, but they let me stay. I sit around and talk, especially with the young teachers.

"I used to do everything on a one-horse New England farm, including the milking. But I don't milk anymore. I still play a little tennis though. They won't let me play singles. So I play doubles. You can't hurt yourself much at doubles."[. . .]

As he talked, the poet seemed as relaxed as time. He filled a big arm chair, his frame buttoned into a gray suit, his feet encased in old-fashioned, high-lace shoes, and a dark tie carelessly knotted under the collar of a white shirt. He exuded serenity, an almost unknown quantity in this jittery world. And he exuded strength, too, in body and mind, and nothing from the New England over-soul to the atomic bomb escaped his shrewd observation and tart humor.

"I don't worry about my soul," Mr. Frost said, his deep-set blue eyes twinkling in his seamed and weathered face, topped by a thatch of snow-white hair. He looked like a particularly literate, shrewd, and kind Foxy Grandpa as he continued.

"What I worry about is my understanding. What makes a poet is a desire to understand what goes on. You don't want to miss any tricks in art or religion or your neighbors or in your representative in Congress."

The poet finds it difficult to gauge man's advance—or retreat—in today's world.

"A scientist like Vannevar Bush must be full of a feeling of progress," he said, "but a man who feels deeply about humanity must feel we are back in ancient Egypt."

Mr. Frost readily admitted he would hate a brave new world in which his security were guaranteed from cradle to grave.

"I'm just a natural gambler," he explained. "I like a life of gambling. I'm willing to take a chance. I've never had a cent's worth of life insurance, mainly because I could never afford it when it was needed.

"But if I had a guaranteed fifty-dollar-a-week life, if there was no uncertainty, I'd get into the Irish Sweeps out of sheer desperation! What we want is the largest possible number of citizens who can take care of themselves. What we need is character."

Mr. Frost has found that the number of persons who read and enjoy poetry remains constant despite radio, television, or the movies. He chuckled again, and recalled a young lady who told the poet she had found her father reading his *North of Boston.*

"She said she was so amazed that she exclaimed, 'But, Papa, I didn't know you ever read poetry!' And her father, equally amazed, cried, 'Is this stuff poetry?' "

· V ·

THE FIFTIES

A Visit to 35 Brewster Street

John Mason Potter prepared this interview for publication in the Boston Post Magazine, *where it appeared on April 27, 1952. It was done at RF's Cambridge home, 35 Brewster Street, which he had purchased in the spring of 1941 and which he retained through the remaining years of his life.*

THE spring afternoon was coming to a graceful end, and the lights were already on in the living room at 35 Brewster Street, Cambridge. The bard of New England's north country, Robert Frost, portly, white-haired, pleasant-faced, with the charm of many years and much accomplishment, sat in a book-lined corner and talked.

It was gladsome talk, rich with a feeling for being an American, a New England countryman—for Robert Frost is that, even though he has a home in Cambridge—for being a poet and a spiritual being. It was serious talk, seasoned here and there with a bit of humor.

It was [as] though the atmosphere of the purposeful, albeit gay, spring afternoon had reached into the room and touched him. Probably it had, for he has recorded many such instances where the spirit of places and hours and things has touched the antenna of his soul.

"The arts are important, but they do not stand alone. They are a part of something bigger, a part of a nation's enterprises. Those enterprises are all sorts of things: business, science, politics, manufacture, and the arts. They all go together, are all part of each other. You can't separate them from each other.

"People sometimes say that America is too commercial, too energetic in its efforts for prosperity. I get very impatient with that sort of talk. Other nations are commercial too, and they seek to prosper. Without prosperity the arts suffer. I don't know why it is, but the periods of prosperity are also the periods of our greatest strides in art.

"The arts serve as a permanent record of a nation. What we know about our past, about a country, we learn from the written word and from architecture. They record permanently. You can't separate them from the things they record.

"If the arts become separated from these other things, they fail. If the arts get left out, there is no record. They say that Carthage had everything except the arts, so now no one knows anything about it."

It is the belief of many persons that in future ages people will be able to know what life was like in America—in the part of America formed by the northern half of New England—by reading the poetry of Robert Frost. There are many who esteem him as America's greatest living poet and one who within his own lifetime has taken his place beside Bryant and Whitman and Emerson and the other immortals of verse.

It is the country life that Robert Frost loves and of which he writes—of farms and trees and rural lanes and of birds and small animals and of country people.

"There are people who don't like such things, and sometimes they are. . . . Well, you mustn't call them Communists because then they can sue you, but I know what they are.

"Sometimes I hear someone say that he does not like poetry about nature, the country, that it should be about the city and machines and man-made things. When he says that I know what's inside of him. He is as clear as can be to me then, and I know what he is, whether he does or not."

The poet has little patience, either, with the obscurantists in art.

"I met a young man from South America recently, an Argentine, and he asked me if I had ever read any of the works of a certain Argentine poet. I hadn't. (I don't read much in translation, because you lose so much.) He said to me, 'He writes in code.' I asked him, 'Who supplies the code?' 'Another man,' was the answer."

Mr. Frost chuckled, and several times after he referred to writing poetry in code as a big joke.[. . .]

"I've only written one book, really. It has come out in sections, but it is really only one book. You know I'm really not much of a writer. I've been writing poetry for sixty years now, and the book has six hundred pages, and so I have averaged only ten pages of poetry a year. That is not very much.

"I write when I feel like it. Sometimes I can sense that feeling coming on for a couple of days, and then I find that I have to versify.

"I do it sitting down in a chair with a piece of paper lying on a book on my knee. I never use a desk. I write wherever I happen to be. Once I wrote a poem in a hotel in Wilkes-Barre. It was the only time I was ever there. It was 'The Heart Begins to Cloud the Mind.' It was a sort of reflection of myself and the New Deal.

"I usually do a poem in one sitting, and the longest ones in never more than two sittings. You either go ahead or you get stuck. If I am exhausted from doing it at twelve or one o'clock, I stop, if I am not near the end of it."[. . .]

"I don't like to stop for fear that I won't come back to it. But I have got back to it in every case. I am always afraid that I will get distracted and break the back of it.

"I always use a pen. I have never learned to typewrite and have never used one."[. . .]

At seventy-five he still reads his Poe, declaring, "I have never outgrown anything that I ever liked. I have never had a hobby in my life, but I have ranged through a lot of things. I have a cursory interest in life."

As for the poetry that has been his life, he says, "I don't like a too technical interest in verse, even though I am a versifier. It is the tune that I am interested in."

Craft and Courage

Although the United States Senate had by formal resolution extended to RF the "felicitations of the Nation" in 1950 on what was presumed to be his seventy-fifth birthday, a long-standing error in reckoning his age had by 1954 been straightened out. Accordingly, the poet was in that year feted as he rounded out his eighth decade.

The text that follows is drawn from three separate accounts published at the time of the eightieth-birthday celebration in New York.

By Ira Henry Freeman,
The New York Times, March 26, 1954:

ALL his life, Robert Frost, famous American poet, said yesterday, he has been trying by "craft or courage" to temper the "hurry and overcrowding" of the world. In just that way he sailed serenely and modestly through a long, crowded day of public celebration of his eightieth birthday.

The bulky, white-haired, sun-tanned, plain-spoken man seemed as comfortable in a Waldorf-Astoria Hotel suite filled with reporters and television crews as he would be mending wall on his farm at Ripton, Vermont.

Mr. Frost's birthday is not until today. But the observances began about nine o'clock yesterday morning with television interviews that filled the hotel room with cameras, glaring lights, and non-literary questions for nearly three hours. During the noon hour the poet answered more questions of two dozen reporters, remaining on his feet the entire time without fatigue.[. . .]

He was asked yesterday what he thought about McCarthyism, the atomic age, juvenile delinquency, the "situation in Washington," politics today, labor's rights, human freedom, contemporary education, and whether he would advise youth to "take up" poetry. He disposed of all these subjects in a non-controversial, genial, often humorous, way.

As to his "feeling" about Senator Joseph R. McCarthy, Republican of Wisconsin, Mr. Frost said:

"I'm past feeling anything at all about McCarthy. Why don't we leave his name out of the conversation, for once?"

The situation in Washington, the poet said, looked "more confused from there than it does from here." He was not "excited" about the atom bomb, and politicians were "slinging the word 'fear' around" so much he hardly knew what it meant any more.

Freedom he defined as "feeling easy in your harness." As for "juvenile delinquency"—well, he had been a juvenile delinquent himself, but people didn't call it that seventy years ago.

Then he returned to his moral: a man must learn by "craft and courage" to keep the world from hurrying and crowding him too much.

"That's the only way you can live your own life: do what you want to do," he noted. "Like writing a poem, for instance. I've been trying to do that all my life.[. . .]

By John G. Rogers,
New York Herald Tribune, March 26, 1954:

[. . .]Mr. Frost was asked to confirm the impression that he was an optimist.

"No labels," he replied.

Well, was he hopeful in a time when some people were not?

"It goes on," he said, meaning life. "It goes on. I don't hold with people who say, 'Where do we go from here?' I wouldn't get up in the morning if I thought we didn't have a direction to go in. But [an admonishing wag of forefinger here] if you ask me what the direction is, I don't answer.

"Like Aaron Burr when somebody asked him, 'Burr, how is it with your soul?' I'm a little coy about that. I'm a little coy about where the human race is headed. As a matter of fact, whenever you can't pin me down on some specific point, it's due to my quality of uncatchability."

"The way of understanding is partly mirth," Mr. Frost wrote in one of his gentle, reflective poems, and there was good humor on his face and in his voice throughout yesterday's interview.

He was asked, inevitably, to name the "best" American poet.

"Aren't you asking a good deal?" he replied. "You name him."

"Well," said the questioner, "Joyce Kilmer."

"Oh," said Mr. Frost.

Somebody decided to ask, "Why do you write poems?"

"I write 'em," said Mr. Frost, "to see if I can make 'em sound different from each other."[. . .]

Could he sum up his philosophy briefly?

"No, that would take quite a while, but when I hear anyone say that we're all going to the dogs I say, 'Oh rats!' "[. . .]

By Mary Hornaday,
The Christian Science Monitor, March 26, 1954:

[. . .]His attention called to the fact that he belies the old adage "poets die young," Mr. Frost reversed the concept of dying and lifted the question onto another level. He said the phrase didn't mean "dying into the grave."

Most poets, he said, "die into something. They may die into critics or philosophers. Certainly they have a tendency to become more rational." Then he added, "But it's none of my business what I'm dying into. That's up to others to say. I don't say that any more than I say, 'I'm going to be a poet, watch me.' It's up to others to say whether I am a poet."

At the press conference when someone asked him which was his favorite part of the country, Mr. Frost recalled he had lived in California, Massachusetts, New Hampshire, Vermont, Michigan, Iowa, and Florida, then added: "I feel perfectly content if every so often I see the American flag. I know the things I'm saying won't need much explanation in the U.S.A."

He refused to say anything derogatory about so-called "difficult" poets, such as the late Dylan Thomas.

"Some wildness," he explained to this query, "belongs to all poets. Poetry is the place where wildness lives, though in some poets there is an excess of this uncatchability."

In his refusal to expound on Senator McCarthy or the atom bomb, Mr. Frost made it clear that he has never been an ivory-tower poet. He recalled the night back in 1884 when he rode on a fire engine in the Cleveland victory procession in [. . . California].

"That is," he recalled, "I rode the fire engine until they put some pretty girls up there and made me walk.

"The thing about it was that there were troubles then, too. There was fighting between the Republicans and the Democrats in the street that night."[. . .]

"I find my greatest freedom on the farm," he said. "I can be a bad farmer or a lazy farmer and it's my own business."[. . .]

He was asked to define poetry.

"It's like a wild-game preserve," he answered. "It's where wild things live. This is the ultimate in poetry, and it has to be there."

"I've never written poetry by the week or by the month, but just a little every year. I've always been afraid of facility. If I got down to writing every day all year around, it would all probably be the same poem."[. . .]

From Beyond the Andes

In August of 1954 RF flew to South America as a delegate, sent by the United States Department of State, to the World Congress of Writers at São Paulo, Brazil.
This interview, which was published in the August 18th O Estado de S. Paulo, has been translated from the Portuguese by Prof. Joseph B. Folger, an emeritus member of the Department of Romance Languages at Dartmouth College.

SOME days ago we had the opportunity of bringing into focus in these columns, through a rapid conversation, the complex personality of the poet Robert Frost[. . .]. Last evening, at the end of this São Paulo winter and its absence of cold, we had the honor of being received once more by the illustrious visitor.

In one corner of the salon of the Hotel Esplanada we found Frost, simple and cordial. In his patriarchal aspect there is nothing that reminds one of his semi-official position as dean of North American poets, crowned by the Washington Congress and recipient four times (four!) of the Pulitzer Prize. He has lived eight decades, but he continues to have a youthful spirit.[. . .]

Previously, in our first interview, we tried to reflect various aspects of the personality and the work of the writer who is now visiting us. Meanwhile, figures like Frost ever offer us new facets to awaken the curiosity of those who come near them.

"Have you written much lately, Mr. Frost?"

And he, with his customary good nature and simplicity, explains (What a beautiful example that old young man gives to young writers!), "I'm always writing. Just a few days ago I finished two poems: 'Waste' and 'One More Brevity'. . . ."

And, replying to another question of one of those present, he clarifies his statement.

"I write anywhere: on the street, on trains, when out walking—except in airplanes! And speaking of that, a curious thing, I never did have, properly speaking, what you would call a workroom; that is, a table, an easy chair, and so forth: things that many writers find indispensable in order to get to be a great writer. . . ."

The clear eyes of Frost shine mischievously—with frank, reinvigorating mischief that does one good. And without changing his tone, he addresses to the group of newspapermen and admirers around him a question that at first takes them by surprise.

"Is it true, what I have heard out there, that you Brazilians have certain preconceived ideas about us North Americans? In certain circles they assured me that you see us with the same eyes with which you face the Russians. . . ."

Everybody present protests, denying such a thing. . . .

"I know, I know," adds Frost, with a broad gesture of a man of experience. "Yes, I recognize that we have in the United States certain groups whose tendencies, particularly in the world of Big Business, aren't at all attractive. But there's no reason for you to worry about them. . . . You don't need to keep an eye on them. . . . We ourselves will take care of them."

Everybody laughs, and Frost, pretending surprise, adds, "For Heaven's sake, interpret carefully the meaning of my words! I think that men of Big Business and the 'trusts' are as necessary as those of other classes. And you here who have such a big, beautiful city, how could you have built it without the help of Big Businessmen? So," he goes on, "the silent campaign that has been carried on at certain times against specific groups of North Americans has no justification. It's ridiculous.

"That reminds me of what I was told: that North American participation in the exploitation of petroleum would constitute a danger, for after the wells were sunk battalions of Marines would come in to guarantee their operation. . . ."

This waggery, so unexpected in a man like Frost, who seems to live always far removed from everyday problems, provokes laughter among those present.

He goes on, after this, to talking about the new generation of North American poets, and Frost reveals something.

"To me one of the most talented young North American poetesses is living right now in Brazil. I'm talking about Elizabeth Bishop, whom I had the happy experience just a few days ago of seeing again in Rio.

"Besides her, I could mention other individuals of great worth in the younger generation, like Karl Shapiro, Robert Lowell, Richard Wilbur, Leonard Bacon. . . . But it is still early to make assertions. They're all 'in the field.' It remains to be seen how many will cross the finish line."

They ask the great poet if he knows the work of any of his Brazilian colleagues.

"Unfortunately for me, I don't understand Portuguese. I feel ashamed of that. No one regrets that more than I do! And I confess that I have no liking for translations. The translator always ends up betraying the author. But now, on returning home, I intend to learn Portuguese—at least in order to understand the message of your poets. . . ."[. . .]

The conversation becomes general. The most diverse subjects come up.

"Can a poet live in the United States on what he writes?"

Frost retorts, "I have lived well. . . . It's true that in the first forty years of my life my poems brought me only five hundred dollars. Meanwhile, in these last forty years, I have been rewarded with generous sums for that initial poverty.

"At present my greatest sources of income are the 'readings' of my poems, which I do on trips across the United States, generally under the financial auspices of literary clubs. And I confess that the amount I earn with these talks and readings is nothing to be scorned. In addition to that, I have the royalties, so-called, on my books.

"I have to add to that my income as a professor at Amherst College. Theoretically I have to give annually a two-months' course on literary composition. . . . And I religiously spend two months every year at the college mentioned, promoting literary gatherings, encouraging this or that student. But I'm going to tell you a secret. The administration pays me—and royally—on one condition: that I not conduct any course at all. . . ." And with an air of secret complicity he confides, "I suspect they are afraid that any course of mine would turn out to be a real disaster!"

The hours slip by. It is now night outside in the city that obstinately resists receiving the winter of 1954. As a farewell gesture those present ask Frost, "Don't you have a message to send to readers in São Paulo?"

"Message?" he repeats thoughtfully. "No. No, I have no message, for I have set it down already in my works. But now I do remember a story. Years ago—many years ago—someone asked me what my definition of poetry was. And I replied poetry is something 'necessary' [a term which in English has two essential meanings: necessary and unavoidable!].

"Yes," he goes on, while we shake his distinguished hand, "tell your readers that without poetry it is impossible to live, especially in today's world. And say also that in spite of everything, and counter to all that there is ugly and unpleasant on the earth, there still remains for us this hope and this incentive: that poetry is unavoidable in the contemporary world!"

"Deeds that count are liberties taken with the conventions."

This discussion between RF and Dr. Reginald L. Cook of Middlebury College was tape-recorded at Ripton and then broadcast by the British Broadcasting Corporation on July 16, 1954, to commemorate the centennial of the publication of Thoreau's Walden.

The text, minus introductory remarks originally included, is now reprinted from the August 26, 1954, issue of The Listener.

COOK : Mr. Frost, we are celebrating the birthday of one of the great books, *Walden*.

FROST : Yes, and when we happen on it once and so often like this, what a reminder it is of how many good books we have in our own language without going outside to read foreign books in the unhappiness of translation. I say we leave the foreign books waiting till we learn their language and can read them in the original. They might serve as an incentive to us to get an education.

COOK : You would favor putting off foreign books till we have mastered our Greek, Latin, French, and German, as we no doubt will have some fine day. Meanwhile we have *Walden* in English.

FROST : And plenty besides, but *Walden* will do for an example. For there we have a book that is everything from a tale of adventure like *Robinson Crusoe* and *The Voyage of the Beagle* (the three have a special shelf in my heart) to a declaration of independence and a gospel of wisdom.

: 142 :

A man may write well and very well all his life, yet only once in a lifetime have such luck with him in the choice of a subject—a real gatherer, to which everything in him comes tumbling. Thoreau's immortality may hang by a single book, but the book includes even his writing that is *not* in it. Nothing he ever said but sounds like a quotation from it. Think of the success of a man's pulling himself together all under one one-word title. Enviable!

COOK: What would you say if one of the great foundations we look to for our long vacations should come to you and, in recognition of your weakness for the book *Walden*, offer you a free year to think things over by the pond Walden?

FROST: To qualify as a Thorosian I might well offer them in reply some good reasons for staying where I am in Vermont and refusing the chance to go anywhere else. In the imitation of a hero it may be hard to decide just what he did that he would have his followers do after him—live by a pond or live on hasty pudding or refuse to pay taxes when out of sorts with the government.

But, anyway, Thoreau was the chief advocate since the Old Testament of making the most of the home town and township. Make of the stones of the place a pillow for your head if you hope to see angels ascending and descending. The opposite doctrine is to desert your country because you do not seem to be accepted in it as a prophet.

Thoreau saved himself a journey to the Arctic to see red snow by waiting at home till red snow fell in Concord. At last accounts he was still waiting for elephants and tigers to cross his path in the woods of Concord. He taught John Burroughs to versify, saying, "My own will come to me."

Then, too, I fear he might be against my submitting to a benefaction, though I lack chapter and verse for that; and he did say once that perhaps the town poor lived the happiest lives of all, because they were great enough to receive alms without misgiving.

And, again, you knew very well when you as good as invited me to a year off at Walden Pond that I couldn't go back there now except for a glimpse to contrast it with the lonely wild place it used to be when he played the famous game with the diving loon on it that autumn day long ago. (I wish I had time to read the passage about the loon.) The pond is simply swarmed over by the popularity he so feared in life for his ideas and books. The only thing commonness has not done to it is change the good old folk word "pond" into the fancy one of "lake."

COOK : Do you mind telling me where you get this word "Thorosian" you take to yourself so cheerfully? It sounds dangerously like a neologism. Did you get it up?

FROST : All poetry is neologism in being either new words or old words in a new sense—chiefly and preferably, of course, old words in a new sense. "Thorosian" is, I admit, a new word—so new I haven't decided how to spell the second "o" sound in it—but it is coining even as you and I converse, and so on its way into the dictionary.

COOK : How would the word "Waldensian" do for your purpose? "Waldensees" for any of the brotherhood, and "Waldensian" for their behavior? There you have two perfectly good words already in existence.

FROST : I am afraid few would know what they meant. Thoreau might enjoy them for their odor of Puritanism.

Which reminds me of a story a boy handed in in college about pressing his unromantic sister, a scorner of shrines and shriners, into a pilgrimage to Walden. But when his teacher objected he could improve it by turning the sister into a lady love, Hollywood fashion, the boy wanted to know what that sort of love had to do with *Walden*. No girl is mentioned in the book. The teacher stood rebuked. Nor is any girl mentioned in the fine sketch of Thoreau by Emerson, one of the best biographies of anybody by anybody.

COOK : But for a nickname like Thorosian to stick there must be someone answerable to it in nature.

FROST : There is a whole class of society that would answer to it if it shouted from the doorway to call them home from the field at last for supper: naturalists and sages, scientists not too strictly scientific, philosophers not too professional.

You, Doc, are more one than ever I was—you listener to thrushes, you walker alone. (Thoreau said he had no walks to waste on company.) And there's Viola White down here in the Abernethy Library, keeper of his relics, the books he made and the pencils he made. (He made pencils, you know.)

Our friend the poet, Robert Francis, has given more years to

Waldensian hermitage than anybody. W. R. Brown, if he were here, might be murmuring over any liberties I take with the Thorosian text. In England there is Jack Haines, who boosted me up a cliff to look at an ebony spleenwort by matchlight. And there was Edward Thomas, best of friends and best of poets—a natural naturalist if there ever was one. He derives more, however, from Jefferies, Borrow, and White of Selborne than from any American. And there are several journalists right on New York newspapers I could claim, but I must stop somewhere.

COOK: I don't believe you are as serious as you might be about these Thorosians. They don't congregate, do they? They have no meeting place that I ever heard of under the green trees Bryant spoke of as God's first temples. They wouldn't be Thorosians if they had.

FROST: Yes, Thoreau had an impatience with membership and sometimes even of citizenship. His theme was freedom in a way, but it was a freedom within freedom; that is to say, an independence that seems to stop short somewhere of Liberty with a capital "L." I called it myself once a one-man revolution. A statue to it would be of less stature than one of Liberty in New York harbor.

Thoreau hated slavery. For him, John Brown was one of Plutarch's worthies. He predicted a great poem about him some day. But he was not interested in the liberty brightest in dungeons and on the scaffold, as much as he was in the daily liberties he could take right under the noses of the high and mighty and the small and petty.

It must have bothered him somewhat that though he was theoretically free to go to jail for delinquency in tax paying, he was not free from the friendship that would not let him stay there. He had to let Emerson buy him out.

We know well enough what we mean by freedom in practical politics, but it is a subject apt to get more confused when gone too far into. It seems to break down into a number of freedoms that conflict. Thoreau was content to settle for something less difficult that I call independence.

Between the tyranny of being handled and judged by general laws and statistics at the large end and the tyranny of being handled and judged by gossip and fashion at the small end, there should be room for any real fellow with a little effrontery to take his liberties more or less at ease. They usually open in form with an "I dare say" or "I venture to say" or "I make bold to say."

The best word in any poem is a liberty taken with the language. Deeds that count are liberties taken with the conventions.

COOK: It was a considerable liberty he and Emerson took in being almost Buddhists in a Congregational New England village, wasn't it, Mr. Frost?

FROST: Yes, Thoreau told them it was fit he should live on rice mainly who loved so well the philosophy of India. The book is strewn with the wise sayings of Asia. Both he and Emerson seem more possessed of the religions of the Far East than of the Near East.

COOK: But no one in the village molested them. They weren't tried for heresy. Of course, they were in a position to appeal from the little world of Concord to the big world of Boston twenty-five miles away. And at least one of the famous pair was already getting famous.

FROST: And Concord itself was no ordinary village. It was highly civilized. A great civilization in its greatness can afford to indulge in all sorts of deviations and aberrations: individuality to the extent of eccentricity, thrift to the extent of miserliness, privacy to the extent of secrecy—about how much money, for instance, you had in the bank or strong box. (Old men liked what they had saved to be a surprise to the world when they died.)

The opposite of civilization is not barbarism but Utopia. Utopia can let no man be his own worst enemy, take the risk of going uninsured, gamble on the horses or on his own future, go to hell in his own way. It has to concern itself more with the connection of the parts than with the separateness of the parts. It has to know where everyone is; it has to bunch us up to keep track of us. It can't protect us unless it directs us.

COOK: Mr. Frost, are you thinking of Brook Farm when you speak of Utopia like that?

FROST: No, but I should be. There you had exhibited all the tyranny of the commune. But in Thoreau's declaration of independence from the modern pace is where I find most justification for my own propensities. He said he went to the woods to live deliberately.

Come to think of it, that is why I have gone to a number of places: to live deliberately. Give me the speed of a perfectly geared automobile that I can slow down to half a mile an hour, to tell one flower from another. My intolerance has been for the throng who complain of the modern pace yet strive to keep it. There is the widest choice of companions you will fall into step with, be they living or dead. There is no such thing as a prescribed tempo—at any rate, not in civilization.

"If you would have out
the way a man feels about God,
watch his life, hear his words."

The interview from which the following text is drawn was done by reporter John Sherrill for Guideposts, *a nondenominational, inspirational monthly publication. The text originally appeared in the magazine's issue for August 1955.*

THE poet, dressed in a gray suit and white shirt open at the neck, was finishing breakfast. His first words were keynotes. Frost looked up. His great eyebrows moved upwards as he spoke.

"I hope you won't ask me to put names on things," he said. "I'm afraid of that."

Yet that was what I had come to do. And one of the first topics we discussed was what God meant to him in his poetry, as for example in "Bereft"[. . .]:

> Where had I heard this wind before
> Change like this to a deeper roar?
> What would it take my standing there for,
> Holding open a restive door,
> Looking down hill to a frothy shore?
> Summer was past and day was past.
> Somber clouds in the west were massed.
> Out in the porch's sagging floor,
> Leaves got up in a coil and hissed,
> Blindly struck at my knee and missed.

Something sinister in the tone
Told me my secret must be known:
Word I was in the house alone
Somehow must have gotten abroad,
Word I was in my life alone,
Word I had no one left but God.

Frost folded his massive hands—he is a large, well-built man—
and spoke softly.

"People have sometimes asked me to sum up my poetry. I can't
do that. It's the same with my feeling about God. If you would learn
the way a man feels about God, don't ask him to put a name on
himself. All that is said with names is soon not enough.

"If you would have out the way a man feels about God, watch his
life, hear his words. Place a coin, with its denomination unknown,
under paper and you can tell its mark by rubbing a pencil over the
paper. From all the individual rises and valleys your answer will
come out."

We reviewed, a little, what I knew about Frost's life. Perhaps
from its rises and valleys a picture would emerge.[. . .]

Reflecting on those days [of his early life], Frost spoke of how
no one had confidence in his future.

"Where is it that confidence and faith separate?" he asked.
". . . We have confidence in the atom. We can test the atom and
prove that it is there.

"I have seen an old New England farmer try to test God in this
same way. He stood in his field during a thunderstorm and held his
pitchfork to Heaven and dared God to strike him. You just can't
prove God that way."

Robert Frost must have had faith in his poetry. It certainly
couldn't have been confidence. He submitted to magazines time and
again. Most of his work was returned.

And all this while, pressure was great to pin Frost down, to get
him to commit himself to a career. Frost evaded the efforts.[. . .]

Often Frost has been asked to interpret the philosophy behind
his poetry before a group of students. Each time Frost refuses. He
says that the poem's meaning is as the individual reader interprets
it. "It must be personal with you," he says.

So I won't try to pin Frost down and say, "This is what he has to say." But I can say what meeting Frost, learning about his life, reading his poetry, talking with him about his views on religion has meant to me.

When I went to see Frost that day I was hoping, I can see now, to put him quickly into a pigeon-hole in my mind; I'd have liked to pin him down and classify him. Robert Frost refused. And that is precisely why his interview haunted me so.

Let me put it this way: Imagine that you see a butterfly, and its beauty is something you want to capture and take home with you. You catch the butterfly and place it carefully on a cardboard under glass. And to your sorrow, you haven't caught the butterfly at all. You can examine the thing that you have under glass, and give it a name. But your relation to it is changed. Where once the butterfly had a subtle, vibrant aliveness, the very act of pinning it down has destroyed it for you.

As we make more and more progress controlling and classifying the material world, we are tempted to try to capture more elusive qualities of the spirit in the same way. It just can't be done. And that to me was Robert Frost's message.

Frost, through his poetry—his life—was saying: There is a point beyond which the spiritual side of life must be protected, kept sacred as a personal experience, not captured or tested like the farmer with his pitchfork tried to do.

As Frost himself said, "You can't test a stirring. You can't pin down the God within you."

Something Brave to Do

"Something Brave to Do" was printed in The Christian
Science Monitor *on December 21, 1955. The interview,
which took place at Cambridge, was prepared for publication
by Mary Handy of the* Monitor *staff.*

NEARLY everybody is looking for something brave to do.
I don't see why people shouldn't write poetry. That's brave."

Robert Frost was sitting on a green velvet chair in his parlor
talking to us. Around him were bookshelves and plants. Through
the curtained windows the sunlight filtered. Outside the old house
on Brewster Street blew the cold, fresh air of literary Cambridge.

"If people are looking for something to be brave about, there's
their chance in poetry," he was saying. "It's one of the ways of being brave. Some like hostile criticism. Some like bullets flying
around. You get neglect flying around, too, and you can feel it like
invisible television waves." He stopped, and cupped his hands.

"There's nothing to it except valor and courage. A special kind
of courage for a special kind of punishment. The fun is more than
the punishment if you'll only see it that way.

"There aren't enough poets," he continued. "My advice to young
people is to write poetry." And informally, with frequent sparks of
humor, he began on one of his favorite subjects: encouraging young
poets.

"There are fifteen hundred colleges in this country, and each
year every one graduates, say, ten who have had A's in English.

Some in poetry. Some in prose. Where are they all? Why don't some of them go through with it?

"They're either afraid of it or someone's afraid of it for them. They don't presume to be one of 'those people.' They think it couldn't happen in their family. Or teachers think it couldn't happen in their classes.

"I remember one professor when he heard I'd had a few things published looked down his nose and said to me, 'So we're an author, are we?' I just got up and left.

"It's an old story. Courage and adventure. Courage for that kind of adventure. To write is not the horrible thing. The horrible thing is not having anybody want it for a long time.

"You get jobs for a while. I knew one poet who was a silversmith. So many land in teaching English where they have too many papers to read. That's exhausting."[. . .]

He stopped talking, and looked up and smiled. He asked about us, our work. He remarked that it was nice to have pictures taken without flash bulbs. Flash bulbs made you blind with light. And we asked him which were his favorites among his poems.

"Favorites?" he chuckled. "Parents can't admit any favorites. There are impulsive moments over the last one you wrote that has been very particularly favored. But I have no favorites.

"The pleasure in looking back at them is the moments when the writing was self-propelled, self-driven. You look at places where you had felicity. Not where you chewed pencils. What gives me pleasure gives others pleasure. A lot of people talk falsely about that.

"Recognition is a curious thing. I suppose if you do anything in the arts you either get some while you are alive or you don't get any until you are dead. Some get more while they are alive. You have to think you are in luck if you get in a book on a few shelves.

"The most satisfying part is to write the poem. The next most satisfying is to have people read them. Another very important one is to see poems turn up in quotations, become part of people's lives. Maybe turn up in a Presidential campaign."

Then he told us about his work habits. He has never written a thing in the afternoon, he said.

"But then about eight p.m. I recover from the dullness of the

afternoon and feel fine until about three in the morning. I also like
to write a couple of hours in the morning. Used to like to teach a
class at eleven. But in the afternoon I garden, go on errands, anything that doesn't count too much."

A dog was barking at the door, and he stopped and let it in. It
was a tiny little dog that seemed to love him well. It curled up
comfortably at the poet's feet as he went on talking.

"Our times? People say ours is not a good time for poetry. I look
back over the past and see some of the most remarkable writing
went on as if nothing were happening in the world when really
there were revolutions going on. Think of Jane Austen during all
the Napoleonic disturbance.

"You can take part in all these things or you don't need to. Life
will go on. Cruelty will go on. Happiness will go on.

"That doesn't mean you don't care a lot. But everybody that
gambles, gambles just the same. We're all gamblers. So far as society is concerned it may end any minute. People say something
might happen to the sun any time. But you make your peace with
things.

"The world's never had anything but little pieces of peace. So
you can't wait for that. People ask what right Nero had to fiddle
while Rome burned. People have always done that.

"Is this a good period for poetry? I can't complain. It's different
with different families. I have a friend whose mother read poetry
aloud a lot. Mine did. I remember a good deal of verse. I never
learned any of it on purpose.

"I have a friend who says he could recite poetry all his waking
hours between here and Europe on an ocean liner. Some people
never read a poem.

"I never took any thought about it. Some people think of it as
their battle—the world against me and poetry. Like Hitler and
Mein Kampf. Poetry gets neglected and gets hurt.

"People ask, 'Is this the worst time for poetry?' Is it worse than
the Middle Ages? I wrote a poem about that, 'The Lesson for Today.' I don't know how to measure. In our time, anyway, you are
such a rank insider. You can't tell."

We got up and thanked him. He smiled, thanked us, talked
about some mutual friends, and told us to come back for another

chat sometime. As he walked with us to the door he grew serious again.

"One thing people fear about is that we may be terribly material-istic," he said. "We are the richest nation in the world. That could mean we are very material—and it might not.[. . .]"

On Liberties and Freedom

On December 23rd in 1956 RF appeared on the National Broadcasting Company's television program "Meet the Press," to be interviewed by a panel consisting of Lawrence Spivak, Inez Robb, Clifton Fadiman, David Brinkley, and Ned Brooks.

The questions that were asked him and the poet's answers are here reproduced from their publication in The Boston Sunday Globe *of December 30th.*

SPIVAK: Mr. Frost, few words have had their meaning so distorted as freedom and liberty. It seems to mean different things to different people in different countries. Now will you tell us what freedom means to you, a poet?

FROST: First of all it means the freedom my country gives me and I suppose the freedom that everybody's country gives him. There ought to be, of course, no comparative freedoms, but I like mine best; and I think [. . .] the reason for it probably is that it's like old clothes or old shoes. Mine fits me, and that's as far as I can go.

SPIVAK: Mr. Frost, do you think there is any relationship between freedom and great poetry, or do you think that a great talent expresses itself regardless of the political climate of a country?

FROST: I don't believe the political state of affairs matters too much. I think that the personal freedom that you get from the country is something you assume. Your real anxiety day by day is your own freedom of your own material, your own condition, your own mental condition and physical condition that gives you command of what you want to think of when you want to think of it. And then I'm more interested in the liberties I take than in the big thing you call freedom or liberty: the little liberties socially, in poetry, art and little trespasses and excesses and things like that.

FADIMAN: What you are saying perhaps ties down to the question I wanted to ask you.

We hear a good deal these days about economic and political freedom, the kind of freedom guaranteed to us by law. Do you think economic and political freedom in itself is very much good without the kind of freedom that's inside your head? I mean the mental freedom that comes from having enough character and intelligence to make proper choices?

FROST: The economic freedom of course is something. . . . You're asking me do I think it makes any difference to a poet whether he hears the wolf at the door all the time, and I don't believe it makes too much difference.

If you are talking about poverty and wealth I think sometimes wealth has its bad things and poverty has its bad things and limits to our freedom. Poverty has done so much good in this way in the world that I should hesitate to abolish it.

ROBB: In the world in which we live, Mr. Frost, there is a great yearning for what people think of as security, and that usually means economic security. Do you feel that you would have written any better poetry if you had been endowed from the beginning with an ample income?

FROST: I don't think so, no. You see, I'm on the other side. I know what you're talking about, what you're leading up to. I'm on the side of adversity.

I once drew up a little story about that. It said just how many disadvantages does a person need to get anywhere in the world— disadvantages. And I said here's a man born to too much money, and that's disadvantage number one. Then his mother is a very dominant person, very fond of him. That's disadvantage number two. No father in it; that's disadvantage number three.

He goes to Groton, and that's disadvantage number four. Then he goes to Harvard, and that's disadvantage number five. Then he begins to kick around among the politicians in Albany and Washington. That's disadvantage number six. (Have I got six?)

And then God says, "I'm going to make something of that boy; I set my heart on him." And, "He hasn't amounted to anything yet, but I'm going to give him one more disadvantage." And He gives him polio, and then he sits on top of the world along with Stalin and Churchill!

That row is forever in my mind.

ROBB: May I ask another question?

You once wrote, Mr. Frost, "Originality and initiative are what I ask for my country." Are those the two things that you still ask for your country?

FROST: Say those again.

ROBB: "Originality and initiative."

FROST: Yes. That's what I want in art, and I want that so much that I am inclined to favor young poets and artists too much. It's their funeral you know, not mine; but I make their funeral mine.

BRINKLEY: Mr. Frost, I think most of us tend to think of the poet as being a kind of agent of the free spirit. I wonder how you in that light would feel about the increasing pressure in this country toward conformity, toward having people think and act and dress and live alike?

FROST: I don't know how to answer that, because I don't feel that pressure. I think we're the freest people that ever were free. I don't know what the pressure is.

Take this pressure of haste, you know, that they talk about: the pace. If you want to see the opposite from haste come up to Ripton, Vermont. We live on "procrastinity" up there, I call it. We just put everything off.

FADIMAN: You do have a lot of haste down here, Mr. Frost; we have a monopoly on it.

FROST: But you don't have to join in it. I didn't meet any last night in the hotel where I am. And I used to visit my daughter in Bank Street, and I couldn't even hear the murmur of the city down there. It was as quiet as it is in Vermont.

BRINKLEY: I'd like to ask one more brief question on the same line.

Do you think non-conformity is as much admired in this country today?

FROST: Yes, I think we're paid for it.

SPIVAK: Mr. Frost, do you seek to do anything through your poetry or do you just write because you must, or because you love to do it?

FROST: I do it because I like to do it. I have always done what I liked to do. I never did anything I disliked to do very long at a time.

SPIVAK: Which of your poems do you like the best?

FROST: The one that was last praised by some friend.

SPIVAK: Which one is that?

FROST: The last one that was praised very much by people was too long for me to recite to you so I can't help you there; but it was called "One More Brevity."

SPIVAK: Have you a short one that's been praised?

FROST: Yes, I have one on this subject of freedom. (What gives us our freedom is having a territorial basis, belonging to the land.) That's one of my favorite poems. Because other people seem to like it. Shall I recite it? It's short.

SPIVAK: Yes, if you will.

FROST:

> The land was ours before we were the land's. . . .

It all lies in that first line.

> The land was ours before we were the land's.
> She was our land more than a hundred years
> Before we were her people. She was ours
> In Massachusetts, in Virginia,
> But we were England's, still colonials,
> Possessing what we still were unpossessed by,
> Possessed by what we now no more possessed.
> Something we were withholding made us weak
> Until we found out that it was ourselves
> We were withholding from our land of living,
> And forthwith found salvation in surrender.
> Such as we were we gave ourselves outright
> (The deed of gift was many deeds of war)
> To the land vaguely realizing westward,
> But still unstoried, artless, unenhanced,
> Such as she was, such as she would become.

It all lies in the first line.

FADIMAN: It's a beautiful poem you just quoted and is of course a severely limited thing that it is bound by the rules of meter or measure. And people talk about freedom in poetry as if that were a thing very much to be desired; but isn't it true that great poetry becomes great in part because of its limitations, and may it not be true that freedom, even politically and socially, emerges the same way?

FROST: And that's no paradox that we gain in freedom on a higher plane by sacrificing agents on the next plane below it. All the way up. That's our freedom.

When it says "the truth will make you free" it means that you get a new enslavement that will free you from all your other enslavements.

FADIMAN: The notion of unfettered, unrestricted freedom is really a Utopian and windy idea, is it not?

FROST: Excuse me?

FADIMAN: I say, the notion of unfettered freedom some people talk about—complete freedom—is meaningless.

FROST: To me it's unchartered freedom. You want something in balance, form. It comes to everything. It's just as much in the phrase as it is in the verse, isn't it? You need your freedom by phrase, and that's a kind of formality.

The dictionary is a limitation, isn't it? I'm awfully limited by the dictionary, and I'm awfully limited by the need of phrase and grammar; and I just have the feeling I can take all that and then some. Freedom of rhyme and meter.

ROBB: What we are saying then, Mr. Frost, is that both poetry and freedom have their own discipline?

FROST: Absolutely. And in limitation, yes. But one rises above another to higher and higher freedom all the way to the freedom of the spirit.

BRINKLEY: You are a teacher. You know, of course, there's a great cry in this country now that we should train more scientists in our schools, because the Russians are. I wonder if you see in this any danger we might train too many people to split atoms and not enough to write sentences?

FROST: No, no, I'm not afraid. They're advertising for those boys in the *Scientific American* and all around all the time. They don't seem to be able to get them. I don't know where they are. I should think that's been drawn that way. My imagination would have been caught by all that's going on in there, and I wonder that we don't—that they don't swamp that.

Where do they go? Do you know?

FADIMAN: Do you think they are going into the humanities more, Mr. Frost?

FROST: I'm afraid not so much into the humanities as into sociality. Humanity in another sense of the word. The humanities means, you know, the Latin, Greek, and all that sort of thing.

BROOKS: Right along that line, Mr. Frost, we seem to find a great many people in the world today who are deeply depressed by all the conditions we find around us, but you seem to be very much of an optimist, and I wonder how other people can acquire the same optimism that you seem to have?

FROST: I do not believe I am quite an optimist, but I believe there is a lot that is so good in it that it is worth going on with. There is a lot of bad about it.

This matter of confusion. I think the thing that confuses the mind is loss of a sense of form, and if you lose the sense of form, the doctor can restore it by teaching you how to make a horseshoe or a basket or something like that, or to blow smoke rings or anything to restore your sense of form. And as long as so many of us, nearly all of us, have a chance to make a little rounding out of something— of family life or a magazine or an article or a poem or a basket or a horseshoe or a tumbler—that is what keeps the sanity and that is what keeps and saves us from the sense of confusion.

When I hear people talk about confusion—at commencement addresses, you know—I just think it is getting into a bad habit. They don't mean it. Someone said it that was confused probably, and the rest of them are not confused but just go on saying it.

SPIVAK: Mr. Frost, in the minds of most of us, Christmas has come to be a happy season, and yet very few of us believe we are really happy. Do you consider yourself a happy man?

FROST: That would be self-praise, if I said it.

SPIVAK: Well, what then does happiness mean? I am trying to find out what you think happiness means.

FROST: It is an expression that lost its ancient English meaning; it is inward happiness. It is very hard to tell you. You can judge better of it than I can. I cannot even tell what I look like except in a looking glass, and that does not seem to persuade me. And I cannot tell how happy I am. I rather you tell me.

Spivak: Let me put it this way: What are the things in life that really count to you?

Frost: Well, this feeling of everyday that you can handle it, that you can give it shape, you know. Every morning I make up my bed. (I live alone.) Every morning I make up my mind a little bit before I begin to read the morning papers. Then I alter it a little bit, but that is going on all the time. What a busy world it is that way. How attractive it all is to have so much to re-handle day by day—the question of international affairs.

About this question of poetry and prose, you have not asked me if poetry has half a chance in a world like this—the making of poems and giving them their shape.

Fadiman: I often wonder whether we have an audience for poetry. I know your books are widely read, Mr. Frost, but is it not true that many other great poets are [not] equally fortunate? Have we lost the great audience that Whitman said was necessary for great poets?

Frost: I think the best audience the world ever had, probably, is the little town-and-gown audience that we get in the little college towns in the U.S.A.—two thousand towns, very pretty towns, too. They may not teach anybody anything, those colleges, but they do make pretty towns, and they do make a nice town audience!

Fadiman: Along that line. . . .

Frost: Better than Homer ever had or Ossian ever had or the troubadours ever had. I am just a wandering bard myself.

Fadiman: You are a wandering educator, too, Mr. Frost. Do you feel that poetry can [be] taught?

Frost: In this loose way: I made up some lines the other day—

> It takes a lot of in and outdoor schooling
> To get adapted to my kind of fooling.

Poetry is a kind of fooling that you got to get the hang of, and I go around playing that. You cannot preach about it; you get in a little wisecrack and you read a poem and so on.

There is a certain amount of teaching; that is, from the teacher's desk, too. At the same time, it cannot be too direct. It is shooting all around it and playing all around it, and it is outdoors and indoors, in school and out of school.

You can say a snobbish thing about it, if you want to, but St. Mark said, "These things are said in parables" (that is, poetry, figures of speech), "so the wrong people cannot understand them, and so get saved."

BROOKS: Mr. Frost, you must at various times have had young ambitious poets come to you for advice. Perhaps some of them had talent. What encouragement do you give these people?

FROST: Well, I always say to them, "This is what we want, but you have to have a snout for punishment. You are going to take a lot of punishment for it." And then I would say, "I wish you the greatest things for my country and for you and for me, but it is your funeral, not mine."

ROBB: In other words, the way of the poet is still hard?

FROST: Yes, it is meant to be. The way of everything is still hard. I have heard people quote me as saying that one thing will never change in the world no matter how easy we make it with all sorts of science and everything else. One thing will always be hard. That is saving your soul, Inez, saving your decency.

ROBB: One other question. This is the question that you yourself asked, Mr. Frost, and I am going to ask you to answer it.

It is a quatrain and is called "A Question," and you say:

> A voice said, Look me in the stars
> And tell me truly, men of earth,
> If all the soul-and-body scars
> Were not too much to pay for birth.

FROST: You bring up another thing, the mood. That is a mood, when you sometimes wonder if it is worth it, all the pain.

ROBB: Well, was it?

FROST: Sometimes I feel one way, and sometimes I feel the other. In the many movements of a poet's mind you do not have to have one doctrine running all through the work, optimism or pessimism. Sometimes it seems too bad.

I made a prayer the other day. (You say things against God and the whole thing sometimes.) I made a prayer like this: "O God, if

You'll forgive our little jokes on You—all our little jokes on You—we'll forgive Your one great big joke on us."

BRINKLEY: I have one short question, Mr. Frost.

I believe I have seen you quoted as saying that a poem in one respect is like a love affair, in that it begins in delight and ends in wisdom. I wonder if you found any other similarity?

FROST: Yes, that is true about everything. You know what God's great big joke on us is? The answer is the spring of the year. It begins in delight and ends in we don't know what kind of a crop.

SPIVAK: You once wrote that courage is the human virtue that counts most. Why did you say that?

FROST: I said that to tease the lady, so she would say: "Isn't it a sad world where courage has to be the chief virtue."

SPIVAK: You do not quite believe that?

FROST: I don't think it is sad. I do believe it, yes; I think it is. But I wanted to hear her say it is a sad world where the chief virtue had to be courage; that is, in all things—the daring.

SPIVAK: Do you believe that virtue, courage, is the human virtue that counts most, though?

FROST: Yes, I will stick to that, tonight.

SPIVAK: Only for tonight?

FROST: I will stick to that.[. . .]

A Tour in Britain

In the late spring of 1957 RF made a goodwill mission to Britain for the United States State Department. It was, in a phrase he used in this and similar connections in the closing years of his life, "a rounding out" for the poet, a visit to the land where he had first won literary acclaim four decades before.

During a period of nearly a month RF talked and read before audiences, visited old friends and made new ones, saw once again a few of the scenes of his 1912–1915 adventure, and received the highest academic honors that England and Ireland could bestow.

This interview, which appeared in The Scotsman *of Edinburgh on May 22, 1957, records RF's arrival at London.*

MR. Robert Frost, doyen of American poets, arrived here yesterday to give readings of his works at universities and to receive honorary degrees at Oxford and Cambridge. Mr. Frost's shrewd blue eyes and rugged countenance do not fit the conventional idea of a poet. Neither do his edge of wit, his disarming chuckle, and his tolerant approach to the problems of modern living.[. . .]

In his London hotel today Mr. Frost confessed to surprise—he cannot, though he tries hard, conceal his innate modesty and friendliness—that so warm a welcome should have been prepared for him here. This week he is lecturing at the universities of London, Cambridge, and Durham, and on May thirtieth at Manchester University.

"It was difficult to make up my mind to come," he said. "You see, they will be such different audiences here, whereas in America people know me and my gruff voice and I know them. I did not expect to be remembered here as I am."

He is determined to visit both Edinburgh and Glasgow but cannot say when, because of the many official engagements in his itinerary. The son of a New England father—much of his work reflects life in New England, where he has lived for many years—his mother was a Scot who came from Alloa, the daughter of a sea captain who sailed from Leith and lost his life at sea.

"She used to read Robert Burns to me," he said, "and I remember well some of her sayings. She had no patience with snobbery and pretence, and if anybody was boasting she would say he was surely 'the cousin of the Duke of Argyll's piper's son's wee laddie.' "[. . .]

Asked if he thought if some of the more incomprehensible poets of the English school reflected in their work the dissonance of the age in which they lived, Mr. Frost's eye glinted. He raised an admonitory hand.

"Poets who seek to conceal their meaning have usually something so commonplace to say [. . .] it is no more worth bothering about than some adage, as 'a stitch in time saves nine.' "

To the young poet of today he would say, "There is a danger of forgetting that poetry must include the mind, as well as the emotions. . . . The mind is dangerous and must be left in. . . . The poet can use the mind in fear and trembling. But he must use it."

Asked about some of his writing in which sensitivity to the beauty of nature is allied with poignant awareness of the suffering within the natural order, Mr. Frost responded with another question.

"Where is there any benevolence of purpose?"

Yet he is hopeful about the future of mankind.

"When a tree is cut down, another grows."—So he sees individual lives and even, perhaps, civilizations.

Of the problems of injustice in the human pattern he had this to say:

"We must cry a little and laugh a little, but neither cry nor laugh too much."

He wants, as befits a poet, to see more poetry in his country and the world.

"But I tell the young people who come to me that they have got to be prepared for work and sacrifice."

Then Mr. Frost's mood changes.

"I have never been an assiduous worker."

The warm chuckle comes again.

"I don't like British central heating and cold streets, and I am not one for sightseeing. But when I came to Britain years ago for the first time, it was because I wanted to visit the cradle of lyric poetry—and also to live under a thatch, and I hope to see a thatched cottage again this time."[. . .]

To the People and the Press

Manchester was among the several university cities RF visited in England. The text that follows is drawn from the Manchester Guardian *of May 31, 1957. It captures the typical character of RF's interviews and public appearances during the course of his highly successful English tour.*

I'LL tell you a story," said Robert Frost, his blue eyes twinkling under his famous thatch of white hair. At once all nearby conversation stopped in the lounge of the Manchester hotel yesterday to enable everyone to eavesdrop on the great American poet, whose stories about the people of New England are the subject of some of his most famous poems.

"Eighteen years ago I was very ill, and a minister came to see me. His son had just been born, and he wondered if it was good to bring someone into the world at a time like this. So I told him that you didn't go down to a tennis court to criticize the layout or what it's like. You go down to a tennis court to see if you can play or not, or at least I do.

"Well, I saw his son at college, a fine boy, just recently, and his father told me he had been brought up on my story about tennis."

This was the Robert Frost of *North of Boston,* the same voice which Padraic Colum once likened to the bark of an eagle.

Frost has more than once pointed out that

> Most of the change we think we see in life
> Is due to truths being in and out of favor.

He himself had hardly changed since his last visit to England in

1928—he still does not look anything like his age, which is eighty-three—and during his present tour, arranged by the United States Information Service, he has not found England greatly changed either. There has been a depression, a world war, and a welfare state since his last visit, but as a poet he has always dealt in the most durable things of life.

"The country does not seem to have changed much, except the farmers look more progressive. I remember a rick being burned because a farmer had some new machinery in."

He was sure the people had not changed either. Friends like Edward Thomas had gone—"he died at Vimy Ridge, you know"—but he was shortly meeting Mrs. Thomas and other old friends.

He told the large crowd at Manchester University last night:

"Edward Thomas was one of the greatest friends of my life, and I am always hoping to hear that more people know about him. That is one of the wishes you have for a poet, a gentle poet, that he may be thought of."

He was going to collaborate with Eleanor Farjeon on another edition of Thomas's poetry, "to see if we can give it another little shove."

He had persuaded Thomas to turn from prose to poetry.

"That was the only time I ever influenced anybody. I taught school, but I have never succeeded in teaching anybody to be a poet."[. . .]

At eighty-three Robert Frost was as full of wry asides as forty years ago when Wilfrid Gibson described him as going

> . . .on and on and on,
> In his slow New England fashion, for our delight,
> Holding us with shrewd turns and racy quips,
> And the rare twinkle of his grave blue eyes

When he first arrived at Manchester someone asked him at the station if he would see the controversial English play, *Look Back in Anger*, which was showing in the city. But he said he wanted "to see the simple folk of Manchester who did so much to keep England from going in on the side of the South in our Civil War."

Would he like to see the Lincoln statue in Platt Fields? No, he didn't want to see any of the show places. He wanted to see the city "just as it happens."

How many of the "simple folk" were there now? He did not wink an eye when told there were at least eight hundred thousand.

He said over a ginger beer at the hotel that he was "quite good at scraping up acquaintanceships" and added:

"In the train I saw a lady writing. So I said aloud, 'Do you think she's writing something for the *Manchester Guardian*?' She looked up and then we got talking. She was a Tory M.P.'s wife and had been educated at Bryn Mawr College."

Mr. Frost's eyes twinkled.

"Sometimes I wonder if all the girls educated at Bryn Mawr don't come over and marry your Tory M.P.'s."

Following his own principle that "all truth is dialogue," he questioned the reporters who questioned him.

"Are you a Manchester boy? It is good to belong to a home town," he said to one reporter.

"I come from a part of America like this. All dependent on cotton and woolen goods, at one time, but now they've had to get more diversified to survive."

He had missed the reception committee at the station and so he waited at the platform barrier with his friend Prof. L. Thompson, of Princeton University.

"I guess you thought I'd come up third class, but I came up first class today and fooled you," Mr. Frost said.

I asked him if it was true that of all the great men of the past he would most like to meet Theocritus, and he took me to task for it, as he took the professors to task for other things in his lecture at the university. He told the audience of at least five hundred:

"Someone suggested today that I thought Theocritus was best. But I guess someone a long time ago put that one in my mouth. They were just referring to my admiration for him and for the eclogue style of poetry which you find, say, in Virgil.

"I write two kinds of poems: long blank verse ones like the eclogues and short lyrics."

Did he speak his poetry aloud as he wrote?

"No, I just try to catch a voice I hear. Speaking it aloud imperfectly as I would might spoil it. That's why I used to like to go to the theater to hear the voice."

He didn't like reformers, he confessed, but he counted Lord

Beveridge among his friends—"and I guess you'd call him the father of your welfare state." He had met Lord Beveridge the day before and asked him where the Liberals had all gone to.

"When I was here last they were a big party. Now they're just a handful."

He seemed pleased to know the Liberals still won some votes in elections.

He said his definition of a liberal was "someone who is unhappy because he is not as unhappy as other people."

Wry and typical comments such as this were very much appreciated by his large audience, and his style was proof enough that poetry could be made much more widely popular than it is at present. But you need a Robert Frost to do it. No one who heard him could doubt the uniqueness nor the greatness of the man. The temptation, as with his poetry, is merely to quote his wry asides as he pokes fun, perhaps at the press or at the "professors."

I had asked him about the progress of his "one-man revolution," and he told the audience about this and added:

"I don't mind a revolution if I start it. The kind of revolution I don't like are those someone else starts. I guess you'd call it vanity."

He introduced several of his lyrics as "a sing-song rhymey thing" and on one occasion added:

"They may not be deep enough. This question of how deep is deep. The things that are done with poetry! You bother people with your poetry, and then they bother you back with it. That's what the professors do. It evens up."

He quoted Humpty Dumpty—"one of those nice brevities I like so much"—and described it as "very deep." And he warned his audience to be careful about Mother Goose—"a very deep lady or woman: be careful as well because there's a social distinction there."

In his famous poem "Stopping by Woods on a Snowy Evening" he has his horse ask a question. He recalled that a professor had asked the famous Texan horseman, Frank Dobie, if a horse could ask a question, and he approvingly quoted Dobie's reply: "A horse can ask better questions than most professors."[. . .]

Even after he had been reading and talking for over an hour the audience would not let him go.

He offered to answer questions as he believed that was the practice in Britain. A woman asked him to sketch the background of his poem "Dust of Snow," and he said that the heart-warming incident he described in the poem was similar to "good news in the morning paper" (and he gave another sly peek over at the reporters) . [. . .]

No one in the audience as they cheered him as he slowly walked out could think him either old or a conservative. He merely had the appearance of a great man.

It Takes a Hero to Make a Poem

Before leaving England to fly to Dublin, where he was to receive an honorary doctorate from the National University of Ireland, RF tape-recorded a conversation with the author-critic Cecil Day Lewis. Later broadcast over the BBC's Third Programme (on September 13, 1957), the interview was printed in the Spring 1958 number of the Claremont Quarterly *under the title used here.*

D AY LEWIS : Mr. Frost, when I think about the way you write, the language you use seems entirely a language of your own; and in your first book you seem to have started writing this way without apparently any influence from anyone else.

FROST : You can see in some poems some lingering words like "fain" and "list" that I was getting rid of, that I was ashamed of to begin with.

DAY LEWIS : Yes, but you got rid of those pretty fast, I think.

FROST : Yes.

DAY LEWIS : But the—the poem "Mowing"[. . .]

FROST : "Mowing"? Yes, now that's perfectly clear, straight goods—mine.

DAY LEWIS : But that seemed to set the style, and you never felt any need to alter it much?

FROST : No, I don't remember thinking much about style except that I was ashamed at "thee" and "thou" and "thine" and such things as that: that I'd dropped them without any—without thinking much about it.

D AY LE WIS : Yes.[. . .] When I re-read your poems to write an introduction to some of them I noticed one or two Augustan phrases almost. Or they might have been Augustan as altered a bit by Crabbe. One of them was—the "highway where the. . . ." (How does it go?) The "highway where the slow wheel pours the sand." And then there was one phrase: that famous one about

> To warm the frozen swamp as best it could
> With the slow smokeless burning of decay.

That seems to me very like a good Augustan, or at any rate a good line by Crabbe. Did you read him?

F R OST : No, I had never read Crabbe when I wrote that. But I'd read, you know, so scatteringly—so at large—that I can't put my finger on any particular thing. I didn't know about Crabbe until somebody called my attention to him, and then I felt some kinship. I have two first editions of him now.

D AY LE WI S : Yes, yes. And another thing, do you not think that the language of the American countryside, of the country folk you lived amongst so long, has got into your poetry?

F R OST : It must have a good deal, though I'm aware of another— of a vocabulary a little below any I use, you know: a little more—a little rough, a little cruder. But I think there's nothing in our country talk of the sort of rustic kind that didn't come from some quarter in England.

D AY LE WIS : Yes?

F R OST : There'll be a word like "clide." The cattle—the cattle get clide. That's "cloyed" really, and that's a word that you wouldn't use for animals, you know, like "sorrowful and cloyed." But they use it about the cattle: The cattle get clide, when they're overfed. Things like that I haven't played with. They're curiosities, but I haven't played with them.[. . .]

D AY LE WIS : Now there's another thing that interests me very much. I've forgotten where you said it, but somewhere or other: that you write a poem to clear up some confusion in your own mind.[. . .]

F R OST : Yes, I suppose that's a good deal backward-looking theory, that I can see in nearly every poem some answer to some doubt or some question, you know, that's come up in my mind—

even in argument with people or something—a difficulty in a situation, you know, that needs a phrase to finish it off. The same as in diplomacy they find a phrase. It's just like diplomacy—you find a phrase.

DAY LEWIS: Yes.

FROST: It's a way *out* of something. Now that's not very obvious in the poems. Not as obvious to anybody else as it is *to* me. I could probably name twenty or thirty poems that were just answers to somebody that had—somebody that had left me unsatisfied with the last thing he said in an argument.

DAY LEWIS: Yes, yes.

FROST: A year afterwards.

DAY LEWIS: I suppose most of us start off in a kind of fog. We have a feeling that there is a poem asking to be written and one makes moves into this fog to see the right direction to follow, but I noticed in the—I think it's in your introduction to your collected poems—you made a difference between the way the scholar works with his accumulation of facts and the way a poet works. I think you said the poet just allows whatever sticks to him to stick to him, like burrs when you walk through a field. But I've been looking into this lately, and it seems to me that—that at a certain stage, at any rate, of their work scholars—I mean historians, philosophers, or scientists—have very much the same imaginative jump as poets do. I think it was Collingwood, the Oxford historian and philosopher, who said that he—he starts in a fog, and he doesn't know what the problem is until he is halfway towards solving it. Well, that is true for us, isn't it—for poets?

FROST: Yes, yes, that's a good description—another good description of a way a poem happens.

DAY LEWIS: Yes.

FROST: But it seems to me there's a difference here about the material. You can see the deliberateness with which the scholar seeks his material after he gets going, but a poet never lives in that way at all. All the best things he ever uses are things he didn't know he was getting when he was getting them. A poet never takes notes. You never take notes in a love affair.

DAY LEWIS: Yes. Do you find that subjects have to lie about in your mind for a long time before you can use them or. . . ?

FROST: Oh, no. The thing is that the scattered material that's been making in various ways—thrown ahead of me, all round me; and all of a sudden some day I see a way across some of it, and that is a little theme—a little idea. It gives me a start and a direction so that I can use some of this stuff. That's all. You never—you never cease: you never rest from sort of little ideas and things that don't seem to start to be poems. They're just scattered thoughts, you know. But some day, all of a sudden, there's one that looks as if it's just struck like lightning across a lot of this stuff.

DAY LEWIS: Narrative poems, you've written quite a lot of them. Have you come across any narrative poems written in our time that seem to you true narrative? They seem so often to me to be really dramatic monologues or ballads or something concealing themselves as narratives.

FROST: Yes, I guess that there's a good deal of that in mine, too. Can you think of one that seems to you pure narrative? I think every poem, even a little lyric, ought to have a progress through it; it ought to go to an end and have something of a narrative movement in it.

DAY LEWIS: Yes, yes.

FROST: Not stand still and pirouette on one leg.

DAY LEWIS: I've tried to write narratives myself, and I'm not at all sure. . . . I mean we're so overawed now by critics and, indeed, other people who tell us that the work of the narrative poem is all done better by the novel or the short story or the films, and so on, that I tend to get rather overanxious, I think, when I'm writing a narrative poem.

FROST: I think there's always someone talking. I even look, when I approach a novel, to see if it's unbroken prose, without any conversation in it. I don't read it then, I want it to be broken with talk. I want drama in the narrative—a lot of talk. I suppose mine just runs over with these things. There's always somebody—nearly always somebody—talking.

DAY LEWIS: Yes.

FROST: I remember someone said to me once, "What you're trying to write is the short story." But I thought that was rather doubtful.

DAY LEWIS: It seems to me that possibly you have an advantage in the writing of narrative by living in a fairly remote place: in the country, where small things that happen—things that are gossiped about—are extremely important. I should think that is a good foundation, isn't it, for telling the sort of stories that you tell? In the next village but one, they would refuse to admit that you existed, and you refuse to admit they exist; so in the country you're in a close circle of a community, and anything that happens there is potential drama and story.

FROST: Yes, I've picked up many of them all my life. And they're all dialogue, aren't they, nearly?

DAY LEWIS: Quite a lot of them.

FROST: Yes, there's a story implied in every case. They are rather the sort of thing you speak of; they're gossip. And one of the three great things in the world is gossip, you know. First there's religion; and then there's science; and there's—and then there's friendly gossip. Those are the three—the three great things. Philosophy is just a thing that trims religion, you know—that prunes it and all that. And you've got science. And you've got this: the biggest of all, is gossip—our interest in each other.

DAY LEWIS: Yes, which is really based on a kind of hero-worship, isn't it? Or rather a lot of hero-worship is based on that, isn't it?

FROST: Yes, yes.

DAY LEWIS: And I suppose that anyone who is going to write a narrative poem now has to have the kind of interest in human beings that often comes out as hero-worship.

FROST: That's it. It is hero-worship, you see, and one of the things that makes you go is making a hero out of somebody that nobody else had ever noticed was a hero.

DAY LEWIS: Yes, exactly, yes.

FROST: You pick up the unconsidered person.

DAY LEWIS: Yes, and of course that is what gossip does, in a small community: it makes heroes, doesn't it—or villains—out of our neighbors? But they're big anyway.

FROST: Yes. Do you know, that's interesting to hear you use the word that way, when people are saying there's no such thing as heroism left. Some of the talk is that way. I know of a book of history that says heroism is out of date. But it's in everything. It's in making a book, you know. And it takes a hero to make a poem.

A Poet and a National Symbol

*The association with official Washington which was a promi-
nent element of the final years of RF's life began in the latter
part of the 1950's. During this period his fame as a poet-
philosopher-sage and as a public figure enlarged to staggering
dimensions. The much-beloved octogenarian took on, more
and more, the character of a national symbol, and the Capital
was for him, in accordance, increasingly a place of appropriate identification.*

Here James Reston devotes one of his regular columns for
The New York Times *to a Washington visit by RF in the
fall of 1957. The text was published in the* Times *on October
27th.*

Every time Robert Frost comes to town the Washington
Monument stands up a little straighter. The old gentleman was
here this week just when everybody was down in the dumps about
the Russians, but he was full of bounce and confidence.

The beauty of life, said he, looking out on the golden maples on
R Street, lies in struggle and change and taking tough decisions.
When he heard people complaining about the Russians and the
Sputnik and the endless standoff with Moscow, he said he had
trouble suppressing a mocking frivolity.

"We ought to enjoy a standoff," he remarked. "Let it stand and
deepen in meaning. Let's not be hasty about showdowns. Let's be
patient and confident in our country."

At eighty-three, Mr. Frost is still full of poetry and plans, still
wandering about the world talking to kids about what it means to

be an American, still taking long walks through the Northern woods, and still urging everybody to talk up and be sassy.

He is against everything and everybody that want people to rely on somebody else. He is against the United Nations. He is against the welfare state. He is against conformity and easy slogans and Madison Avenue, and he hasn't seen a President he liked since Grover Cleveland.

"I keep reading about old Grover, and after sixty years I have to admit there were one or two things that could be said against him; but I concede it reluctantly. As Mencken said, Cleveland got on in politics, not by knuckling to politicians but scorning and defying them. He didn't go around spouting McGuffy Reader slogans or wanting to be liked."

The United Nations, disturbed by Mr. Frost's opposition, suggested to him recently that he might like to write a poem celebrating the ideal of the interdependence of the nations. Sweden had given the U. N. a huge chunk of solid iron, and somebody thought that this should be built into the U. N. building as a symbol of nature's strength and unity.

Frost was not interested. Iron, he said, could be used to strengthen the U. N. building, or it could be used for weapons of war. That was the way with nature, he said: always confronting mankind with decisions. So he rejected the invitation with a couplet:

> Nature within her inmost self decides[*]
> To trouble men with having to take sides.

His pet project at the moment is to band together all men and women who want to stamp out "togetherness." The glory of America, he says, has been its pioneers, who celebrated "separateness" and who were not always seeking protection. "There is," he remarks, "no protection without direction."

Mr. Frost is still a physical phenomenon. There is a comfortable, shaggy look about him but great physical and mental power. He has a pair of shoulders like a Notre Dame tackle, a shock of disobedient white hair, and a vast solidity, like a great natural object.

---

* The error in this quotation, wherein the first line of the couplet ends with the word "decides," rather than "divides," is evidently referred to in RF's birthday interview in 1959, as reported on page 196.

His idea, one gathers, is that America should act in the face of the Communist challenge as a great man would act. It should not be dismayed. It should not be boastful. It should be calm and watchful and industrious. It should avoid pretension and sham. It should say clearly and calmly what it means and do what it says it will do.

"The question for every man and every nation," he says, "is to be clear about where the first answerability lies. Are we as individuals to be answerable first only to others or to ourselves and some ideal beyond ourselves? Is the United States to be answerable first to the United Nations or to its own concept of what is right?"

Once we get this straight, he believes, the United States will be less entranced and preoccupied with the Soviet world, more self-reliant, more prepared psychologically for the endless struggle of existence.

Transition and change do not bother him. He is pleased with Dean Inge's reminder that when Adam and Eve were kicked out of the Garden of Eden, Adam was heard to remark, no doubt by a reporter of the *Times*, "We sure are living in a period of transition."

"All life," he says, "is cellular. We live by the breaking down of cells and the building up of new cells. Change is constant and unavoidable. That is the way it is with human beings and with nations, so why deplore it?"

To Mr. Frost most of the political pronouncements of the day are just "corn-meal mush," put out by politicians who think their "first answerability" is to what will get them re-elected, instead of what is right and true.

But he isn't worried.

"I stand here at the window and try to figure out whether American men or women swing their arms more freely. There cannot be much to fear in a country where there are so many right faces going by. I keep asking myself where they all come from, and I keep thinking that maybe God was just making them up new around the next corner."

Washington Has a
New Kind of Bureaucrat

Thus did one newspaper herald the naming of RF in 1958 to be Consultant in Poetry at the Library of Congress.
This article by John Barron was published in the Washington Evening Star *on May 22nd, the day after the news conference held to announce the poet's appointment.*

ROBERT FROST yesterday promised to become a lobbyist in Washington for the arts.

The poet, perhaps America's most honored and beloved, has been appointed consultant at the Library of Congress. At a press conference here following announcement of his appointment he let his wit, kindness, and intelligence play over a diversity of topics, including Ezra Pound, President Eisenhower, and American education.

If his new duties at the Library, which begin in October, are hazy to others, they are quite clear to him. He declared his mission in Washington would be to make "statesmen and politicians more aware of their responsibilities to the arts."

Asked how he proposed to accomplish this, he replied, "I guess I'll have to ask them to dinner once in a while."

He also said he might give politicians copies of his books. Later, the eighty-four-year-old farmer and teacher added, "If you only knew all of my wiles."

Alluding to his recent role in obtaining release of poet Ezra Pound from confinement in St. Elizabeths Hospital, Mr. Frost said he feared he was acquiring more of a reputation as a lawyer than as a poet. But he thought his experience with officialdom had left him better prepared for his new job here.

"I wouldn't have so much confidence in myself if I hadn't been so successful in a Washington law case recently," he said. "I surprised myself."

Then he referred to a poem by Kipling which begins, "If only my mother could see me now. . . ."

Mr. Frost said he had not seen Pound since 1915. He explained that he sought freedom for the poet, who had been charged with treason, "on general principle and out of sentiment for a good poet in trouble with himself, the world, and the law."

He said Pound had complained that he did not act fast enough.

Through his negotiations with Attorneys General Brownell and Rogers and other officials in the Pound case, Mr. Frost said he gained a new impression of government. He said he found no "buck-passing," but was met everywhere with frankness, directness, and honesty.

The poet described President Eisenhower as "a very, very fine man, even if he doesn't read too many books." He said he had a book, the complete works of Robert Frost, which he intended to give the President "as a gift from one farmer to another."[. . .]

Concerning American education, Mr. Frost thought the most harmful deficiency lies in the high schools. He advocated establishing named chairs in them to create tenure and prestige for teachers.

He said that at parties and receptions attending his travels about the country, he seldom meets a high-school teacher.

"They aren't thought of as anything in the community. No one would think of having them there."

White-haired, handsome, alert, Mr. Frost responded to questions with humor and a logician's perception of their implications. He evinced some difficulty in hearing, but otherwise was fit and vigorous.

Once, during a momentary lull in the questioning, he called for more queries from reporters, saying, "We want to make this lively."

He quoted poetry and made couplets. About adult education he said:

> What are you doing back here?
> My name is adult, I went to school without result. [. . .]

"Poet in Waiting"
Bids for a Rating

These were the headlines for Bess Furman's account in The New York Times *of RF's press conference in Washington as he took up his duties as poetry consultant at the Library of Congress. The story was published on October 16, 1958.*

ROBERT FROST wants to borrow four American paintings for a year to create a discriminating atmosphere in his federal office. The eighty-four-year-old poet would have them on the walls of the Library of Congress office into which he has just moved as Consultant in Poetry in English for the year 1958–59. He titled his job "Poet in Waiting."

He told a news conference today that the four paintings, which he said couldn't be beaten, would help him "get out of the small-potatoes class."

He listed them as: "Winslow Homer's 'Four Bells'; Andrew Wyeth's 'Sea Wind'; Thomas Eakins' painting of boatmen on the Schuylkill; and James Chapin's—that Negress of his, that girl singing."

This later sent librarians scurrying to their art reference books. The Chapin picture was easily identified as "Ruby Green Singing" and Wyeth's as "Wind From the Sea." But Eakins apparently had a whole series of Schuylkill paintings.[. . .]

"I never knew Eakins or Homer. I did know Jim Chapin, but no intimacy that I could be accused of. But I think those four pictures I could go on—I'd stand by them."

Mr. Frost said that three of the pictures are now in public galleries, and the fourth, Wyeth's, is privately owned by Charles Hill Morgan III of Amherst, Massachusetts, "who once put it into my hotel room at Amherst."

The white-haired poet said that he also wants a bookcase in his office, to be filled with his own choice of this country's poetry—"My Little Anthology." This selection, he said, would be for his visitors to enjoy, whether he were present or not.

He noted that only about two thousand books of poetry in English are copyrighted each year, and that half of them probably were "vanity press" (the printing paid for by the author).

Mr. Frost made it clear that he is not giving accolades either to the abstract in art or the obscure in poetry.

"A man I know owns a painting of a head with three eyes which he considers priceless," he said. "Three eyes!" he snorted.

He said that Ezra Pound, the poet whom he helped to get released from a mental hospital here, had written some fine verse, both rhymed and free, as a young man.

"But the Cantos, those lengthy things," said Mr. Frost. "I don't say I'm not up to them, I say they're not up to me. Nobody ought to like them, but some do; and I let them. That's my tolerance." [. . .]

Mr. Frost gave his first lecture in his new position tonight. It was limited to high-school seniors in this area.

The poet said he wouldn't want to have too sumptuous working conditions.

"If I had a beautiful studio, I'd never paint. I'd have ladies visiting."

He glanced about the room and added, "Might as well be candid."

He Himself Is Perhaps the Biggest Metaphor of All

This interview-article by Milton Bracker, originally entitled "The 'Quietly Overwhelming' Robert Frost," appeared in the November 30, 1958, New York Times Magazine.

ROBERT FROST is a poet whose work and personal appearances have moved thousands of Americans to a demonstrativeness that might easily be associated with the presence of a heroic athlete or a movie star. When he says his poems (the verb he insists on—he never "reads" them), it is to standing-room-only audiences. And the response is based not on superficial idolatry but on a deep-set and affectionate admiration often bordering on awe.

At eighty-four, Robert Frost has won four Pulitzer Prizes and been cited by more institutions of higher learning than there are in any college football conference. He has jested that he would rather get a degree than an education; but this is simply to be gracious to the donors. Actually, he has not only had an education of his own (though never a baccalaureate degree), but as a teacher, both fixed and itinerant, has contributed preferred shares of stock to the educational portfolios held by several generations of scholars.

But the impact of Robert Frost on poetry and on those who love it is possibly less than his impact as a personality on anyone who gets near him. If you have had considerable experience in "interviewing" people, you are still not prepared for this white-haired New Englander (who, improbably, was born in San Francisco), because he is like no statesman, celebrity, or ordinary human being you have ever interviewed. Robert Frost, newly honored by appointment as poetry consultant to the Library of Congress, is quietly but unmistakably overwhelming.

"There's nothing in me to be afraid of," he will assure you. "I'm too offhand; I'm an offhander."

But there is a deadly joke in his offhandedness. As he says, slipping it in casually, in another connection, "I bear watching." Moreover, he will let you know disarmingly that, "I'm not confused; I'm only well-mixed." And he might have added of himself, as he frequently remarks of certain of his most-quoted and picked-apart poems, that he is "loaded with ulteriority."

"You have to look out for everybody's metaphors," says Robert Frost. He himself is perhaps the biggest metaphor of all. He even *looks* like a symbol.

His hair is really white and really silky; a mass of it tends to sift down to the left side of his forehead like snow to one corner of a window. His eyes are pale blue, cragged by heavy brows with white curls wintering them. His lower lip is the thicker; it juts a little. In the over-all he is massive, often understandably likened to rough-hewn granite.

He had an "altercation with a surgeon"—there is a virtually imperceptible scar on his right cheek. But the real scar is the scar of living, and no man ever wore it more proudly or with more stunning effect, as photographers have discovered.

Even in the impersonal formality of a New York hotel room, he would prefer to be tieless. He wears high black shoes and is apt to leave them half unlaced. His hands show virtually no spots of age. His grip is firm and wholly unself-conscious. And when he walks down an aisle to a stage or platform, he strides strongly and directly, as completely in command of the situation as of the loyalty and awe of those in the audience. His voice is resonant to the level of being gravelly; he may use it to repeat things he has said many times before. But he is psychologically incapable of speaking a cliché or of arranging words in a commonplace manner.

Still, an interview has to have a "plan of campaign," Robert Frost acknowledged. So what more natural than a little starter about his new job? He seized upon the word "consultant" in his new title.

"As the greatest living authority on education," he began, with a twinkle, "I particularly want to be consulted by the foundations."

Robert Frost has had one publisher for forty-three years. His books have sold more than four hundred thousand copies, and he has actually made a living out of poetry, although he once had to give up buying a painting he wanted because he could not get it for one thousand dollars. But the implication was clear: If, through his new post, he could interest those who might assist other poets, he was eager to do so.

He passed a hand over his face and injected a mild qualification.

"I'm not to advocate anything," he said. "I can describe better than I can advocate. I'm a reporter; you should have seen me at Rutgers. . . ."

He was referring to an occasion where—as at the New School for Social Research a few nights later—poetry, as personified by Robert Frost, "gets mobbed."

But (with no specific reference to either audience) Robert Frost, the reporter, was not to be taken in by the externals.

"You want to watch for those people who seem to enjoy what they don't understand," he said. The "partisans" of Ezra Pound, for example, and "I can't be called that."[. . .]

"You can't make a poem without a point."

He laughed, remembering having said it another way: "You've got to snap the quip to make Pegasus prance."

Robert Frost is much too human not to be pleased by his own phrase-making.

"Snap the quip," he repeated, with a chuckle. "I could make up a joke at a banquet, use it in a different way at another banquet. I'm very instructive; I'm very accidental. I go barding around, and all that. Barding around."

He frequently "bards around" with college presidents and has warm regard and great respect for several.

"But I'm aware that some of them have no interest in it, and that's all right," he said.

Again the raised brows, the fleeting laugh that lights up the weathered face like a sudden shaft of sunlight.

"They *have* to be present when they decorate me," he added. Then, more seriously, "I'm not as anxious about poetry as I am about these poor college presidents."

Apart from the problems faced by the educators, there was a

criterion he liked to apply: "He's on our side." He mentioned four of whom that might be said, then fretted a little lest he had left out some others. He is always elliptical in his language; never in his sense of friendship.

Robert Frost has defined poetry as "that which is lost from prose and verse in translation." As for the great poets, Shakespeare "knew more about psychiatry and people like Othello and Desdemona" than any twenty-five-dollar-an-hour man.

Robert Frost considered the Moor for a moment as an analyst's patient.

"The psychiatrist would advise him not to smother her," he decided.

Then his quick eyes changed reflectively.

"But some of them are awful good at it," he admitted.

He was reminded of his own insights—his incredible exactness with words, as when, in "Blue-Butterfly Day," he wrote of the wheels that "freshly sliced the April mire," thus choosing the absolutely correct verb, the one so uniquely evocative as to renew and fix for many readers the experience of observing such a wheel in such mud for all time. And the other exactnesses: the swimming buck pushing the *crumpled* water; the ice crystals from the birch branch *avalanching* on the snow crust.

Robert Frost's browned face crinkled at the references.

"That's what I live for," he said—the appreciation, in detail, of the essential purity of his work. "It cuts a little edge across your feelings," he said.

Then he talked of the American attitude toward poetry, of the time he and a distinguished scientist met and he had begun, "Let's you and I compare science and poetry; that's what I live for."

The other said, "You mean the exactness of science and the inexactness of poetry?"

" 'Oh,' I said," said Robert Frost, " 'you mean poetry is inexact. If you mean that, I'm going home.'

"He said, 'Let's change the subject.' "

And he told of the diplomat who had spent a lot on modern art and liked to be regarded as something of an expert on it, but who remarked of a young relative with poetic inclinations, "We hoped he'd get over it." Robert Frost had not enjoyed that.

On the other hand, he knew businessmen who really had "this same gentle weakness for the arts."

"A man will say, 'I'm just an engineer,' " he went on, "yet he will read more poetry than anyone I know."

And he linked this to the "greatest triumph in life; that's what everything turns on: to be reminded of something you hardly knew you knew." He said it gave you the feeling, "Oh, what a good boy am I."

Then, inevitably, I brought up "Stopping by Woods on a Snowy Evening." He had "said" this a few nights before at the New School, pronouncing it a little rapidly—a little too rapidly to permit the emotion of those in the audience (who had been gripped by it for anywhere from thirty minutes to thirty years) to break out in applause. There is of course a growing literature about these sixteen lines; and Robert Frost took it in stride.

"Now, that's all right," he said; "it's out of my hands once it's published."

His protagonist might have said:

> But I have promises to keep,
> And miles to go before I sleep. . .

simply because he was having a pleasant social evening, and it was time to go home. Yet Robert Frost knew it had often been taken as a "death poem."

"I never intended that," he said, "but I did have the feeling it was loaded with ulteriority." He said it was written one night back in the Twenties, when he was a "little excited from getting over-tired—they call it autointoxicated."

In the second stanza he made what he has called an "unnecessary commitment"—the line

> My little horse must think it queer

But he rode it out; he "triumphed over it."

And, he went on, there was "that thing about every poem. I didn't see the end until I got to it. Every poem is a voyage of discovery. I go in to see if I can get out, like you go to the North Pole. Once you've said the first line, the rest of it's got to be."

Robert Frost leaned heavily toward his visitor, as on a rostrum he seems to move gradually closer to each individual in the hall.

"The glory of any particular poem," he continued, "is once you've tasted that arrival at the end. That's what makes all the difference."

But in poetry, as in other struggles, the defeats need not be "inglorious." Again, as always, with Robert Frost, it was doing what had to be done and doing it bravely. It was the triumph of spirit over matter. It was people "not believing, and then having to believe."

Robert Frost has one "ruthless purpose" and that is poetry. But he is as aware of the police story on page one of the morning paper as of the so-called advent of the space age. He takes it all in perspective.

He was at Kitty Hawk in 1893, before the Wright Brothers. Some time after their historic flight he wrote a poem called "Kitty Hawk." Thus, early aeronautics and recent rocketry are in a sense the same to him; they are both part of the "great enterprise of the spirit into matter." Science is the great "lock-picker." Science goes "on, on, on; but the wonder of philosophy is that it stops."

Since man knew all along that the moon and the planets were there, it was inevitable that scientists would be "risking spirit" to get there. And that poets would write of where they were trying to get, and why.

As for Robert Frost himself:

"About one-tenth of my poems are astronomical; and I've had a glass a good deal of the time." (He meant a telescope but, as in so many things he says, the figurative interpretation was at least as accurate.)

He said the young missile men were doing a "fine, daring, bold thing." They were sharing the "great event of history"—science. And science meant the "dash of the spirit into the material," no matter how remote.

But Robert Frost has always had his feet on the earth, too. And as for the two powers that seemed in contention for this planet (as well as in a race to the moon), he saw their opposed systems as evidencing "two great ideas—who's to say they're not both valid?

"I don't look to the time when they're going to throw away their dream of Utopia," he said, without naming the Russians.[. . .]

Robert Frost had not read Boris Pasternak; he preferred not to discuss the case of the Soviet Nobel Prize winner as an individual. But in general terms:

"What they're ridiculing him for is from selfishness. They don't want their own thing reflected on—it's treason. We stand all that better than they do."

He glanced back to 1954 and the late Senator Joseph R. McCarthy, and resumed:

"We do stand it perfectly. Poor McCarthy. He seems to me like a soldier boy who couldn't bear to hear parlor pinks sitting around and talking the way they did. . . .

"Our freedom allows us great extremes of thought, and we almost let our people plot against us. But I don't see how you can help doing something for your own existence. All you have to do in court is prove the other fellow was about to shoot you. You can have a pretty good time in court if you can prove that."

The conversation narrowed back to Robert Frost himself. He spoke of sleep.

"Just as I feel I never have to go to sleep," he said, "little dreams begin to come over me—voices, sometimes—and I know I am gone. There is a curious connection between reverie, meditation, and dreams."

The very night before, he had dreamed of stumbling and falling. And often he would dream of a boyhood experience when, mistaken in thinking "I bore a charmed life," he got a "terrible dose of hornets." Now he dreams of the hornets, yet never so deeply as to be unaware of his actual situation. "I'm aware of the blankets," he said, a little wonderingly. Safe in bed, he pulls them up over his head and thwarts the dream-swarm.

He said a magazine had recently listed him as "one of the oldest living men."

"Funny, isn't it, about living on?" he mused. "They didn't educate me when I was young—the doctor said I was delicate and wouldn't live long. That's probably what prolongs life."

He went further into paradox.

"I'm not the kind of man who thinks the world can be saved by knowledge. It can only be saved by daring, bravery, going ahead. . . .

"I have done many things that it looked as if it was impossible to do—like going on the platform. I did it because I didn't have to face bullets."

He said he wondered what it must be like to stand before a firing squad.

I told him I had seen a German general face one in Italy in December, 1945.

"Did he do it bravely?" Robert Frost asked.

I told him he had done it very bravely.

There was a television set in the corner, and it seemed reasonable to ask if he took any interest in the medium.

"I do a little of it," he said, meaning being viewed, rather than viewing. "It's so when I see Peter at the gate, and he says, 'Have you lived modern?' I can say, 'I've flown and I've been on TV.' "

How about the Beat Generation?

"They're not even beat," said Robert Frost.

The Consultant Complains
at Not Being Consulted

In December of 1958, after less than two months in office, RF held a second news conference as Consultant in Poetry. This account by Mary McGrory is drawn from the Washington Evening Star *for December 10th.*

IN the scant two months he has been here, Robert Frost, the Library of Congress Consultant in Poetry, has caught a slight case of Potomac Fever. He would like to stay here in elective office.

The eighty-four-year-old poet told a press conference, which he called for another purpose, "I don't want to run for office, but I want to be a politician."

"I knew I couldn't run for office with all these opinions," said the blue-eyed sage. "I am not a practical campaigner like this or that politician. However, I wish that some good Senator would resign about six months before the end of his term and let me finish it out."

Someone suggested that ex-President Truman had given voice to the same thought.

"Then he stole it from me," Mr. Frost rejoined comfortably, crossing his high black shoes.

His first act in office, he said, would be to introduce a bill "to give this office of mine a real standing in government." And this was the purpose of the meeting.

Mr. Frost told the reporters that as the Library's Consultant in Poetry his full talents of consultancy were not being utilized by the government. Since he assumed office, he reported, he has been consulted three times by the White House, once by the Supreme Court, and once—and then only "in a way"—by the Senate.

"I wondered if I hadn't come down here on a misunderstanding. I thought I was to be poetry consultant, and I expected to be consulted in everything—poetry, politics, religion, science. I'll tackle anything."

On his first call on the White House, he related, "I said to the White House that since Mrs. Roosevelt and Walter Reuther and all my educated friends think that socialism is inevitable—we have got to have it—why don't we join up and hurry it along. It won't last, and we'll get it over with."

"The White House," he said, "laughed and said he didn't agree with that policy."

The second White House summons found him picking the name of one poet from a list of thirty. The one he chose was, like himself, a member of "no coterie or gang."

"I didn't know whether it was for execution—to be shot against the wall—or to be made king of the dump," he said.

His one inquiry from the Supreme Court was in relation to something he once said to Justice Cardozo: "You have to distinguish between being a referee and a handicapper."

Did this have to do with the integration crisis? Mr. Frost said yes, it did.

"I think the legislative department has been delinquent. Congress ought to have tended to things that the Supreme Court was driven to in desperation," he said boldly.

"That's tellin' them, isn't it?" the consultant asked.

Mr. Frost has not been consulted about education, on which he regards himself as "the greatest living expert." If he were, this is what he would say:

"I have long thought that our high schools should be improved. Nobody should come into our high schools without examinations— not aptitude tests, but on reading, 'riting, and 'rithmetic. And that goes for black or white.

"A lot of people are being scared by the Russian Sputnik into wanting to harden up our education or speed it up. I am interested in toning it up, at the high-school level.

"If they want to Spartanize the country, let them. I would rather perish as Athens than prevail as Sparta. The tone is Athens. The tone is freedom to the point of destruction. Democracy means all the risks taken—conflict of opinion, conflict of personality, eccentricity. We are Athens, daring to be all sorts of people."

Does the would-be Senator feel the present Administration is sympathetic to the arts? It was "much more so," he rejoined promptly, "before a recent sad event" (by which he meant, he eventually said, the departure of Presidential Assistant Sherman Adams).

"He really cares about the arts," said his fellow New Englander.

He recalled that, when Governor of New Hampshire, Mr. Adams drove down to Boston to hear Mr. Frost read his poetry at a meeting.

He knows that President Eisenhower reads his poetry, too.

"I would like to see in the President of the United States, or anyone presiding, a real weakness for poetry or the violin—in his nature—like wine, women, and song," said Mr. Frost.

Mr. Frost would also consult about religion.

"The one thing I consider a curse," he said, "is to be an agnostic. Don't say, 'We don't know.' We know a hell of a lot."

Frost Predicts Kennedy
Will Be President

Facing the press on his eighty-fifth birthday, in 1959, RF made a statement that produced, all across the country, headlines like the ones quoted above. It drew, also, from Senator John F. Kennedy of Massachusetts a letter which began: "I just want to send you a note to let you know how gratifying it was to be remembered by you on the occasion of your 85th birthday. I only regret that the intrusion of my name probably in ways which you did not entirely intend, took away some of the attention from the man who really deserved it—Robert Frost."

Maurice Dolbier summarized RF's March 26th birthday session with newsmen for the April 5th number of the New York Herald Tribune Book Review.

COFFEE and croissants were served in an outer office at Henry Holt and Company, but the real refreshment was in an inner office, where Robert Frost, just turned eighty-five, held a birthday press conference.

"Pour in!" he advised the thirty-or-so reporters and reviewers. "Everybody quiet outside! Now speak right up! . . .And don't put any words into my mouth unless they're brighter than mine!"

The questioners spoke right up.[. . .]

With the rise of science, poetry seems to be playing a lesser role. Has Mr. Frost any comment on that?

"Poetry has always played a lesser role. . . . When you're in college, half of all you read is poetry. When you're out, not so. Funny, isn't it? Out of all proportion.

"When I was young, my teachers used to recite, not knowing that I was going to be a poet, a little rhyme:

> Seven cities claimed blind Homer, being dead,
> Through which the living Homer begged his bread. . . .

It's only luck when a poet gets too much notice.

"I may say I've never got on by setting poetry in opposition to science or Big Business or academic scholarship, although some poets seem to live on that contrast. . . . Science cannot be scientific about poetry, but poetry can be poetical about science. It's bigger, more inclusive. . . . Get that right, you know," and Mr. Frost repeated it.

A questioner said that Mr. Frost had once written a poem:

> Nature within its inmost self decides. . . .

Mr. Frost broke in: " 'Divides,' not 'decides.' It was a misprint:

> Nature within its inmost self divides
> To trouble men with having to take sides.

I was thinking when I wrote of that lump of iron in the United Nations building, that stands for unity. But, even as you look at it, it seems to split. You think of tools that can be made of it, and you think of weapons. . . .

"We think that if people were all the same, they wouldn't want to hurt each other. But in the arts, we want all the differences we can get. And in society, too. I don't want to be always meeting people who've been everywhere I've been. I've never been to the Taj Mahal. I want to meet people who have been there. We really want people to be different, even if it means a risk of fighting with each other.

"I'm beginning to hate the word 'peace,' the way it's being thrown around today. The word is becoming spoiled. Everybody wants pieces of peace, but we don't expect to have eternal peace, except in the next world; and we don't know what's going on up there. Or down there. . . . We need enough peace to consolidate our gains."

Do these large birthday celebrations bore him?

"They don't bore me, but sometimes they make me feel too old. The question of desserts might bother me at night. But I like to be made of, you know. I like to be made of."

Has he any wish for the world and his country that he'd like to state on this eighty-fifth birthday?

"For the world, no. I'm not large enough for that. For my country? My chief wish is for it to win at every turn in anything it does.

"A few years ago, I summoned my family and friends and swore to them that if we lost the Olympic Games at Melbourne, I'd turn Communist. We lost. My family and friends reminded me of the oath, and asked what I intended to do about it. 'Break it,' I told them.

"I like to win. I hate to lose at chess."

The Russians feel the same way.

"Yes, they do. Don't they? . . . People say that there's always room at the top. There isn't. There's only room for one at the top of the steeple."

Cannot Mr. Frost afford to say this, because he's at the top, and sitting pretty?

"I was down under for many, many years, with no prospect of winning."

There was a twinkle in the frosty eyes.

"Sneak up on things. And never be caught looking as if you wanted them."

Is Mr. Frost in favor of help or self-help?

"Self-help mostly, but it would be ungenerous not to let people help you some."

Isn't this a revision of the Vermont attitude?

"I," says Mr. Frost, "was born in San Francisco."

Is New England in decay?

"People ask me that on my travels. Often they ask me in the South. And I ask, 'Where did you go to school?' And they say Harvard—or Yale. And then I say the successor to Mr. Dulles will be from Boston: Mr. Herter. And the next President of the United States will be from Boston. And then I ask, 'Does that sound as if New England is decaying?' "

About this next President? Whom does Mr. Frost mean?

"Can't you figure that one out for yourself?"

We would like to hear it from him. Mr. Frost shrugs.

"He's a Puritan named Kennedy. The only Puritans left these days are the Roman Catholics. There. I guess I wear my politics on my sleeve."

Told by a Holt executive that his poems, counting all editions, have sold over a million copies:

"That's good. Gee, if my grandfather could have lived to hear that! He'd think I must have been working hard."

The new book of poetry?

"It's coming along. . . . I still write about ten pages a year, without counting those I throw away.

"There are two dangers for poets. One is to be made of too much. The other is to increase in facility—know-how. I try not to know how too well. I have to contend with something."

Of an article about him in *Horizon* by Francis Russell:

"I don't know Mr. Russell, but I wish he could have consulted me before writing in that article that I was going to die soon. It's an odd thing. Every man who has said that about me, since I was a baby, has died right off."

Of his late friend Ahmed Bokhari of Pakistan:

"Once when he was visiting me, I said I was an old-time Yankee and could look back ten or eleven generations to the founder of my family in America, an adventurer on the coasts of Maine, Nicholas Frost. He said he knew all the names of his male ancestors for fifty generations. I said, 'Why, that must take you back to the time of the Prophet.' He replied calmly, 'Yes, we are of that family.' "

Of America and England:

"When I was in England last year, I said to an English friend, 'All your colonies are going, the way we went.' And he said: 'Ah, they're ripening off. You fell off green.' "

Of America:

"I am always happy to be under our flag when I go to sleep."

The Craft of Poetry

*In 1959, immediately after his eighty-fifth-birthday celebra-
tion, RF recorded with poets Cleanth Brooks and Robert Penn
Warren a discussion centering upon technical aspects of verse,
made for inclusion in a tape entitled "Conversations on the
Craft of Poetry," which was issued by Holt, Rinehart and
Winston, Inc. to accompany their third edition of Brooks and
Warren's book* Understanding Poetry. *Also participating in
the session was Holt editor Kenney Withers.*

*The following extracts are drawn from a printed transcript
that was published in booklet form as a companion piece to
the recording.*

WITHERS : Mr. Frost, I once heard you say that for a poem
to stick it must have a dramatic accent.

FROST : If it doesn't, it will not stay in anybody's head. It won't
be *catchy*.[. . .]
Catchiness has a lot to do with it, all of it, all the way up from the
ballads you hear on the street to the lines in Shakespeare that stay
with you without your trying to remember them. I just say catchy.
They stick on you like burrs thrown on you in holiday foolery. You
don't have to try to remember them. It's from the way they're said,
you know, an archness or something.

WARREN : Well, I'm sure you're right about the dramatic quality being the basic quality of good poetry. That would bring up the
relation of meter and rhythm to the dramatic moment—moment by
moment—in a poem, wouldn't it?

FROST : That's right.

WARREN : I'd like to hear you say it in your way, how meter enters into this picture—the dramatic quality.

FROST : The meter seems to be the basis of—the waves and the beat of the heart seems to be basic in all making of poetry in all languages—some sort of meter.

WARREN : The strain of the rhythm against the meter. Is that itself just a dramatic fact that permeates a poem?

FROST : From those two things rises what we call this tune that's different from the tune of the other kind of music. It's a music of itself. And when people say that this will easily turn into—be set to music, I think it's bad writing. It ought to fight being set to music if it's got expression in it.

BROOKS : Yes, there's something resistant and unique in it; you can't just turn it into something else. This is to overstate the matter, but I do want to get it clear, if I can for myself: Would you say that even though the meter is based on the human pulse or some kind of basic rhythm in our natures, still for the poet it's something to be played over against—it's something to be fought with, to be tussled with? It's not directly expressive—ta-DA, ta-DA, ta-DA, ta-DA, ta-DA.

FROST : No, it's doggerel when you do that. You see, and how you save it from doggerel is having enough dramatic meaning in it for the other thing to break the doggerel. And it mustn't break *with* it.

I said years ago that it reminds me of a donkey and a donkey cart; for some of the time the cart is on the tugs and some of the time on the hold-backs. You see it's that way all the time. The one's doing that and the other—the one's holding the thing back and the other's pushing it forward—and so on, back and forward. . . . I puzzled over it many years and tried to make people see what I meant. They use the word "rhythm" about a lot of free verse; and gee, what's the good of the rhythm unless it is on something that trips it—that it ruffles? You know, it's got to ruffle the meter.

BROOKS : Isn't this the fault of—to name the name of a man who did write some very fine poems, I think: Vachel Lindsay depends too much on just the doggerel—the stamp of the. . . .

FROST : Singsong, yes. And you know when he had something else, he thought he ought to put a note about it in the margin. Did you notice that?

BROOKS: Yes, to tell you know to read it.

FROST: "Say this in a golden tone," he says. You ought not to have to say that in the margin.

BROOKS: No, no. It's built in.

FROST: That ought to be in the meaning. This is why you have to have a meaning, 'cause you don't know what to do with anything if you don't have a meaning. It makes you act up; you've got to act up.

"What sayest thou, old barrelful of lies?" Chaucer says. What d'you say, "old barrelful of lies"? And you can hear it talk just the same today—and all of it. That's why it exists. It's beautiful, anywhere you look into Chaucer:

> Since I from love escaped am so fat,
> I never think to have been in his prison lean;
> Since I am free, I count him not a bean.

This is Chaucer talking too. It's just the same now. I hear the country people talking, England and here, with these same ways of acting up. Put it that way—call it "acting up."

You act up when you talk. Some do more than others. Some little children do: some just seem to be rather straight line, but some switch their whole body when they talk—switch their skirts. *Expressiveness* comes over them. Words aren't enough.

And of course all before words came the expressiveness—groans and murmurs and things like that emerging into words. And some few of these linger, like "um-hnm" and "unh-unh" and "mmm" and all our groans. By myself sometimes I groan at something already done that I'd like to avert.

WARREN: From a groan to a sonnet's a straight line.

FROST: Yes, that's right.

WARREN: You are distinguishing, then, the meaning in the most limited sense from the over-all, felt meaning of the whole thing. Is that it?

FROST: That's your whole guide, the over-all meaning.

WARREN: That's your guide and your end product.

FROST: Yes, your end product. And also, you know, one of the funny things is that this *mood* you're writing in foretells the end product. See, it begins sort of that way and a way of talking that foretells the end product. There's a logic of that sort of thing.

Somebody said to be a master writer you don't have to wait for your moods. That'd be like Browning as he got older. You get to be a virtuoso, and you aren't a poet any more. He'd lost his moods somewhere. He'd got to be a master. We don't want to be masters.

WARREN: In other words you don't want even to be master—is that right?—of the particular poem. Before you start you're moving from mood to the exploration of the mood, is that it?

BROOKS: Poem is a discovery. . . .

FROST: Yes, that's right. You're on a little voyage of discovery. And there's a logic in it. You're going to come out somewhere with great certainty. And you can tell whether you've lost it on the way. And you throw the poem away—if you lose it.

WARREN: Yes.

FROST: Down the years, looking back over it all. And you see, a good many who think they're writing free verse are really writing old-fashioned iambic. A good deal of Whitman's like that, and a lot of Masters is like that: he just never got away from blank verse—the sound of blank verse.

And so there are places where this thing takes place that I'm talking about—there's both the meter and the expressiveness on it—and so we get a poem.

Ezra Pound used to say that you've got to get all the meter out of it—extirpate the meter. If you do, maybe you've got true free verse, and I don't want any of it!

WARREN: Well, you can go at it another way: I guess it's Winters who said that behind all good free verse—I may be misinterpreting him, but I think that's what he says—behind all good free verse there's a shadow of formal verse.

FROST: That's right. And if we hadn't had the years of formal verse, this stuff wouldn't be any good, you know. The shadow is there; that's what gives it any charm it has. You see, I'm hard on free verse a little—too hard, I know.

BROOKS: Would you be hard, Mr. Frost, also, on the business of the beatniks and chanting poetry to jazz? Is that letting too much of music—of the wrong side of music come in?

FROST: Yes, absolutely. Death! Hang 'em all!

This fellow that's going to talk with me (A. P. Herbert from London) tomorrow, they've told me what his prejudices are, you know, to see if they couldn't rouse me to say something to him. He's in favor of hanging delinquent children. That's the funniest prejudice. And he'd be in favor of exterminating the free-verse writers, I'm pretty sure. I'm not as bad as that.

Let's put it this way, that prose and verse are alike in having high poetic possibilities of ideas, and free verse is anywhere you want to be between those two things, prose and verse. I like to say, guardedly, that I could define poetry this way: It is that which is lost out of both prose and verse in translation. That means something in the way the words are curved and all that—the way the words are taken, the way you take the words.

WARREN: The best-order notion: the old Coleridgean best-order notion.

FROST: Yes, I'm pretty extreme about it.

You know, I've given offense by saying that I'd as soon write free verse as play tennis with the net down. I want something there—the other thing—something to hold and something for me to put a strain on; and I'd be lost in the air with just cutting loose—unless I'm in my other mood of making it prose right out, you know, and I don't write much of that. But that's another thing.[. . .]

BROOKS: Speaking of tune, Yeats said that he started a poem with a little tune in his head.

FROST: Yeats said a good many things, and I've talked with him about that. He said that nothing he hated more than having his poems set to music. It stole the show. It wasn't the tune he heard in his ear. And what this other thing is. . . . If he meant a tune, it doesn't seem to go with that, does it?

Burns without any doubt had old music—old songs—in his head that he wrote from. But I don't think that of Yeats; I don't know what he meant by that. But if he meant a tune. . . . I have a tune, but it's a tune of the blend of these two things. Something rises—it's neither one of these things. It's neither the meter nor the rhythm; it's a tune arising from the stress on those—same as your fingers on the strings, you know. The twang!

WARREN: The twang.

FROST: The twang of one on the other. And I don't know what he meant. I think he must have meant what we mean: from a result of something beginning to rise from it right away when you're playing one on the other; that's what he carried. There must be a oneness as you're doing it. You aren't putting two things together—laying them together. It isn't synthetic like that; no.

BROOKS: No, it's growing a plant, not building a wall.

WARREN: Growing in terms of this dominating mood—is that right?—that you referred to as a germ of the poem?

FROST: Yes.

WARREN: The tune is the mood groping for its logic, is that it? Something like that?

FROST: That's right; that's right, yes. I'm glad that we feel that way together. Yes, you know that, when I begin a poem I don't know—I don't want a poem that I can tell was written toward a good ending—one sentence, you know. That's trickery. You've got to be the happy discoverer of your ends.

BROOKS: That's a very fine way of phrasing it, "the happy discoverer of your end." Because otherwise it is contrived. You can see it coming a mile off.

FROST: A mile away.

I've often said that another definition of poetry is dawn—that it's something dawning on you while you're writing it. It comes off if it really dawns when the light comes at the end. And the feeling of dawn—the freshness of dawn—that you didn't think this all out and write it in prose first and then translate it into verse. That's abhorrent![. . .]

One of the things that I notice with myself is that I can't make certain word sounds go together, sometimes; they won't say. This has got something to do with the way one vowel runs into another, the way one syllable runs into another. And then I never know—I don't like to reason about that too much. I don't understand it, but I've changed lines because there was something about them that my ear refused. And I suppose it has something to do with this vowels and consonants.

You know what I've thought sometimes: that the mouth and throat are like this, that it's certain sounds are here, and you can't go right from this one to that one; you've got to go like this. The mouth's got to be doing that inside. I don't know.

But gee, you know, I don't want any science of it. It's got to be—not trial and error. You don't correct it if you're going well—if you're felicitous—if you're having a happy day.

Well, we've come a good way. And it's fun. I don't often sit with somebody to talk about it this way. Sometimes from the platform I say some of these things, you know. And I used to do it more than I do it now. I had a notion I had to tell the public how to read lines. Then I decided no; that's in them anyway. They all had Mother Goose and everything. Don't you see that you throw them back on their Mother Goose? And then all with the play of ideas in it; how deep the Mother Goose is, you see:

> Pussy cat, pussy cat, where have you been?
> I've been to London to see the Coronation!

To pervert a little:

> Pussy cat, pussy cat, what did you see there?
> I saw nothing but what I might have seen just
>   as well by staying right here in Nashville!
> I saw a mouse run under a chair.

And that's very deep. But it's so pretty the way it's set off, you know, and nobody need see it at all unless they're any discerning. "I saw a mouse run under a chair." That's meant a lot to me, that has, all my life.

WARREN: That's a good one.

FROST: That's what makes regionalists, you see. You could stay right at home and see it all.

You know another thing I think belongs to poetry is fresh observation, don't you? All the time, little insights. They say "nothing new," but there is all the time. For instance, I was saying about women the other day—they were plaguing me to leave some boys I wanted to talk to; they thought I was getting tired or something. Finally I turned on them, and I said, "A woman would rather take care of you than listen to you think."

WARREN: That's a mark of a good woman.

FROST: And then I softened that to them by saying, "That's why we like you, my dears. You see, because we know that what we think doesn't amount to much anyway, we men." You see, that was a fresh observation.

WARREN: Well, the mere observation of just the facts of the

world is a constant refresher for poetry. It's a waking up of yourself when you get the least little turn of an observation of the way a leaf or a light is, or something.

FROST: Little insights into a character and a little observation of something growing. You know how it does, something with life.[. . .]

Of Passionate Preference

On September 29, 1959, RF participated in a symposium on "The Future of Man," sponsored by Joseph E. Seagram & Sons and held at New York's Waldorf-Astoria Hotel. Milton S. Eisenhower served as chairman of a panel which included, in addition to RF, Julian Huxley, Devereux C. Josephs, Ashley Montagu, Hermann J. Muller, and Bertrand Russell. A question-and-answer period with journalists Douglas Edwards, William L. Laurence, and Inez Robb followed formal statements made in turn by each of the distinguished panelists.

Here reprinted from the symposium's proceedings is a transcript of approximately the final half of the interview period. It contains substantially all of RF's remarks in that part of the program, as somewhat revised by him subsequently for publication.

SIR JULIAN: [. . .]I think we've got to supplement the present idea of adult education for leisure with the planned provision of more opportunities for people to use their leisure. We've got to look forward beyond the concept of the welfare state, which aims at ensuring a minimum maintenance level for everyone, to what I may call the "fulfillment society," which would be planned in such a way as to give more opportunity for disciplined freedom in the realization of all sorts of human possibilities.

MRS. ROBB: I would like to ask Sir Julian about the "fulfillment society," which he recently said would supersede the welfare state. How do you define fulfillment, Sir Julian?

SIR JULIAN: That would take too long to define properly,

though I think most of us have a pretty good idea of what it means. Anyhow, the question is how are we going to achieve this aim, isn't it?

MR. FROST: Well, the balance is between our being members of each other and being individuals. You see, we're members of each other—that's what you're all talking about, insisting on—and civilized society is a society that tolerates all sorts of divergences, to the point of eccentricity and to the point, even, of doubtful sanity.

DR. EISENHOWER: Lord Russell, did you start to say something?

LORD RUSSELL: Yes, I do want to. I want to say what I was thinking about in the matter of education. I wasn't thinking of conveying knowledge, I was thinking of conveying ways of feeling.

Now, in almost all civilized countries at present the school child salutes the national flag. He ought instead to salute the flag of the United Nations. He ought to salute some international symbol and not a national symbol, and I feel that in all our education—I'm not saying this about one country or another but about all of them—they go on glorifying their own country, which is no longer the right thing to do.

DR. EISENHOWER: I hope some member of the panel is going to disagree with what's just been said.

MR. FROST: Is this Lord Russell?

DR. EISENHOWER: Yes, this was Lord Russell who said this. Did you hear it, Mr. Frost?

MR. FROST: I remember introducing him once in America and praising him and excusing my being there to introduce him, because he said in a preface to a book of his I'd just read that he hastened to publish it before he changed his mind about everything in it.

DR. EISENHOWER: Mr. Laurence?

MR. LAURENCE: I would like to ask Mr. Frost about two things: A.) He mentioned the words—beautiful phrase—"passionate preference." I presume he still believes that love and affection will still have a place in future society and that future methods of procreation will still not include the test tube. And furthermore, he also said....

MR. FROST: My description of what steers it all was answered in what I have already said—if I understand the question.

But let me say something about science. (I'm lost among scientists here, you know. I don't want to seem at variance with them. I'm lost in admiration for science.) It's the plunge of the mind, the spirit, into the material universe. It can't go too far or too deep for me.

But you have to stop and think who owns it. It's a property. Science says, "It belongs to me." No. It's the property of the race. It belongs to us.

And who are we? Science can't describe us; it contributes very little to our description—a very little bit in all this newness [and] wonder of science that they talk about; it's very slight. The wonderful description of us is the humanities, the book of the worthies and unworthies through the ages, and anything you talk about in the future must be a projection from that.

DR. EISENHOWER: Mrs. Robb?

MRS. ROBB: I think what we wanted to ask you especially, Mr. Frost, was whether your testament to man was an affirmation that he will need love in the future as he has in the past and in the present.

MR. FROST: Look! Look! Man has come this way. Shakespeare himself says the best children are love children.

MRS. ROBB: Thank you.

MR. FROST: That sinful enough for you?

MRS. ROBB: Just one more question along this line. . . .

MR. FROST: Shakespeare says the other is got between sleeping and waking.

DR. EISENHOWER: Mrs. Robb?

MRS. ROBB: I wanted to ask reassurance that the test tube will not replace the heart.

MR. FROST: The chief guide in the world for us in the long way we've come is some more or less intelligent handling of that inexorable thing in us—Biblical thing, you know—passionate preference for something we can't help wishing were so, wishing were true.

All your guidance in politics, religion, and love is something way at the middle of your heart that you can't help wishing was so. All the time. That's what we're talking about here: what we can't help wishing were so.

MR. EDWARDS: I would like to ask Dr. Montagu what his idea is. What is the key to the future of man?

DR. MONTAGU: Well, I would put it in a nutshell, as follows:

The realization of his evolutionary destiny, his potentialities for being an individual who can co-operate in a creatively enlarging manner with his fellow men everywhere.

MR. EDWARDS: How are we going to go on with finding this key to the human destiny, Dr. Montagu?

DR. MONTAGU: You see, Mr. Frost keeps on telling me that all the things that I am saying would be terrible, and I am under the apparent misapprehension that I am supporting him in everything he has said.

MR. EDWARDS: Dr. Montagu, love is one of Mr. Frost's keys to the continued good future of man. How are we getting along with finding this key to our destiny?

DR. MONTAGU: We're getting along by the remarkable discovery, rather late in the day, that man's own nature is as capable of investigation, even though it's more difficult, as the particles that make up the nucleus of the atom. And we have now a sizeable, though proportionately very minute, quantum of knowledge about the nature of human nature.

For example, we have learned in the last fifty years that man is virtually the only creature on the face of the earth without any instincts, that everything he knows and does as a human being he has to learn from other human beings, and that therefore whatever genetic capacities he is endowed with, these will be conditioned, insofar as their realization is concerned, by the processes of education which they are made to undergo.

SIR JULIAN: And by the environment as a whole.

DR. MONTAGU: Precisely.

MR. EDWARDS: Dr. Montagu, would you give us in a nutshell —and this can be really nutshellized—what is your definition of mental health?

DR. MONTAGU: Mental health, I think most investigators would agree, is the ability to love and the ability to work.

But what is love? We've had a vast number of authorities who have told us: the church, *True Romance* magazine and its equivalents, our contemporary troubadors, the crooners, and, of course, that supreme of all the authorities, Hollywood. But these, of course, are not authorities. These are mass-culture confusionists on the subject.

Those who have taught us most about love are newborn babies and small children, who show, as it were, in high relief, the potentialities for love. We have learned from them that adults are nothing more or less than deteriorated babies.

Sir Julian disagrees, but give me. . . .

LORD RUSSELL: May I speak for a moment?

DR. EISENHOWER: Please do, Lord Russell.

LORD RUSSELL: I just wanted to say that it seems to me that some of the discussion has brought in big words and difficult things to achieve. And the problem before us is really a rather simple one. The problem is: Would we rather that the human race continue to exist even though that may involve some happiness to people that we don't quite like, or would we rather have the whole thing exterminated? That is the whole question.

DR. EISENHOWER: Since a member of the scholarly panel of specialists has become an interrogator, I think it would be fair to direct this question toward the interviewing panel, if one of them would like to answer it.

MRS. ROBB: I think Lord Russell is right. What he is saying is that we have to learn eventually to love our enemy, and we are civilized. It's what Mr. Frost has been saying; it's what the poet, who is always the truthteller, has been telling us all afternoon.

DR. EISENHOWER: Mr. Frost, did you want to make a comment on this point?

MR. FROST: Well, I was just going to say that these philosophers, you know—they have always wanted to be rulers—they always wanted to be philosopher-kings. And they have been once or twice. And one or two college presidents have been. And in these philosopher-kings philosophy has once or twice got as formidable as science. We have had to give some thinkers hemlock or burn 'em at the stake. And I hope Lord Russell feels as if he'd lived a formidable enough life to have been burned at the stake.

DR. EISENHOWER: Mr. Laurence?

MR. LAURENCE: I want to address this question to Mr. Frost, because that's pertinent to this particular problem. Mr. Frost believes in conflict as a force to keep human progress going. Now, what is the surest way, in his mind, to keep us in conflict that would be constructive rather than destructive?

MR. FROST: The certainty of conflict is originality, that's all—the bursting power, the bursting energy and daring of man. And it's always there, always there. You can't hope for anything that doesn't include that.

DR. MONTAGU: But why give it the name "conflict"? Why not the name of "interthinking" or "co-operation"?

MR. FROST: Oh, yes—unless you're so in earnest about it that you'll either die, kill or be killed, for it, you haven't really got down to where the truth is.

SIR JULIAN: Well, there always will be conflict.

MR. FROST: That's all, I think.

DR. EISENHOWER: Ladies and gentlemen, when this panel was planned, the promise was made that we would adjourn at three o'clock. I must say it does seem almost downright criminal that such eminent people as we have—both our interviewing and responding panel—should be brought together and remain together for such a short time, because, really, we've had nothing but a few introductions to great ideas.

I would like to break over on the prerogatives of a chairman and pose one concluding question myself, which may involve Lord Russell and several members of the panel.

It seemed to me, when the question of nationalism came up, that it was left with the assumption that nationalism is evil in itself, and I just don't think this is so. It seems to me that true love of country, like love of family, can be one of the greatest forces for progress in the world.

Historically, when we developed allegiance to the tribe and then the nation, we didn't give up any allegiance to the family. Although we exist as a nation to which we show allegiance, we still recognize loyalties to our families, to our churches, and to our local and regional communities. And today, now that we have to build a peaceful world in co-operation with other nations, this doesn't imply that we must give up nationalism or love of country. Indeed, nationalism or taking national pride, in this sense, can be a highly constructive motivating force.

It seems to me that this was left in a rather bad way, and I wonder if Lord Russell wants to quarrel with the chairman before we conclude?

Lord Russell: Yes, I certainly do. I should like to say about nationalism that it has two entirely distinct aspects.

On the one hand, there is cultural nationalism, and there is love of your native soil. And against that I have not a word to say.

On the other hand, there is the view that your nation is so much better than any other that it has a right to fight and kill people of other nations whenever it happens to suit its interests. And that is the sort of nationalism that I don't like.

Dr. Eisenhower: I'll call the kind you are talking about "blind nationalism."

Any other member of the panel—Mr. Frost?

Mr. Frost: One more question to Lord Russell. Since we all agree that we're now smart enough to go on with what we are in an evolutionary way, we ought to be smart enough to stop where we are. And I am in favor of stopping where we are, because I like all this uncertainty that we live in, between being members and being individuals.

That's the daily problem: how much am I a member; how much am I an individual; how comfortable am I in my memberships? It's an endless problem that you can hire psychiatrists about. And they can't help you!

I like the layout. Do you, Lord Russell?

Lord Russell: Yes, very much.

Dr. Eisenhower: Ladies and gentlemen, it does seem really shameful to bring this to a close, but we must; and on your behalf I want to thank Lord Russell, Dr. Muller, Dr. Montagu, Mr. Josephs, Sir Julian Huxley, Mr. Frost, Mr. Edwards, Mrs. Robb, and Mr. Laurence. And now we will say good afternoon.

·VI·

THE SIXTIES

"I was always a bookseller."

RF on the eve of National Library Week made these observations, reported by W. G. Rogers for release by the Associated Press on April 3, 1960.

LIBRARIES," said Robert Frost, "are in the same game I'm in. That's the game of surrounding people with books—getting people coated with books."

With the celebration of National Library Week beginning officially tomorrow, the oldest, best-known, and best-loved of contemporary American poets sat down at a lunch table, managed to forget about a stiff knee that had been bothering him, and gave his opinions of libraries, books, bookstores, and education.

"I'm in favor of great libraries," he said in that gravelly unpoetic voice so perfectly suited to the reading of his poems. "I've heard the greatest [academic] library is at Harvard, then the next at Yale, maybe, and then the University of Illinois in Urbana.

"A good library is something," he continued, "but I want books to stick to people. And I have to admit I've used libraries a lot to get them to buy books on trial so I could see if I want to buy them myself."

That led to the subject of his personal library. How many books did he own?

He shook his head. Some are in his home in Cambridge, Massachusetts, some on his Vermont farm, and they are not catalogued.

"That's the trouble," he confessed. "When a book gets in there with the others, I can lose it. But I'm a great ranger over my books.

At midnight I get the idea of going over them, and I always find something I didn't know about.

"You've heard about that snobbish old New England lady? There were some neighbors she didn't approve of. And she explained, 'What would you expect? They were brought up in a bookless home.'[. . .]

"The first book I remember reading through was *Scottish Chiefs.* I suppose we had it because my mother had some Scottish blood in her. It was about Robert Bruce and William Wallace. I was fourteen. I had to start that several times before I went on to the end, for I saw Wallace's execution coming and I couldn't endure it.

"But I remember a still-earlier book, brought home for my mother to review for my father's paper. It was poetry of Robert Herrick's, published in 1882 when I was eight. It must prove I was interested in poetry without knowing it."

Frost once explained to an Amherst audience where for forty years, on and off, he has taught, "You go to college to learn that there's a book side to everything."

He recalled his first visit to a college.

"Three students had read a poem of mine printed while I was in high school and invited me to visit them. I never had seen such an array of books as they had in their rooms. And I have never forgotten.

"As I have taught in one place or another, I often moved into the house of the man I was substituting for, while he was on a sabbatical. Some of these sabbatical houses had no books at all. I am a terribly hard judge on people without books.

"But really," he expanded on the subject, "I was never teaching anywhere. I was always a bookseller. I once said to a class at Amherst that any boy who bought one hundred dollars' worth of books would get the mark of A, or B for fifty dollars' worth, and the rest would fail.

"I could not teach in a town without a good bookstore. At Amherst I fall back on the Hampshire Bookshop in Northampton. It's wonderful[. . .]. There's a fine bookstore at Dartmouth. I speak with enthusiasm of the Vermont Bookshop in Middlebury[. . .]. Two of my daughters used to work in bookstores[. . .].

"All thinking, and all stories, go on in books. The movies made from them are just illustrations. And I don't like illustrated books.

"Look at a book. From scrolls to what we have today the shape has never changed. They get ramps instead of stairs in the new buildings, and curves instead of good square corners, but a book is always a book."

He shook his finger to prepare for a word of warning.

"But of course I'm not for the bookworm. Here's a word of caution you might want to note. In my 'Death of the Hired Man,' that I wrote years ago, there's this line: 'He hates to see a boy the fool of books.'

"It's interesting to see how country folks are sometimes wise without books."[. . .]

"What I want is an assurance from Washington that our government is aware of the arts...."

On May 5, 1960, RF appeared before a United States Senate subcommittee in Washington to favor legislation for the establishment of a National Academy of Culture. Excerpts from his testimony are here drawn from the printed record of the hearing, which was conducted by the Hon. Ralph W. Yarborough, senior Senator from Texas.

SENATOR YARBOROUGH: The Subcommittee on Education will come to order.

This morning the Subcommittee on Education is holding a hearing on S. 2207, a bill introduced by the esteemed junior Senator from South Dakota, Senator Francis Case, to provide for a National Academy of Culture.

The subcommittee is highly honored to have as a witness on this bill a great American and a distinguished man of letters whom we will ask Senator Case to introduce.

We welcome you to the subcommittee, Senator Case, and ask you to proceed in any manner you deem appropriate.

SENATOR CASE: [. . .]Mr. Chairman, since a member of your committee, Mr. Prouty, is a Senator from the State of Vermont, which is the legal residence and the long-time residence of Mr. Frost, with your indulgence I would ask him actually to make the presentation of Mr. Frost.

SENATOR YARBOROUGH: We would like to hear from Senator Prouty of this subcommittee. He is a very able and hard-working member of the Education Subcommittee of the Senate Committee on Labor and Public Welfare.

SENATOR PROUTY: Thank you, Mr. Chairman.

I should correct the chairman. I am not a member of the Subcommittee on Education.

SENATOR YARBOROUGH: You are a member of the full committee, and I see you there so regularly that I feel as though you are a member of this subcommittee.

SENATOR PROUTY: Thank you, Mr. Chairman, you are very kind.

I am also a member of the Calendar Committee, and the Calendar Committee is to be called very shortly on the floor, so it will be necessary for me to leave quite soon.

I am, however, very grateful for the opportunity to present to the subcommittee certainly one of the most-distinguished men of American letters. He was not born in Vermont, but we are most proud that he claims it as his legal residence.

I have heard on occasion that he has democratic leanings—I am using the small "d"—but I am sure as the years go by he will become a convert to republicanism, which is quite a liberal philosophy itself.

It is sometimes suggested also that one who has not been born in Vermont cannot claim to be a Vermonter, but in the case of Mr. Frost that certainly is not true. We claim him as one of our own and are very happy to have him in the Green Mountain State. He is one of the greatest and best-known poets writing in the English language. His life and his works have become a part of contemporary American history.

I commend him most highly to the members of the subcommittee. I am sure you are going to find his views are very persuasive, and I think the mere fact that he is here is going to give this bill substantial support in the Congress and from the committee.

Thank you very much, Mr. Chairman.

SENATOR YARBOROUGH: While I take it that the distinguished Senator from Vermont would claim anyone north of Boston as a Vermonter, I have a message from another one of the members of the full committee; that is, from Senator John F. Kennedy, of Massachusetts, who sends his regrets and desires that these words be given here in the record:

"I keenly regret that other duties prevent me from being present today to welcome the distinguished son of Massachusetts.

"I know of no one who is better qualified to set for us new coasts and horizons. Mr. Frost is a poet laureate of the Library of Congress, which is fortunate to have his counsel and wisdom."

Mr. Frost, it seems each of the New England states is claiming you as a native son. California has no Senator here this morning to lay claim to being the state of your birth. It must be a source of pride, as well as amusement, to you that you are claimed by so many states. I would like to put in a claim for Texas, but we are outnumbered this morning.

It is a great honor and a great privilege to this subcommittee to have you here to testify on behalf of this bill to create a National Academy of Culture. You are the most-distinguished witness who has appeared before this committee in its history, and the Subcommittee on Education is very proud to hear your testimony this morning.

You may proceed in your own way. No one can tell you how to proceed anyway. You would proceed in your own way, but we want you to know that you comply with the rules when you do proceed in your own way.

MR. FROST: Well, I want to throw the weight of all the nice things that have been said about me on the side of this bill. I don't need to go on insisting on my way after all this. But I'm like Homer —you make me feel like Homer: the seven cities claimed the Homer, dead, "through which the living Homer begged his bread."

I came near being a Texan once, and I came near being a Pennsylvanian. I've been so scattered; I've about decided I am an American—U.S.A.

SENATOR YARBOROUGH: Congratulations.

MR. FROST: Of course, you know from all that's said about me that I would be on the side of this bill. I have long thought of something like this. My mind goes back over talks I've had with various people in Washington, but it's only lately that I have come to know Washington. I feel the pleasure of being in these great affairs, this last year and this year.

I've always said it would be sad if a great nation like this got so great and prosperous and famous without the help of the arts at all—like Carthage. My respect is always for nations that have had art and literature, language of their own—Japan, you know.

You think of some nations—China—that have had their own literature, and then you think of those that have had none—nothing. I heard someone say sadly the other day, "You know, I'm of a nation that has no literature at all, no art—no particular art." Africa has had nothing—no written language.

What I want more than anything—the encouragement, that's all right—but what I want is an assurance from Washington that our government is aware of the arts: aware of us artists, writers, sculptors, and all.[. . .]

And the awareness is the great thing.[. . .] I was at a poetry affair lately in New York where about a thousand poets were present (I think it was a thousand) at the Waldorf, and I was able to say that it seemed to me in the length of the evening that nearly everybody had a prize. So there's quite a little going on.

The foundations are getting aware of us. But I want my country officially to be aware of us, so that we feel our equality. I do want you to declare our equality. We will take care of the rest.[. . .]

What would the Academy do? It would be like any institution; it would have its corruptions. But you know we'd have to allow for those, and everybody would be—get to scheming. [. . .]I'm always hearing about who's at work to get what for whom. The thing gets going that way, and that would all be in it.

But never mind that. We would still get this recognition—the recognition, the awareness. That is what I ask for. We want to be aware of it.

This last year I got acquainted with Washington, and I've grown very, very proud of myself. It set me up. You don't know all—I'll not go into all the story of it, but it has been wonderful; and I just want this great city to establish something like the Academy.

The greatest monument in the world stands here, of course, to one of the two or three greatest men that ever lived. But I want some—I want the state to show some feeling for these arts.[. . .]

Senator Yarborough: Mr. Frost, do you think this National Academy of Culture would be something like the French Academy in France? Is that the kind of academy you advocate?

Mr. Frost: Yes, it would have those defects.

As the French say, "You can't have virtues without their defects." It would have the defects of the virtues. That's an interesting expression, isn't it? Very French.

SENATOR YARBOROUGH: Now this measure provides that the members of the Academy are to keep a life membership in the National Academy of Culture, but that the commission to select the members shall be named by the President and shall serve for a period of three years.

I have a question on that. Do you not think that as an artist is picked as a member of the National Academy then he, too, should vote on the future membership in the Academy?

MR. FROST: There are many modifications of this, you know. For instance, I wouldn't quite call it an academy of "culture." I don't like the word very well. I'd call it the Academy of the Arts. But little things like that don't matter too much.

And then the way people would be elected to it. I think it sounds fine to make them permanent members once they're in and all that: no more contention—have tenure. But that could all be worked out.

The great thing is the establishment, the institution.[. . .]

SENATOR YARBOROUGH: Mr. Frost, you have talked of scholarship and poetry, pointing out that scholarship was a matter of study but that poetry involved an inspiration of something that had not been thought of before. In reading biographies of you I have noted, if those biographies were correct, that you had a pretty hard time economically, at least up until you were about forty years of age. Money was pretty scarce.

I want to ask you, do you think it important in the inspiration of poetry—do you think there is any connection between adversity and the spark of genius, or do you think that ease would kill the spark of genius? Do you think an easy time would not produce poets? If everybody had it easy, would we have good poets?

MR. FROST: It's necessary to make a distinction. You know, this would not help beginners. They take their lives in their hands in the arts, and nothing can prevent that.

Nobody knows the story of people who succeeded against all that. Their beginnings, most of them, very, very, very sad—shoestring start. Somebody tells me there are no more shoestring starts in America. But that's all there is in America. There will always be shoestring starts in the arts. That's a rhyme!

Then, this thing would just radiate a certain atmosphere over the country. It's something to know that the arts are not slighted.

Many, many other countries have a contempt for the arts.[. . .]

Gamble is what you want. That would not remove that. You would not find babes by intelligence tests, you know, who were going to be artists. You don't know where they would come from.

The same for science, too. There's something going on right now. They think [. . .] we spend a lot of money and all of a sudden we could beat the Russians in science. It's not impromptu like that. It has to be all the time—an atmosphere, a general favor.

This would be a center of general favor to the arts. That's all. Treatment as if they were something.

You know it's not fair to say they aren't treated pretty well now. I've had lots of favors.[. . .]

SENATOR YARBOROUGH: Senator Clark of Pennsylvania, a member of the full committee, has joined the hearing.

Senator Clark, do you have any questions or comments?

SENATOR CLARK: Mr. Frost, let me first express my own joy that you are here today in support of this bill and express my appreciation. . . .

MR. FROST: Thank you very much.

SENATOR CLARK: . . . express my appreciation to Senator Case for having arranged this meeting.

I am not a member of the subcommittee, but when I heard you were here I left another meeting to come, hoping to hear you before you had finished.

I think one of the great tragedies of American life is the lag between the men of inspiration and genius in the world in the field of the arts, and also in the fields of science, and the public understanding expressed through members of the legislature as to what needs to be done to keep our brain power and our artistic feelings alert and alive. I can think of nothing which would be better to make some compression of that lag than to create, as you suggest, a National Academy of Culture.[. . .]

I wonder, Mr. Frost, if you have ever thought of de Tocqueville's proposition that it is very difficult for democracies to breed excellence?

MR. FROST: Yes.

SENATOR CLARK: That it tends to breed mediocrity. And whether we who live in a democracy should not be alert to encouraging excellence, whether it were in the arts and sciences; and whether this bill which you advocate would not be a most appropriate vehicle toward that end?

MR. FROST: Yes, damn de Tocqueville. He condemned us to mediocrity. We can't do that. It's all wrong.

I was saying last night that one way in our education—one way out of education—would be to give everybody C. You can't give them all A's, of course, but you must get down to some dead level— what they used to call the "gentlemanly C" and an average—the mediocre thing.

The boys say to me lately, "Are you selective?"

Am I selective? Would I prefer one to another?

I say, "That's all I do." And I've been a very free selector, and this is all toward that, you know.

You say, "He won the Pulitzer Prize," you know. Everybody knows that that means something, but not too much. Maybe a better one got left out and so on. But it's got to go on. We've got to choose; we've got to prefer.

As I said, talking to some scientists lately, I said to them, "Have we come up?"

They said, "Yes," rather reluctantly. They did not know whether we had come up or not, but they said, "Yes."

And I said, "What's brought us up?" And they thought it was more or less an accident, I guess.

I said, "I think it's passionate preference." Passionate preference. It's done in all ways—in the arts more than anywhere else. That's where it rings: passionate preference. And we can just bless that by having an institution like this. We can't make it, you know. This comes out of that. But we can bless that. We can approve of it.

SENATOR CLARK: Could I ask you one final question? Is not really the major purpose of your bill to encourage in the arts that pursuit of excellence which tends to be denigrated in a democracy?

MR. FROST: Yes, that's a good way of putting it. But I've never particularly felt that; I've always resisted the idea that we were going down in this thing. This thing is going fine, you know. We put on a glorious show the last two hundred years. A little more. I'm not correcting anything. A little more; a little more, that's all.

SENATOR YARBOROUGH: Mr. Frost, in your study of peoples and poetry have you formed any opinion about whether the great poets are recognized while the nation is young or in its full maturity or in its old age? Knowing in history that nations are like people, with a younger age and middle age or older age before they lose their special period in the world, is there any special period in the nation that tends to cause this blossoming forth of poetry more than any other period of history in a nation?

MR. FROST: You know the Greek story of a singer in the very ancient times—a singer with the army. And then singers all the way along, and we have had them. We have always had some of it.

Right in the town where I live a good deal, I pass Longfellow's old home, and crowds stop by there. I remember hearing that when Charles Sumner brought him into the Senate the Senate adjourned to welcome him. And have I not been treated well? It may be a mistake in either case.

SENATOR YARBOROUGH: Mr. Frost, as this National Academy is established and poets and artists are elected, you would not expect them by election to the Academy to change their ideals and their methods; you would not expect them to succumb to what was called winning the arts just for a piece of silver or just for a ribbon to stick on their coat?

MR. FROST: No. I told you to begin with there would be some corruption. It goes with everything. And there would be people that would sell their souls for a ribbon to stick on their coats. And they would catch it. . . . You know who that was that sold—that Browning had thought had sold—his soul for a ribbon. That was Wordsworth.

We sometimes misjudge each other. One of the strange things is that all our lives we're guessing at each other. They call that psychology.[. . .]

The great thing, you see, is the recognition this would give, spread over the country—always in the story something to think about—that you're thinking about us up here. That's all.[. . .]

I might say that I'm not here to clinch any argument. It's just to give an impression of how I feel. That's all. I've been very personal, but without selfish motives. I'm not asking for anything for myself, but for the country—for our country.

SENATOR YARBOROUGH : Bills have been introduced in session after session of Congress by different legislators to create a national academy. I think your appearance here will give impetus to these bills and will help push them forward where in the not-distant future we will have such a National Academy of Culture created by act of Congress, having thereby the stamp of approval of the whole American people on that Academy.

Thank you for coming here and adding your influence in this matter.

MR. FROST : Thank you.

"The whole thing is performance and prowess and feats of association."

Richard Poirier, then a member of the English Department at Harvard, tape-recorded this interview with RF. It originally appeared in Number 24 (Summer-Fall 1960) of The Paris Review. *Roughly one-third of the text as there published is included in the following extracts.*

INTERVIEWER: Some of the early critics like Garnett and Pound talk a lot about Latin and Greek poetry with reference to yours. You'd read a lot in the Classics?

FROST: Probably more Latin and Greek than Pound ever did.

INTERVIEWER: Didn't you teach Latin at one time?

FROST: Yes. When I came back to college after running away, I thought I could stand it if I stuck to Greek and Latin and philosophy. That's all I did those years.

INTERVIEWER: Did you read much in the Romantic poets? Wordsworth, in particular?

FROST: No, you couldn't pin me there. Oh, I read all sorts of things. I said to some Catholic priests the other day when they asked me about reading, I said, "If you understand the word 'catholic,' I was very catholic in my taste."[. . .]

INTERVIEWER: When you started to write poetry, was there any poet that you admired very much?

FROST: I was the enemy of that theory—that idea of Stevenson's that you should play the sedulous ape to anybody. That did more harm to American education than anything ever got out.

INTERVIEWER: Did you ever feel any affinity between your work and any other poet's?

FROST: I'll leave that for somebody else to tell me. I wouldn't know.

INTERVIEWER: But when you read Robinson or Stevens, for example, do you find anything that is familiar to you from your own poetry?

FROST: Wallace Stevens? He was years after me.

INTERVIEWER: I mean in your reading of him, whether or not you felt any. . . .

FROST: Any affinity, you mean? Oh, you couldn't say that. No. Once he said to me, "You write on subjects." And I said, "You write on bric-a-brac." And when he sent me his next book, he'd written "S'more bric-a-brac" in it. Just took it good-naturedly. No, I had no affinity with him. We were friends. Oh, gee, miles away. I don't know who you'd connect me with.

INTERVIEWER: Well, you once said in my hearing that Robert Lowell had tried to connect you with Faulkner, told you you were a lot like Faulkner.

FROST: Did I say that?

INTERVIEWER: No, you said that Robert Lowell told you that you were a lot like Faulkner.

FROST: Well, you know what Robert Lowell said once? He said, "My uncle's dialect—the New England dialect, *The Bigelow Papers* —was just the same as Burns's, wasn't it?" I said, "Robert! Burns's was not a dialect. Scotch is not a dialect. It's a language." But he'd say anything, Robert, for the hell of it.

INTERVIEWER: You've never, I take it then, been aware of any particular line of preference in your reading?

FROST: Oh, I read 'em all. One of my points of departure is an anthology. I find a poet I admire, and I think, well, there must be a lot to that. Some old one—Shirley, for instance: "The glories of our blood and state"—that sort of splendid poem. I go looking for more. Nothing. Just a couple like that and that's all.[. . .]

I'm very catholic, that's about all you can say. I've hunted. I'm not thorough like the people educated in Germany in the old days. I've none of that. I hate the idea that you ought to read the whole of anybody. But I've done a lot of looking sometimes, read quite a lot.[...]

INTERVIEWER: I've been asking a lot of questions about the relationship of your poetry to other poetry, but of course there are many other non-literary things that have been equally important. You've been very much interested in science, for example.

FROST: Yes, you're influenced by the science of your time, aren't you? Somebody noticed that all through my book there's astronomy.

INTERVIEWER: Like "The Literate Farmer and the Planet Venus"?

FROST: Yes, but it's all through the book, all through the book. Many poems—I can name twenty that have astronomy in them. Somebody noticed that the other day: "Why has nobody ever seen how much you're interested in astronomy?" That's a bias, you could say.

One of the earliest books I hovered over, hung around, was called *Our Place Among the Infinities*, by an astronomer in England named Proctor, noted astronomer. It's a noted old book. I mention that in one of the poems: I use that expression "our place among the infinities" from that book that I must have read as soon as I read any book—thirteen or fourteen, right in there I began to read.[. . .]

INTERVIEWER: Would you agree that there are probably more good prizes for poetry today than there are good poets?

FROST: I don't know. I hate to judge that. It's nice for them— it's so nice for them to be interested in us, with their foundations. You don't know what'll come of it. You know the real thing is that the sense of sacrifice and risk is one of the greatest stimuli in the world. And you take that all out of it—take that away from it so that there's no risk in being a poet—I bet you'd lose a lot of the pious spirits. They're in it for the—hell of it. Just the same as these fellows breaking through the sound barrier up there, just the same.

I was once asked in public, in front of four or five hundred women, just how I found leisure to write. I said, "Confidentially—since there's only five hundred of you here, and all women—like a sneak I stole some of it, like a man I seized some of it, and I had a little in my tin cup."

Sounds as if I'd been a beggar, but I've never been consciously a beggar. I've been at the mercy of. . . . I've been a beneficiary around colleges and all. And this is one of the advantages to the American way: I've never had to write a word of thanks to anybody I had a cent from. The colleges came between.

Poetry has always been a beggar. Scholars have also been beggars, but they delegate their begging to the president of the college to do for them.

INTERVIEWER: I was suggesting just now that perhaps the number of emoluments for poets greatly exceeds the number of people whose work deserves to be honored. Isn't this a situation in which mediocrity will necessarily be exalted? And won't this make it more rather than less difficult for people to recognize really good achievement when it does occur?

FROST: You know, I was once asked that, and I said I never knew how many disadvantages anyone needed to get anywhere in the world. And you don't know how to measure that. No psychology will ever tell you who needs a whip and who needs a spur to win races.

I think the greatest thing about it with me has been this, and I wonder if others think it: I look at a poem as a performance. I look on the poet as a man of prowess, just like an athlete. He's a performer. And the things you can do in a poem are very various. You speak of figures, tones of voice varying all the time.

I'm always interested, you know, when I have three or four stanzas, in the way I *lay* the sentences in them. I'd hate to have the sentences all lie the same in the stanzas. Every poem is like that: some sort of achievement in performance.

Somebody has said that poetry among other things is the marrow of wit. That's probably way back somewhere—marrow of wit. There's got to be wit. And that's very, very much left out of a lot of this labored stuff. It doesn't sparkle at all.

Another thing to say is that every thought—poetical or otherwise—every thought is a feat of association. They tell of old Gibbon; as he was dying he was the same Gibbon at his historical parallels. All thought is a feat of association: having what's in front of you bring up something in your mind that you almost didn't know you knew. Putting this and that together. That click.

INTERVIEWER: Can you give an example of how this feat of association, as you call it, works?

FROST: Well, one of my masques turns on one association like that. God says: "I was just showing off to the Devil, Job." Job looks puzzled about it, distressed a little. God says, "Do you mind?" And, "No, no," he says, ("No," in that tone, you know: "No") and so on.

That tone is everything, the way you say that "no." I noticed that—that's what made me write that. Just that one thing made that.

INTERVIEWER: Did your other masque—*Masque of Mercy*—have a similar impetus?

FROST: I noticed that the first time in the world's history when mercy is entirely the subject is in Jonah. It does say somewhere earlier in the Bible, "If ten can be found in the city, will you spare it? Ten good people?" But in Jonah there is something worse than that. Jonah is told to go and prophesy against the city—and he *knows* God will let him down. He can't trust God to be unmerciful. You can trust God to be anything but unmerciful. So he ran away and—and got into a whale. That's the point of that and nobody notices it. They miss it.

INTERVIEWER: Why do you suppose, Mr. Frost, that among religious groups the masques had their best reception among Jesuits and rabbis?

FROST: Amusing you say that; that's true. The other—the lesser sects without the law, you see—they don't get it. They're too apt to think there's rebellion in them—what they go through with their parents when they're growing up. But that isn't in them at all, you know. They're not rebellious. They're very doctrinal, very orthodox, both of them.

But how'd you notice that? It's amusing to me too. You see, the rabbis have been fine to me and so have the SJ's particularly, all over the country. I've just been in Kansas City staying with them.

See, the masques are full of good orthodox doctrine. One of them turns on the thought that evil shows off to good and good shows off to evil. I made a couplet out of that for them in Kansas City, just the way I often do, off hand:

It's from their having stood contrasted
That good and bad so long have lasted.

INTERVIEWER: Making couplets "off hand" is something like

writing on schedule, isn't it? I know a young poet who claims he can write every morning from six to nine, presumably before class.

FROST: Well, there's more than one way to skin a cat. I don't know what that would be like, myself. When I get going on something, I don't want to just—you know. . . .

Very first one I wrote I was walking home from school and I began to make it—a March day—and I was making it all afternoon and making it so I was late at my grandmother's for dinner. I finished it, but it burned right up—just burned right up, you know. And what started that? What burned it?

So many talk (I wonder how falsely) about what it costs them, what agony it is to write. I've often been quoted: "No tears in the writer, no tears in the reader. No surprise for the writer, no surprise for the reader." But another distinction I made is: However sad, no grievance; grief without grievance.

How could I, how could anyone, have a good time with what cost me too much agony? How could they? What do I want to communicate but what a *hell* of a good time I had writing it?

The whole thing is performance and prowess and feats of association. Why don't critics talk about those things: what a feat it was to turn that that way and what a feat it was to remember that— to be reminded of that by this? Why don't they talk about that? Scoring. You've got to *score*. They say not, but you've got to score —in all the realms: theology, politics, astronomy, history, and the country life around you.

INTERVIEWER: What do you think of the performances of the poets who have made your birthplace, San Francisco, into their headquarters?

FROST: Have they? Somebody said I saw a lot of them in Kansas City at the end of my audience. They said, "See that blur over there? That's whiskers." No, I don't know much about that.

I'm waiting for them to say something that I can get hold of. The worse the better. I like it anyway, you know. Like you say to somebody, "Say something. Say something." And he says, "I burn."

INTERVIEWER: Do young poets send you things?

FROST: Yes, some—not much, because I don't respond. I don't write letters and all that. But I get a little, and I meet them, talk with them. I get some books.

I wonder what they're at. There's one book that sounded as if it might be good, *Aw Hell*. The book was called *Aw Hell*. Because "aw"—the way you say "aw," you know: "Aw, hell!" That might be something.

INTERVIEWER: Most of the titles are funny. One is called *Howl* and another *Gasoline*.

FROST: *Gasoline*, eh? I've seen a little of it, kicking round. I saw a bunch of nine of them in a magazine in Chicago when I was through there. They were all San Franciscans. Nothing I could talk about afterwards, though, either way.

I'm always glad of anybody that says anything awful. I can use it. We're all like that. You've got to learn to enjoy a lot of things you don't like. And I'm always ready for somebody to say some outrageous thing. I feel like saying, "Hold that now, long enough for me to go away and tell on you, won't you? Don't go back on it tomorrow." Funny world.

INTERVIEWER: When you look at a new poem that might be sent to you, what is it usually that makes you want to read it all or not want to read it?

FROST: This thing of performance and prowess and feats of association—that's where it all lies. One of my ways of looking at a poem right away it's sent to me, right off, is to see if it's rhymed. Then I know just when to look at it.

The rhymes come in pairs, don't they? And nine times out of ten with an ordinary writer, one of two of the terms is better than the other. One makeshift will do, and then they get another that's good and then another makeshift and then another one that's good. That is in the realm of performance; that's the deadly test with me. I want to be unable to tell which of those he thought of first. If there's any trick about it—putting the better one first so as to deceive me—I can tell pretty soon.

That's all in the performance realm. They can belong to any school of thought they want to, Spinoza or Schopenhauer, it doesn't matter to me. A Cartesian I heard Poe called, a Cartesian philosopher, the other day. . . tsssssss.

INTERVIEWER: You once saw a manuscript of Dylan Thomas's where he'd put all the rhymes down first and then backed into them. That's clearly not what you mean by performance, is it?

FROST: See, that's very dreadful. It ought to be that you're thinking forward, with the feeling of strength that you're getting them good all the way, carrying out some intention more felt than thought. It begins. And what it is that guides us—what is it?

Young people wonder about that, don't they? But I tell them it's just the same as when you feel a joke coming. You see somebody coming down the street that you're accustomed to abuse, and you feel it rising in you: something to say as you pass each other. Coming over him the same way.

And where do these thoughts come from? Where does a thought? Something does it to you. It's him coming toward you that gives you the animus, you know.

When they want to know about inspiration, I tell them it's mostly animus.

A Visit in Ripton

This interview by Roger Kahn, originally published in The Saturday Evening Post *for November 16, 1960, was done at RF's Homer Noble Farm in Ripton, Vermont. He had acquired the Ripton farm in 1939 and, with his friends the Theodore Morrisons, continued to occupy it summers and at other times during each year throughout the remainder of his life.*

To find Robert Frost, the great poet who has written so fondly of New Hampshire, one drives deep into the Green Mountains of Vermont. The paradox amuses Mr. Frost. It makes his green eyes twinkle and moves him to soft laughter. Frost is eighty-six years old now, but he wears his years lightly and humor still runs strong and young within him.

If there were an official poet laureate of the United States, he could well be Robert Frost. Frost's poems have won him four Pulitzer Prizes, a special Congressional gold medal, and, perhaps most important, they have earned him the admiration of millions of Americans who find other modern poets obscure and puzzling.

"I never like to read anyone who seems to be saying, 'Let's see you understand this, you damn fool,' " Frost says. "I haven't any of that spirit, and I don't like to be treated with that spirit."

The spirit Frost does possess, warm and rich as a good harvest, reaches out to schoolboys, politicians, and housewives as strongly as it reaches out to professors of English who have spent years studying his poetry. This independent, questioning, truthful spirit reaches out through all the land.

What sort of talk does one hear on paying a visit to Frost? Talk about poetry, to be sure; good talk that stirs the mind. But more than that, one hears about scores of other things: Fidel Castro's revolution and John Thomas's high jumping; the feel of farming and the sight of beatniks; loneliness and love and religion and Russia; and how important it is for a man to know how to live poor. Somewhat sadly, too, one hears talk about the Boston Red Sox.

Frost roots for the Red Sox, but cheerlessly. He feels that they play baseball in the manner of Boston gentlemen, and, although Frost appreciates Boston gentlemen in their place, he does not feel that their place is on the ball field.

"Spike 'em as you go around the bases," he suggests.

Frost is not a poet by accident, and much of what one hears comes in phrases which, like his poems, are vivid and exciting. It is not surprising to find here such sure command of English, but what may surprise you is the freshness with which Frost looks at the world. He once wrote:

> I never dared be radical when young
> For fear it would make me conservative when old.

At eighty-six he is neither radical nor conservative. He is simply Robert Frost, one man unique in his time and in ours.

Come with me then for a visit on a cool, pleasant afternoon when Vermont summer is changing into fall. The route, up from the south, leads past mountains and farmland almost into Middlebury, the college town. Then you turn off the main highway into a side road that runs through the village of Ripton and, for a time, follows the course of a swift-running stream.

A few miles beyond Ripton, approaching a spine of the Green Mountains, you turn down a dirt road, and when the dirt road stops, you get out of the car and walk up to the brow of a hill. There, in an unpretentious house of weathered timber, Frost lives by himself.

Two old friends, Mr. and Mrs. Theodore Morrison, live in a large farmhouse at the bottom of the hill. Morrison is a novelist and a member of the English faculty at Harvard. Mrs. Morrison is unofficial secretary to Frost, handling his correspondence, screening visitors to provide the privacy he needs, helping the poet with such mundane matters as income-tax returns.

The Ripton farm is Frost's home from May until October. During the winter he lives by himself at Cambridge, Massachusetts, when he is not traveling to recite and talk about poetry.

"Are you going to use a tape recorder?" Mrs. Morrison asked in the farmhouse. She is a sprightly, cultured lady who has been close to, and perhaps suffered, writers for most of her life.

"No, I thought I'd set up my typewriter and just type as he talks."

"Good," Mrs. Morrison said. "He's had a lot to do with tape recorders, and he doesn't like them very much. He feels they make one watch every word, make every word permanent, whether it's really meant to be permanent or not. Come. Let's start up the hill."

Entering Frost's home, one walks into a small, screened porch. The porch leads to a rectangular living room, with a stone fireplace on one long wall and a window, opening onto the countryside, opposite. Above the hearth, two red roses sat in tiny vases.

"We're here," Mrs. Morrison called.

Frost emerged from the bedroom, walking very straight, and shook hands firmly. He was wearing blue slacks, a gray sweater, and a white shirt, open at the throat.

He is not a tall man, perhaps five feet seven, but his body is strong and solid as one might expect in a man who has spent years behind a plow. His hair, once red, is white and luxuriant. His face, with its broad nose and resolute chin, is marked by time, but firm. It is a memorable face, mixing as it does strength and sensitivity.

"No tape recorder," Mrs. Morrison said.

"Good," Frost said. "Very good."

Mrs. Morrison helped set up my typewriter on a table she uses when taking dictation and excused herself. The poet walked to one of two large chairs in the room and motioned for me to sit in the other.

"You're a journalist?" Frost asked.

"Yes, mostly. I write a few other things too."

"Nearly everybody has two lives," Frost said, smiling. "Poets, sculptors. Nearly everybody has to lead two lives at the least."

"What life have you been leading recently?" I asked. "What have you been doing?"

"I never am doing anything, really," Frost said, "and I can't talk about my plans until I see how the plans work out. If I were writing a novel or an epic I could tell you what I've been doing, but I don't write novels or epics."

Frost cannot be sure whether a poem he is trying will find its way into his wastebasket or into an anthology of great verse. He prefers to keep his counsel till he knows, but he is still writing, still an active poet.

"I don't have any routine," Frost said. "I don't have any hours. I don't have any desk. I don't have any letter business with people, except I dictate one once in a while.

"Lectures? Lecture is the wrong word. I'm going to about twenty or twenty-five places from here to California, but lecture is the wrong word. I talk, and then I read. I never wrote out a lecture in my life. I never wrote a review, never a word of criticism. I've possibly written a dozen essays, but no more. You couldn't call mine a literary life."

Frost chuckled and gestured at the typewriter. "You use that thing pretty well," he said.

"Thanks," I said.

"Never learned to type, myself," Frost said a little archly.

"The world," I said, "Khrushchev and Castro—what do you think about what the world's been doing lately?"

"I wonder," Frost said, "if God hasn't looked down and turned away and said: 'Boys, this isn't for me. You go ahead and fight it out with knives and bombs.' "

Frost runs a conversation as a good pitcher runs a baseball game, never giving you quite what you expect. There are semi-humorous answers to serious questions and serious answers to semi-humorous questions. Frost is a master of the conversational change of pace.

"The world," he said, earnest now, "is being offered a choice between two kinds of democracy. Ours is a very ancient political growth, beginning at one end of the Mediterranean Sea and coming westward—tried in Athens, tried in Italy, tried in England, tried in France, coming westward all the way to us. A very long growth, a growth through trial and error, but always with the idea that there is some sort of wisdom in the mob.

"Put a marker where the growth begins, at the eastern end of the Mediterranean, and there's never been a glimmer of democracy south of there. Over east, in Asia, there have been interesting ideas, but none bothered by the wisdom of the mob.

"Our democracy is like our bill of fare. That came westward, too, with wheat and so on, adding foods by trial and error and luck. I think, when corn comes in good and fresh, what would I have done if Columbus hadn't discovered America?"

Again the poet had thrown a change of pace.

"What is this Russian democracy?" Frost said. "Ours, I say, is like our bill of fare—kills a few people every year probably, but most of us live with it. The Russian democracy is like a doctor's prescription or a food fad. That's all there is to that. That finished them off." Frost laughed.

"I have pretty strong confidence that our kind of democracy is better than a trumped-up kind," he said. "I'm pretty sure we're going to win. I'm on our side, anyway."

After Boris Pasternak, the late Russian poet and novelist, won the Nobel Prize for *Dr. Zhivago*, a book reflecting disillusion with the Soviet system, but was prevented by commissars from accepting the prize, Frost was asked to issue a personal protest.

"I couldn't do that," he said. "I understood what it was he wanted. He wanted to be left alone. He could have gotten out and gotten the [Nobel Prize] money, but he didn't want to. He had done what he wanted. He'd made his criticism. He lived in a little artists' colony outside of Moscow, and that was where he wanted to live and be left alone, and I had to respect that. I'm a nationalist myself."

Frost paused then to ask a question.

"Have you noticed," he said, "that every bill up before Congress lately—bills on horses, men, everything—winds up: 'This would tend to promote international peace'?"

It was a short hop from Pasternak and Khrushchev to Castro.

"I'd be in favor of leaving Castro alone for a time," Frost said, "and seeing if he can make it. We've gone past the time when we can fight to protect foreign investments.

"You know what I'd do? I'm protected up to ten thousand dollars on what I put in the savings bank. We could protect anyone who wants to invest in foreign countries up to half a million, a sort of insurance. Then we beg these investors to behave themselves:

Try to make friends; explain to Castro, 'I want to help you help me and your people make money.' If that doesn't work, pack up, come home, prove your failure, and collect your insurance."

The idea delighted Frost. "I'm going to propose that," he said, "the next time I'm in Congress. The general policy of the past—backing foreign investments—is over. Protect them with insurance, but not with army, navy, and diplomacy. That doesn't work any more.

"Belgium was the most selfish of all nations. They're getting their reward for that now. England was a little loftier. The English brought nice Indian boys back to Oxford to see what freedom was.

"Castro is a puzzle to me, but he ought to see that we are a well-meaning nation. He needn't blackguard us all the time."

Frost placed one hand before his eyes, and when he spoke again his voice was very soft

"Unfinished business," he said. "I'm very much in favor of unfinished business. Some of them aren't, but every single heading in the newspaper represents a whole lot of things that have got to stay unfinished, that can't be finished. Us and Russia, that might take a couple of hundred years before it's finished. That's one of the hard things about dying, wondering how the unfinished business will come out.

"Oh, you could go crazy with too much unfinished business. You'd feel unfulfilled. You make a finished article out of this, and I make a finished poem. But take anyone's career. That has got to be suspended and thought a great deal, and you're not saying much about it till you see how it comes out. You suspend judgment and go to bed."

Outside, beyond the window, a lawn stretched down the hill. To the far right lay a brown field, newly turned by the plow. Beyond the valley, mountains rose, deep green.

"Three things have followed me," Frost said. "Writing, teaching a little, and farming. I lived by farming for ten years. I get a queer unhappiness when I don't have a little land to farm. Writing, teaching, and farming. The three strands of my life." [. . .]

"I started life by the ocean," Frost said. "San Francisco. My father was a newspaperman there. He went to Harvard, finished first in his class, but he never talked much about that. Once he got

West he put the East behind him, never mentioned it, died young. My mother was born in Scotland, raised in Ohio."

"Did you grow up amid books?" I asked.

"Didn't you? Didn't you?" Frost said, his voice almost a chant. "Oh, I never got the library habit much. I have an interest in books, but you couldn't call me a terribly bookish man."

There are two bookcases in Frost's living room, and on the window seat between our chairs, books rested in three small stacks. They were his recent reading and ranged from Latin poetry to a work about contemporary architecture. But the room was not overrun with books. The average publishing-house editor lives among more books than does Robert Frost.

"We came to southern New Hampshire after my father died," Frost said. "I escaped school until I was twelve. I'd try it for a week, and then the doctor would take me out. They never knew what the matter was, but I seemed to be ailing. I got so I never wanted to see school.

"The first time I liked it was in New Hampshire. I liked the noon hour and the recess. I didn't want to miss what went on then, and so I became interested in the rest of it, the studies.

"It was a little country school. There was no grading. I could go as fast as I wanted, and I made up the whole eight years in a year and a half without realizing I was doing it. Then they sent me down to Lawrence[, Massachusetts,] to live with my grandfather and go to the high school where my father had gone. It was just the luck of that year in the country, that country school. Otherwise, I might not have made it.

"In high school I had only Greek, Latin, and mathematics. I began to write in my second year, but not for any teacher. There were no English teachers. We had an active school magazine that the teachers had nothing to do with.

"I must have been reading Prescott's *Conquest of Mexico*, because my first poem was a ballad about the night the Indians fought Cortez.

"People say, 'You were interested in Indians the way children are interested in cops and robbers.' But it wasn't that way at all. I was interested in Indians because of the wrongs done to them. I was wishing the Indians would win all the battles.

"The magazine would surprise you if you saw it. We did it for pleasure. When they do it nowadays they have teachers, and that spoils the whole thing. They say, 'I can't finish this, teacher, help me.' That spoils it. We had poems, stories, editorials, and we did it all ourselves.

"I edited the magazine the last year, and I had eighteen assistant editors. One day I got mad at them. They weren't giving me enough material. I got sore and went down to the printing room, and in a day or two I wrote the whole damn thing. I wrote it all. I even made up a story about the debating union and wrote the whole debate. I wrote it all, the whole thing; then I resigned."

Frost smiled at me as he remembered something he had done seventy years ago of which he is still proud.

"Dartmouth is my chief college," he said, "the first one I ran away from. I ran from Harvard later, but Dartmouth first. In a little library at Dartmouth I saw a magazine, and on the front page there was a poem. There was an editorial inside about the poem, so evidently that magazine was in favor of poetry. I sent them a poem, 'My Butterfly.' It's in the big collection. They bought it so easily I thought I could make a living this way, but I didn't keep selling 'em as fast as that.

"The magazine was called the New York *Independent,* and after they bought the poem they asked that when I sent them more, would I please spell the name of the magazine correctly. I'd made a mistake, but they bought my poem."

Although Frost was a straight-A student, he did not linger long at Dartmouth or Harvard and, of course, never received a degree. He has since been awarded two honorary degrees by Dartmouth and one by Harvard.

"When I told Grandfather Frost I wanted to be a poet, he wasn't pleased," Frost said. "He was an old-line Democrat, the devil take the hindmost; and here I was, making good grades, and wanting, he thought, to waste my life.

" 'I give you one year to make it, Rob,' he said.

"I put on an auctioneer's voice. 'I'm offered one; give me twenty, give me twenty, give me twenty,' I said. My grandfather never brought up poetry again."

Frost married Elinor White, his co-valedictorian at Lawrence

High, in 1895 and set about rearing a family and dividing his life among poetry, teaching, and farming.

"I had to find other means than poems," he said. "They didn't sell fast enough, and I didn't send my poems out much. Oh, I wanted them to want my poems. Some say, 'Do you write for yourself entirely?' 'You mean into the wastebasket?' I say.

But I had pride there. I hated rejection slips. I had to be very careful of my pride. 'Love me little, love me long.' Did you hear that? Were you brought up on that? 'Love me little, love me long.' " Frost smiled. "But not too little," he said.

He placed a hand before his eyes again.

"One of the most sociable virtues or vices is that you don't want to feel queer. You don't want to be too much like the others, but you don't want to be clear out in nowhere. 'She mocked 'em and she shocked 'em and she said she didn't care.' You like to mock 'em and to shock 'em, but you really do care.

"You are always with your sorrows and your cares. What's a poem for if not to share them with others. But I don't like poems that are too crudely personal. The boy writes that the girl has jilted him; and I know who the boy is and who the girl is, and I don't want to know.

"Where can you be personal and not in bad taste? In poetry, but you have to be careful. If anybody tries to make you say more— they have to stop where you stop.

" 'What does this poem mean?' some ask.

" 'It means what it says.'

" 'I know what it means to me, but I don't know just what it means to you,' they say.

" 'Maybe I don't want you to.' "

Frost was sitting back comfortably, his mind at work.

"We have all sorts of ways to hold people," he said. "Hold them and hold them off.

"Do you know what the sun does with the planets? It holds them and holds them off. The planets don't fall away from the sun, and they don't fall into it. That's one of the marvels: attraction and repulsion. You have that with poetry, and you have that with friendships."

For a time in his youth, guarding his pride, developing his art,

Frost expected to work as a New England farmer for the rest of his life.

"But people asked me out to read," he said, "and that kind of checked that. Then, when I was teaching in academies, having a successful time, it would be eating me all up, taking me away from poetry too much. Whenever it got like that, I'd run away.

"I didn't have any foundation to help me, but I had a tiny little bit of money saved up, and I went to England. Not for the literary life, I didn't want that. But we could live cheaper there. The six of us went to England, and we stayed for three years for thirty-six hundred dollars, fare and everything. We lived poor, but we had a little garden, and we got something out of it, and we had some chickens. We lived very much like peasants.

"I was thirty-six years old or so, and I'd never offered a book. My poems were scattered in magazines, but not much. Then one day I thought I'd show a little bunch of poems. I left them with a small publisher, and three days later I signed the contract. Funny, it had never occurred to me to try a book here. *A Boy's Will*, that was the book."

This is a time when beatniks, masquerading as poets, recite their work at you, pinning you to the ground first, when necessary. Frost, mentioning his first book, which brims with poems that have become classics, offered no recitations. Only when I urged him did he nod. Then, looking at me intently, he spoke this stanza from his poem "Reluctance":

> Ah, when to the heart of man
>   Was it ever less than a treason
> To go with the drift of things,
>   To yield with a grace to reason,
> And bow and accept the end
>   Of a love or a season?

He speaks his poetry surely, clearly, with perfect command of the cadences. It is poetry written to be heard aloud, and when you hear it in Frost's voice you feel that somehow it reaches its final measure of beauty in these fine New England tones.

"I once thought I'd like to have my lyrics seen as well as heard," Frost said. "I had some booklets made up and given out to audiences who came to hear me. That lasted two nights. The second night so many wanted me to sign the booklets that the police had to get me away.

"Now I sign anything of mine that they type out or write out—without money and without price, you see. There's quite a little of that in me."

After Frost returned from England with his family he had to go back to farming and teaching. He was forty before he gained much recognition as a poet, and he was nearly fifty before his volume *New Hampshire* won him his first Pulitzer Prize.

It struck me then, sitting in the little living room, that Frost has gone from complete obscurity to great fame without changing his way of life. The Vermont house is as simple as the houses where he dwelled when there was no choice but to live simply. One difference is that now a sizable portion of the world tries to beat a path through the woods and up to Frost's door.

"You have to be careful about idolizers," Frost said. "Emerson calls an unwanted visitor a devastator of a day. It's a cranky Yankee poem, but I suppose he was pestered all the time by people who wanted to go deeper into him than he could go himself; and, goodness, he was such an artist they should very well have left it where he did.

"They think, the idolizers, that you've injured them. Whether they injure you or not, the idolizers always think you've injured them.

"How much do you need someone who always thinks you're a hero? How much do you need being thought a hero all the time?

"People say, 'I got over this, I got over that.' They are a lot of fools, the people who say you get over your loves and your heroes. I never do. I don't change very much."

"Has your method of writing changed?"

"If I'm not in shape so I can strike it out, like a good golf stroke or a good stroke of the bat, there's not much I can do," Frost said. "Oh, you get so that some days you can play a beautiful game, but there are always days when you can't. Those days, I can't redo them. They're done—down the sink.

"What some seem to do is worry a thing into shape and have others worry with them. Not to say I don't have the distress of failure, but the worry way isn't for me. There are the days you can and the days you can't, and both are training toward the future days you can.

"Do you know the story about how the bear is born?"

I didn't.

"The bear is born shapeless, says the story, and the mother licks it into shape. That's the way it is with some people's writing. But no good piece is worried into shape. A child is unfortunate that needs to be reshaped just after it's born.

"Is a poet made? A poet might be through all the years of trial and error, but any good poem is not made. It's born complete."

In many of Frost's poems, loneliness is a strong theme. His wife died in 1938, and only two of his five children survive. I wondered how he had come to terms with solitude.

"In the big newspaper office," Frost said, "where everyone sits alongside the other and writes—I couldn't do that. Even reading— I've got to be totally absorbed when I read. Where there are other people reading, too, I don't feel very happy.

"Alone you take all your traits as if you were bringing 'em to market. You bring them from the quiet of the garden. But the garden is not the market place. That's a big trouble to some: how you mix living with people with not living with people; how you mix the garden with the market place.

"I like the quiet here, but I like to have a big audience for my talks, to have a few turned away. I like to feel all that warmth in the room.[. . .]

Suddenly Frost sat up straight. "I'm sorry I can't entertain you," he said. "I'm not set up here for that sort of thing."

He meant drinks, and I asked if he took a drink himself.

"A daiquiri once in a while," he said, "but not much, and not serious. I don't care for those parties where everyone does. They take just a little too much, and they say just a little too much. I've always been shy. I get uncomfortable."

Outside, in the late-afternoon sun, the grass looked bright and fresh.

"Used to play softball out past there," Frost said. "I pitched. They don't let me do all the things I want to anymore; but if we had a ball, I'd pitch to you a little, and I'd surprise you." He grinned.[. . .]

Then we were serious again, and I asked about another strong theme in Frost's work, the theme of God.

"Don't make me out to be a religious man," Frost said. "Don't make me out to be a man who has all the answers. I don't go around preaching God. I'm not a minister.

"I'm always pleased when I see people comfortable with these things. There's a rabbi near here, a friend of mine, who preaches in Cincinnati in the winter. He talks at the Methodist Church here sometimes and tells the people in Cincinnati that he's a summer Methodist.

"People have wondered about him at the Methodist Church. One lady was troubled and said to me, 'How do they differ from us?'

" 'What you got there on that table?' I said.

" 'That's a Bible,' she said.

"I didn't say any more.

" 'Oh,' she said. 'Oh, the Old Testament. Why can't you have a Jew in church?' she said, and she understood."

Frost's voice was strong.

"There's a good deal of God in everything you do," he said. "It's like climbing up a ladder, and the ladder rests on nothing; and you climb higher and higher, and you feel there must be God at the top. It can't be unsupported up there.

"I'd be afraid, though, of any one religion being the whole thing in one country, because there would probably come a day when they would take me down to the cellar and torture me—just for my own good."

He smiled briefly.

"There is more religion outside church than in," Frost said, "more love outside marriage than in, more poetry outside verse than in. Everyone knows there is more love outside the institutions than in, and yet I'm kind of an institutional man."

We turned back to poetry then.

"They ask me if I have a favorite," Frost said, "but if a mother has a favorite child, she has to hide it from herself, so I can't tell you if I have a favorite, no."

I mentioned rhythm in poetry, and how children respond to it.

"Yes," Frost said, "because their hearts beat, and they see the waves."

"Is there one basic point to all fine poetry?" I asked.

"The phrase," Frost said slowly, clearly, "and what do I mean by a phrase? A clutch of words that gives you a clutch at the heart."

His own phrases, his own words, were all about me in the little house. Afternoon was fading, and I realized how much we had discussed, and how Frost had ranged from the profound to the simple —as his own life, which seems so simple, has in reality been so profound. I remembered his poems too.

Some summing up seemed in order, and, for want of a better term, I intended to say that this visit had brought me into the presence of greatness. "I feel as though. . . ," I began.

"Now, none of that," Frost said, anticipating. "We've had a fine talk together, haven't we? And we've talked to some purpose. Come now, and I'll walk with you down the hill."

He got up from his chair and started down the steep path, pausing to look at the sunset as he went.

Helping to Usher in "An Augustan Age"

One of the highlights of RF's public life was his participation in President John F. Kennedy's Inauguration on January 20, 1961—the first time a poet had been recognized and honored by being accorded a prominent role in an Inaugural program.

This interview by Herbert A. Kenny relates to the events of that "day of days," as RF styled it. The text, which here contains corrections by Mr. Kenny, originally appeared in The Boston Sunday Globe *of January 22nd.*

A T the most-solemn ceremony, a touch of informality makes the whole world kin. Thus Robert Frost, eighty-six, dean of the world's great poets, brought the Kennedy Inauguration into human focus with his gruff complaint, "I'm not having a good light at all."

What was his personal reaction to his inability to read the dedicatory lines he had written for the poem that President Kennedy had asked him to read?

"I was never so mad at myself in my life," he responded. Then: "Never again will I attempt to read lines newly written, without memorizing them first."

Over-all, he never had a better time in his life—a life full of honors. He enjoyed the Presidential luncheon at the Capitol, and his box at the armory Inaugural ball was a magnet for the learned and the light-hearted, young and old, friends and strangers alike, all coming to pay tribute to America's greatest man of letters.

His lone regret for the day was his inability to read his lines of dedication—the first occasional lines he has ever written.

The brilliant noonday January sun turned the surface of his paper to the sparkle of a diamond. Vice-President Lyndon Johnson leaped forward to proffer his tall silk hat as a shield.

"It shut out all the light," said Frost, "and I decided not to try to finish the dedication."

He launched into "The Gift Outright," the most nationalistic poem he has ever written, a favorite with him, as it is with President Kennedy. The words rang out on the bitterly cold Washington air and reverberated, not only over the heads of a spellbound audience but in their hearts. The faces of two Presidents and Vice-President Nixon caught by the television camera were the faces of men who were deeply touched.

Until Frost complained of the light, and then took the Texan's hat with an audible, "Here, let me have that," the program had been stilted. Frost brought New England simplicity into it all.

If he had read "The Gift Outright" and sat down, the ritualistic quality of the day might have continued. Had this happened, even the President's classic speech might not have caught the crowd.

Frost's difficulties turned the crowd into a family. People began to fret because the light on his paper was bad. Presidents and Vice-Presidents alike, wives of Presidents, Secret Service men, and others moved around to see how they could help. Mrs. Kennedy, with all the instincts of a perfect hostess, moved uneasily forward to lend a hand.

Frost paused after his reading, and then explained that the lines he had tried vainly to read were lines of dedication, written especially for the occasion. That in itself was a rare tribute from a rare man.

He had previously declined at any time to write occasional lines. When he was first asked to give the Phi Beta Kappa poem at Harvard, he told the university he wouldn't write a special poem but would read something previously written. But he wrote special lines for the Kennedy Inauguration, now printed widely, saluting President Kennedy for giving the arts a place at the Inaugural.

It was the first time in the history of the country a poet had been asked to read.

Frost has criticized the neglect of the arts by the American government and repeatedly has sought the creation of a government academy of the arts.

His role in the Inauguration was a happy precedent and prompted him to write the special lines. The glittering sun on shiny paper prevented him from reading, and the icy weather was no help. But Frost is one of the hardiest breed in the world: a Vermont Democrat.

He acknowledges that at times he hasn't felt at home in the Democratic party since Cleveland, but as he turned away Friday afternoon from his reading he knew he was at home on the platform. The applause was thunderous. President Kennedy stepped forward, tapped Frost's shoulder, and turned him around. He shook his hand. President Eisenhower moved forward to shake his hand.

"They were both very kind," Frost said today. "They were complimentary. I don't remember just what they said."

He had met both before. He had taken dinner with President Eisenhower at the White House.

"We had a great evening," said Frost. "He told me then he feels he is neither Democrat nor Republican."

"The President had to deliver a masterpiece to stand with that poem," one member of the audience later told him.

At the luncheon afterwards, Frost chatted at length with President and Mrs. Kennedy. He complimented the President on his speech and asked for a copy.

"I'd be happy to send you one," said the President. "What is your address?"

"35 Brewster Street, Cambridge," said Frost. "What's yours?"

The President burst into laughter.

Despite his eighty-six years, the wintry weather, and the traffic, Frost managed to turn up at a hotel luncheon that one Cabinet member missed despite a military escort.

At the Presidential luncheon someone informally raised a toast to President Kennedy: "Long may he reign."

"Can't say that of a President," said Frost, "but let's say, 'Twice may he reign.'"

"I think the pleasantest half hour I spent," Frost said, "was with the Mayor of Lawrence, John J. Buckley—that's the city where I was partly brought up, you know. We were on television together reminiscing a bit. It was very amusing."

"I saw some old friends," he continued, "Supreme Court Justice Felix Frankfurter and Earl Warren. I always have a nice chat when I see Mr. Frankfurter."

Chief Justice Warren said to Frost, "Where do you go from here?"

"I'm going down to Georgia to read poetry," Frost told him, "but I may straighten out that situation down there for you."

A very earnest young person came up to Frost's box at the Inaugural ball and asked him what he thought was the significance of a poet's presence at a Presidential Inaugural.

"An Augustan age," Frost replied, a twinkle in his eye.

"An Augustan age?" said the young person.

"Yes," said Frost, "the joining of the arts and power. Make that poetry and power, just for alliteration."

"I could see," said Frost, "he didn't know what an Augustan age was."

What about the weather?

"I didn't object to its being bad," he said. "It was as if we were expected to be sure and remember. It was being rubbed into us a bit. Just so we'd never forget."

Those who attended the Inaugural will never forget the patriarchal figure of the poet on the platform, his hair white as snow, his voice as strong as the Republic itself.

"I'll rumple their brains, fondly...."

In March of 1961 RF flew across the Atlantic on a visit to Israel and Greece—a trip that, homeward bound, included a birthday luncheon in London on March 26th as guest of the American Ambassador to the Court of St. James's.

The texts that follow are extracts from two stories prepared for the New York Herald Tribune, *both reporting on RF's meeting with the press as he was about to depart for Tel Aviv.*

By Earl Ubell,
New York Herald Tribune, March 10, 1961:

AT eighty-six, Robert Frost shows no fear of the press or its minions.

"Go ahead and ask them hard," he challenged them yesterday as he does every audience. And laughter flowed like lava when America's snow-capped volcano of poetry and wit erupted into rhyme (his own), epigrams, and jokes. The occasion was a press conference a few hours before he was scheduled to leave for the Hebrew University of Jerusalem, where he will spend ten days lecturing and "rumpling" the brains of the students. Why Israel?

"I look on all that as an American colony anyway," Mr. Frost quipped. They are practically a colony, he said, because the inhabitants all speak English, many are Americans, and they have so many things in common "with us."

What things in common?

"I don't know," the poet said. "Well, you see I haven't been there."

As the first Lecturer in American Culture and Civilization in the chair established by Samuel Paley of Philadelphia, Mr. Frost has a simple plan.

"I will give two lectures and sit around with the students," he said. "I'll simply rumple their brains, fondly. . . . You have to put in that word 'fondly,' " he said.

"I never say what I plan too long in advance. . . ," an evaluation of himself that proved true at the Presidential Inauguration when he could not say the rhymed preamble to his poem "The Gift Outright." Wind and sun defied him there.

"That was one of the hardest jobs I ever did," the poet said, and that reminded him of some of the lines of the preamble he liked best:

By the example of our Declaration

"You see," he interpolated, "that's a capital 'D'."

It made the least tribe want to be a nation.

And once started "saying" this poem, the volcano rumbled, and out flowed a few more couplets.

Naturally, a science editor challenged him on his possible antagonism of science, since he was going to a country that is betting its future on science.

"My favorite magazine is the *Scientific American*," Mr. Frost said, with a wisp of a grin, "the advertisements in it are more interesting than most other magazines."

He pointed out that his poems are full of astronomy and that he had always had a "glass." In fact, when the Russians launched their Sputnik it made him angry.

"What are they doing in my sky, I wanted to know," he said.

"I have an attraction to science," he admitted; and he once assured his mother, who was worried about Darwin, that the evolutionary theory merely meant that "God had made man out of prepared mud."

However, he prefers the myth to live by—the Garden of Eden, the fall of man. . . . He prefers it to live by, rather than the story of the descent from an albino monkey.

By Maurice Dolbier,
New York Herald Tribune, March 14, 1961:

Last Thursday, just before leaving for Israel[. . .], Robert Frost met the press—and they were his. Many of Mr. Frost's comments have been reported in the news columns, but—as is always the case with the poet's press conferences—there's more, there's more. . . .

He was asked about his widely quoted statement about "poetry and power."

"That was in the *Washington Post*, you know," he said. "They asked me what I looked for in the new Administration, and I said an Augustan age of poetry and power, and they said, 'What's that?' . . . Since then, it's been gone on with and argued about. I never go on with an argument. . . .

"One newspaper deprecated my use of the word 'power.' But I had a letter from the President not long ago, and across it—right across the page—he'd written, 'Power all the way.' "

He was asked about his often-misinterpreted line, "Good fences make good neighbors."

"It's the other fellow in the poem who says that, you know. . . . I don't know. Maybe I was both fellows in the poem. . . .

"All through human history, fences are always being set up, and they're always falling down. Where I'm going, there's a boundary right in the middle of the city. I say that's too bad. Like Berlin. Too bad. Wars come of these things. . . . Quietism is not a thing the human spirit can endure for long."

He was asked about travel.

"I've been in England and a little bit in France. But I'm not a traveler. I've never seen the Taj Mahal. I'm not going to Israel to see the sights. If I see something incidentally, I enjoy it; if I see it on purpose, I don't. A friend wanted to take me to the top of the Empire State Building. I said no; I'd had New York soaked into me, I didn't want to treat it as a sight. . . .

"When I used to come down from Amherst to teach at the New School for Alvin Johnson, my train got in at eight, and I'd walk to the school, zigzagging with the lights so I'd feel like a New Yorker. . . .

"I was in a taxi the other day on one of these crowded side

streets. The driver was damning the jamming and saying unkind things about New York. I told him he shouldn't. I said, 'New York's the greatest city the world has ever seen or ever will see.' 'Yes,' he said, 'I guess you're right. But San Francisco—San Francisco is a *nice* city.'

"I was raised in San Francisco, and with all the Chinese that are there I became an ancestor-worshiper. Later I learned that man was descended from the monkeys, and every day when I come down to breakfast I say to myself, 'How shall I conduct myself today so that I won't disgrace my monkey ancestors.'[. . .]"

He was asked what he thought of "modern American poetry and the cult of unintelligibility."

"I hate it," he said, and then, after a pause, "and I wonder if I'm to blame. . . . Sometimes people say things that dishearten you. I wrote an innocent little poem called 'Spring Pools,' and one critic called it 'a drop of pure strychnine.' Me and strychnine! That takes you down. You think: Is that what's coming? Connection broken right off. . . .

"I think in all my work there's a consistency. It takes serious brainwork to see the consistency. You have to learn how to take me."

How long would he be in Israel?

"Only ten days. I'm coming back in ten days. I've got America to tend to."

Supper with Robert Frost

Leavitt F. Morris did this story for The Christian Science Monitor, *based on his association with RF as a fellow passenger on the plane for Tel Aviv. It was published, with the title as here given, in the* Monitor *of April 6, 1961, shortly after RF's return from his trip to Israel, Greece, and London.*

ROBERT FROST, America's foremost poet, and I had supper together the other evening. It was an impromptu get-together—one which neither of us had planned nor least expected. We both were bound for Israel: he for the more noble purpose of giving a series of readings and lectures at the Hebrew University of Jerusalem and I to cover the opening of the Sheraton Corporation's new hotel in Tel Aviv.

We of the press had been informed earlier that the distinguished poet would be aboard our El Al flight to Israel. It was with great and eager anticipation that I looked forward to seeing and meeting Mr. Frost in person, if only for the moment of a handshake.[. . .]

This was not, as was quite apparent in Mr. Frost's casualness in checking in for the flight, his first long airplane journey. Indeed, he was plainly dressed in a many-seasoned topcoat, a felt hat which might have been bought especially for the trip at the insistence of his daughter, and canvas-top, rubber-soled shoes. A blue woolen scarf hung loosely about his neck. Mr. Frost looked as though he might have just returned from his Vermont village post office rather than soon to leave for faraway Asia Minor.

Mr. Frost is a youthful eighty-seven years. His stride is determined and measured, his step light. He took keen interest in preflight preparations and found the Hebrew inscription behind the ticket counter, "I bare you on eagles' wings" (Exodus 19:4), most assuring.

Moments before take-off the great jet developed mechanical difficulties, and we were forced to return to the Idlewild terminal building, where we were informed there would be a two-hour delay and that during the interval the evening meal would be served.

It was at this interval that Robert Frost and I had "supper" together. At the same table with us was Mr. Frost's traveling companion, New Hampshire-born Larry Thompson, Professor of English at Princeton University. This, I think, is as it should have been. For Mr. Frost, Mr. Thompson, and myself have much in common. We three, while somewhat diversified in our respective professions, hold deeply in our hearts the warmest affection for New England. This unity of feeling, quite unconsciously, I am sure, formed a strong bond between us as was later evidenced throughout the trans-Atlantic crossing and on into Tel Aviv.

This evening meal, referred sumptuously to by El Al as "an eight-course dinner," was served in a room known as the Golden Door. A ramrod-erect waiter "dealed" from under his arm, in a most-dexterous manner, three menus, two by two and one-half feet in size. There was a maze of type offering everything from pheasant under glass to thick steaks.

"That's too big and too much for me," laughed Mr. Frost, handing the menu back. "We just want a little 'supper.' " So Mr. Frost settled for a dish of fresh fruit and I for an omelet.

We talked mostly of earthy things, skipped quickly over politics, touched briefly on the space age, exchanged comments on travel, and aired our feelings on the younger generation.

But it was the earthy things we talked about with such warmth and exuberance.

We talked of the beauty of rambling stone walls that stitch together New England's boundary lines, of lush pasture lands upon which plump cattle feed, of clear, cool mountain streams that nourish the most-delicate meadow flower into bloom and give such vibrant life to a noble elm or sweeping willow tree.

We spoke of the cathedral-like hush of a woodland of maples and birches, of the stanchness and stability of both the White Mountains of New Hampshire and the Green Mountains of Vermont, and the serene little New England villages where neighborliness and friendliness are as much a natural attribute of the people as their ability to make a good living from the land.

"It's the New Englander's uncanny ability to get the most from the least," said Mr. Frost, "that has made him such an independent, hardy individual."[. . .]

In a press interview last year Mr. Frost said he was asked if New England wasn't decadent and if there was any hope for the region.

"I told them we'd always come out all right. Then I reminded them how we've turned out a number of Presidents and that we have here some of the great universities of the world. In fact, I made a prediction that not only would the next Secretary of State come from Massachusetts but that our next President would, too.

"The stories in the papers the next day," chuckled Mr. Frost, "never mentioned a thing I said about New England's economic plight but reported in large type: 'Robert Frost Comes Out for Kennedy.' So you see why I take the credit of nominating John F. Kennedy for President?"

Mr. Frost has been a life-long Democrat, but he describes himself as an "unhappy one." He disagreed with many of the Franklin D. Roosevelt policies but has high hopes that the present Administration can fulfill its pledges.

"There's too much government getting into our lives," he said. "During the last campaign it seemed to me that all the candidates promised to do was to help put the young people into school or the old people into hospitals. People have got to learn to help themselves and take care of their own wherever possible.

"I remember getting a letter from a very wise mother not so long ago. She asked me how she could give to her son the 'hardships' of life which had contributed to making the boy's father a successful man.

"Parents are afraid to give their children some of the hardships of life so vitally necessary in their ripening into maturity of judgment and becoming responsible citizens."

Mr. Frost savored for a brief moment a sweet slice of an orange and before speaking again raked his unruly white hair with strong fingers.

"Look any better?" he asked Mr. Thompson across the table. Then without waiting for an answer he turned to me and asked if it weren't "deplorable" to see the small Vermont and New Hampshire farms giving way to huge combines. When I assured him I agreed, he replied, "There goes your neighborliness: there goes much of the rugged individuality that has made New England what it is."

Mr. Frost still likes to grow things; and on his Ripton, Vermont, farm, near Middlebury, he raises potatoes and other fresh vegetables. He bought his first farm in New Hampshire back in 1915, and, as he so vividly recalls, it was a most unusual transaction.

"I saw this Franconia farm, and it was just what I wanted," Mr. Frost said. "So I went up to the farmer and told him I was thinking of moving him to a larger place up the road a piece.

"The farmer couldn't see how I was going to do that, because he wasn't interested in selling. I offered him one thousand dollars, with no money down, and told him he could get the larger farm, which he needed, for three thousand dollars, no money down. He finally accepted, only to come to me a day later and said he felt he should get eleven hundred dollars for his farm. I agreed, with no money down.

"As it turned out, World War I came along and the man prospered because he was able to provide so many more products from his larger farm."

Late frosts plagued Mr. Frost's crops in Franconia, and he told of one year when he had to sprinkle his beans every day to keep them from getting killed. On one day he had just returned to the house from spraying the beans with water, only to find the ice forming on the leaves in early July. So he started looking for a farm in Vermont. Concord Corners seemed the most desirable place, but at the time he wanted to move there were no farms available. He later found two farms in Concord Corners which he purchased.[. . .]

"Say," he said, nudging me in the ribs, "it must be about maple-sugar time in Vermont. You know, I never could pass one of those dripping spigots without bending down and drinking some of that pure sap. Too much of it can be sickish, but a little bit is good for you."

At this moment El Al announced that its flight was ready for

departure, and we all quickly moved back to the plane and prepared for take-off the second time. Mr. Frost sat across the aisle
from me, and I watched his hands with fascination as he somewhat
clumsily threaded the tongue of his seat belt through the heavy
buckle. They were not the delicate hands usually associated with a
poet. They were the hands of a man used to kneading the soil,
guiding a plow, or milking cows. I can't rightly say that they were
gnarled hands, for they were not. They were thick, strong, firm
hands as you learned from his handshake. These were the hands,
I thought, that knew how to hold the reins of a horse—a certain
horse hitched to a certain sleigh on a certain snowy night in some
New England village.

And then, midst the roar of four mighty jet engines, I remembered these lines from his poem, "Stopping by Woods on a Snowy
Evening":

> Whose woods these are I think I know.
> His house is in the village though;
> He will not see me stopping here
> To watch his woods fill up with snow.
>
> My little horse must think it queer
> To stop without a farmhouse near
> Between the woods and frozen lake
> The darkest evening of the year.
>
> He gives his harness bells a shake
> To ask if there is some mistake.
> The only other sound's the sweep
> Of easy wind and downy flake.
>
> The woods are lovely, dark and deep.
> But I have promises to keep,
> And miles to go before I sleep,
> And miles to go before I sleep.

And thus was I borne into the starlit night and on toward Tel
Aviv.

Morning comes early on these eastbound flights, and within a
few short hours the crew was bustling about preparing a light
breakfast before our scheduled landing in Paris.

Mr. Frost stirred with the rest of us, and as I returned to my seat he leaned forward, eyes alive with a memory, and in a friendly, challenging voice asked if I had ever heard of Vershire, Vermont. He was delighted when I replied that my great-grandmother was married in Vershire in 1853 by a Reverend Hall.

The name Hall immediately set his memory to working, and he recalls a pond near Concord Corners by that name, later changed to Shadow Lake.

"A pity," he said, "to change the name."

So it was to Paris and then on to Tel Aviv that Mr. Frost and I swapped stories on Vermont villages.

Just after we had taken off from Paris, Mr. Frost beckoned me to come across the aisle.

"Know how to peel an apple?" he asked, fondling a bright yellow Delicious, his eyes twinkling. "You never cut the apple from the top of the stem to the bottom," he explained, his knife slicing instead through the apple sideways. "You must see the star shape," he said. "It makes the apple easier to eat, does mostly away with the skin, and there's little waste."

Thus at twenty-five thousand feet over Mt. Blanc I learned from Mr. Frost the proper way to peel—and to eat —an apple.

The stars were out brightly again, and we were within sight of the lights of the sprawling city of Tel Aviv. The stewardesses had distributed our coats and in moments we glided onto the runway at Lod Airport.

As I walked down the ramp behind Mr. Frost he turned to me and said, I thought a bit wistfully, "If I'd have known seventy-one years ago that when I wrote those few verses they would have led to this amount of travel I wouldn't have written them."

As I said good-by to Mr. Frost and wished him success in his lecture series, he stopped and said, "You must come and see me in Vermont this summer."

"It's a promise," I shouted, hoping the venerable poet could hear me above the thunder of a jetliner taking off for New York.

Then he and the jet disappeared into the night.

"I like anything that penetrates the mysteries."

On a spring visit to Washington in 1961 RF, now honorary Consultant in the Humanities at the Library of Congress, held at the national library one of his typically lively and wide-ranging news conferences. Thomas Wolfe reported this session for the May 2nd Washington Post.

AMERICA'S unofficial poet laureate, Robert Frost, invited the Washington press over to the Library of Congress yesterday for "just a little informal coffee hour." Some coffee hour. The old word wizard became so quotable so fast the poor scriveners had to reach for the notebooks and lose a shot at some sociable china-balancing.

Frost recited before a blue-ribbon, black-tie, very-very audience of Cabinet members and other brass at the State Department auditorium last night. But he came to the morning coffee bee wearing summer cloth-top shoes and long johns.

Eighty-seven years old and wise to Washington's notoriously fickle spring weather, this was no doubt some New England sartorial cynicism. So he went on from there.

Frost on education: "Education doesn't change much. It just lifts trouble to a higher plane of regard.

"You know, they put helpless old people in the hospital. Well, they put helpless young people in college.

"College is a refuge from hasty judgment. It's also easy on the family. If a boy goes off to Greenwich Village to paint or write poetry, his family is ashamed when anyone asks about him. But if he does the same thing in college, they can say, 'He's in college,' and it sounds all right."

Frost on science: "Some people worry because science doesn't know where it's going. It doesn't need to know. It's none of its business.

"I like anything that penetrates the mysteries. And if it penetrates straight to hell, then that's all right, too."

Frost on white hair and barbers: "The newspapers are always comparing my hair with Carl Sandburg's. That's absurd. Carl has a hairdo, and I cut my own.

"I cut it at home. I got sick of the barbers because they talk too much, and mostly they talk about how my hair is falling out."

Frost on literary friendships: "You know, it's a great burden to have friends who write. They bring you their manuscripts to read, and you have to say you like it. I'm glad when a friend gets mad at me. Then I can hate his poetry as thoroughly as if he wasn't my friend."

Frost on poetry: "It's a distressing thing to have a poet in the family. That's the one conviction that all nations share.

"I've had a friend apologize and say, 'My boy's a fine lad underneath it all. It's just that he can't get this poetry business out of his system.' Said it right to my face.

"Every now and then I catch a man reading a poem of mine. Catch him dead to rights. He always looks up sheepishly and says, 'My wife's a great fan of yours.' That puts us poets in our place."

Frost on why he likes America: "We've got a good arrangement here. We're minding each other's business a certain amount, and we're minding our own business a certain amount.

"Those fellows [Founding Fathers] who started it did a good job. I say anything I damn please here."

"I'm modestly satisfied.
I've gotten my truth of feeling in."

During the summer of 1961, Mark Harris, novelist and member of the faculty at San Francisco State College, did interviews with both Robert Frost and Carl Sandburg in preparing an article on the two poets for publication in Life. *A part of Mr. Harris's account of his visit with RF at Ripton is extracted from its original appearance in the magazine's issue for December 1, 1961.*

I T was dark, and no moon. Mrs. Morrison lent me a flashlight, and I walked up alone to Mr. Frost's cabin. The schnauzers barked, but when they quieted all was silence, and I asked Mr. Frost if he listened to the radio.

"Not much," he said. "It's an old radio, and it makes a queer, streaky noise."

How, then, did he receive news of the world?

"From people I know," he said.

But didn't he read newspapers? Yes, the *Rutland Herald, New York Herald Tribune, New York Times, Boston Globe.*

"Wherever I am I'll take a little walk and get one. But I'm a book person. Some people talk as if books are going by, but I'm nurtured in books. I'll be reading books after everyone else has stopped."

He asked me about San Francisco. He was born there, eighty-seven years ago, lived there as a boy; and he can still name the order of the streets in the neighborhood of Leavenworth and Washington.

Might we talk about literature? Oh yes, but there were certain questions he had heard too often.

"When Hemingway went down in the plane in Africa I imagined he'd be walking through the jungles when out jumped tourists from behind the trees—'Mr. Hemingway, what do you think of symbolism?'"

But the whole body of Mr. Frost's work is a vast symbolic structure. Isn't it?

"I suppose," he confessed, "I'm always saying something that's just the edge of something more. Symbols are what fly off everything. A little goes a long way. I don't wallow in it. We hate slop, however eloquent."

"Speaking of Hemingway," I said.

Tilting his head slightly backward, Mr. Frost recited some verses he had known long ago, had seemingly forgotten, and then had suddenly recalled the day he'd heard of Hemingway's death. But he could not remember who had written them:

> No tears are needed, fill up with wine,
> Let goblets clash and grapejuice flow.
> Ho, drink me a death drink, comrade mine,
> For a brave man gone where we all must go.

Of his own work he said, "Every phrase, every poem, every whole speech is a dip for depth. I've been playing *only* to score, *only* to win.

"I don't like to talk about myself," he said. "I'd rather hold myself off from myself, in rhyme and meter. That's as near as I want to come to talking about myself.

"People say to me, 'I know what you mean,' but what they want to know is what's eating me. I don't always know. Sometimes it's a hate—somebody I hate, somebody I've argued with makes me write a poem. It's in the poetry I'm always struggling to say it better. It's a kind of gratification that I'm after.

"This," he said—a book, *Complete Poems of Robert Frost*, he meant, his life's labor—"this isn't just amateur apprentice work that I've been writing. With all its imperfections I'll never write any better. I never had this divine dissatisfaction that they brag about so much. I'm modestly satisfied. I've gotten my truth of feeling in."

He was turning pages, looking for a poem he suddenly wanted.

"Sometimes I struggle to say something. Then I remember I've already said it somewhere. I tried not to write anything foolishly sentimental, and when I came near showing it I got a funny feeling. I knew when I was false and when I was true. I'd hate to look back and feel a disillusionment about it, and feel that I'd been false. You often wonder about certain people that let words run away from them."

He found his page—"The Fear of God"—and he removed his hearing glasses in favor of his seeing glasses. He read softly, conversationally. The schnauzers lay at his feet. The night was perfectly still. He leaned a little toward the lamp:

> If you should rise from Nowhere up to Somewhere,
> From being No one up to being Someone,
> Be sure to keep repeating to yourself
> You owe it to an arbitrary god
> Whose mercy to you rather than to others
> Won't bear too critical examination.
> Stay unassuming. If for lack of license
> To wear the uniform of who you are,
> You should be tempted to make up for it
> In a subordinating look or tone
> Beware of coming too much to the surface,
> And using for apparel what was meant
> To be the curtain of the inmost soul.

"That's all I'm answerable to," he said, and he closed the book. But he appeared inclined to talk just a little of himself after all.

"I've been a teacher all my life," he said, "just the same as I'm a Democrat, but I've been a dissatisfied teacher. I can't leave it alone. I'm like some monkeys Darwin tells about. Somebody showed them some snakes, and they screamed and ran away, but they kept coming back. I'm that way about education.

"I've taught every darn year from kindergarten to graduate school, Latin, English, mathematics, history, algebra, philosophy, and one year psychology—well, it was *called* psychology, but what I mainly taught 'em was that it was no good to 'em. (It's all nonsense. I have friends that think everybody ought to be psychoanalyzed. I know someone that's had their child psychoanalyzed ever since it was five years old. My self-respect wouldn't let me do it. I wouldn't surrender. I can take somebody on, but I wouldn't be *taken* on.)"

Still slouching, still peering, he was firm, but never cross, never hostile. There were truths of which he felt certain, but in a quiet voice, his tone somewhat humbly resigned to the probability that regardless of what he said there was little hope of anyone's learning except as he had learned: by living it over the spread of the years.

"Never give a child a choice," he said. "Don't give him a choice of believing in God or not. He can start having choices when he goes to college: they have the elective system there, you know. There's so many courses now where everything you say is right enough—sociology, psychology, contemporary civilization.

"I'm at large, and I'm a civilized man, but school is for *discipline*. A student is an orange pip between my fingers: if I pinch him he'll go far. I'm not violent, but I'm going for the whole damn system. Discipline. Tightness. Firmness. Crispness. Sternness. And sternness in our lives.

"Life is tons of discipline. Your first discipline is your vocabulary; then your grammar and your punctuation, you see. Then, in your exuberance and bounding energy you say you're going to add to that. Then you add rhyme and meter. And your delight is in *that* power."

It was power I had begun by asking him about. This was his answer, was it? Discipline produced power? Discipline in teaching, in writing, in all of life? Form?

"It might be something like that," he said.

I asked him if he would sign my copy of the *Complete*, and he took it now and inscribed it; and I inquired—since Mr. Sandburg had left me doubtful—"Shall I build a bomb shelter?"

He returned the book and capped his pen.

"You shouldn't if I don't," he said. "I hadn't thought about it. Whatever becomes compulsory I'll probably do.

"If we all die together we'll be in good company. On the other side we'll brush the dust off and say, 'Wasn't that something!' "

"That's very depressing," I said, "to think we might not have any future to believe in."

He rose and went into another room. In a few moments he returned with four poems I had never seen.

"The Founding Fathers didn't believe in the future," he said, sitting again. "They believed it *in*. You're always believing ahead of your evidence. What was the evidence I could write a poem?[. . .] I just believed it.

"The most creative thing in us is to believe a thing in, in love, in all else. You believe yourself into existence. You believe your marriage into existence, you believe in each other, you believe that it's worthwhile going on, or you'd commit suicide, wouldn't you?"

He inscribed three of the poems for me, and the fourth for my wife. They were "One More Brevity," "From a Milkweed Pod," "My Objection to Being Stepped On," and "How Hard It Is to Keep from Being King When It's in You and in the Situation."

"And the ultimate one is the belief in the future of the world. I believe the future *in*. It's coming in by my believing it. You might as well call that a belief in God. This word *God* is not an often-used word with me, but once in a while it arrives there."

"That's much more cheerful than what you said before," I said.

"I contain opposites," he said. "I can hold a lot. I can get up a phrase to handle almost everything that happens."

We left the cabin. The schnauzers followed. Mr. Frost lighted my way down the slope.[. . .]

Near the road, I told him I'd promised to return the flashlight to Mrs. Morrison. He offered to do it himself. In the morning I telephoned her to say good-by, and I asked her if he'd returned it to her; and she said he had.

A Visit in South Miami
with Talk of Death and Life

RF whimsically designated 1962 his "year of publicality," because of the several major events it contained which kept him so constantly in the public eye.

The year, at the close of which he was to suffer the illness that, with its complications, led to his death, opened with a touching occasion for the poet: the dedication on January 7th of a school named in his honor at Lawrence, Massachusetts, where he had himself attended high school seventy years before.

Soon after the ceremonies at Lawrence, RF left for South Miami, Florida, where he had regularly spent parts of his winters, beginning in the late 1930's. There, in February, he developed pneumonia and, when his condition became critical, he was hospitalized.

This interview by Charles Whited appeared in The Miami Herald *on March 17th, a month after RF's release from the hospital and during his period of convalescence.*

I THOUGHT I was going to die the other day. I thought: All right, good-by. Then I thought again, that I'd stay around and see who wins the next election."

Robert Frost, poet, relaxed in the small, hot living room of his New England cottage, set in a South Miami pine thicket, and talked and sweated and talked.

"It never occurred to me before that I might die. I was immortal. I would live a long time. A long, long time. Oh, a long time.

: 272 :

"Well, I know now that I can't live more than a hundred and fifty years. After all, there is a limit."

America's poet laureate, as he's sometimes called, is a thickset, paunchy man, with a voice like a dump truck. A week from Monday he will be eighty-eight. And this was his first newspaper interview since pneumonia put him in South Miami Hospital for a month.

His hair is white as a wintry roof top in Vermont. The heavy, broad face is etched with lines of fatigue and flecked with the brown spots of age. But the eyes flash blue under straggling brows, and the words have a scalpel's cleanness.

"Eighty-eight? Why all the fuss about a man being eighty-eight? Ninety maybe, yes. Or a hundred; that would be something. But eighty-eight?"

To celebrate his birthday they're planning a big shindig for him in Washington, March twenty-sixth. But the canny Frost isn't talking about that.

"It's a secret," he said with a sly grin. "I'm not supposed to know anything about it."

So he talked instead about a multitude of things. He talked slowly: good talk, while his mind leaped ahead clearing a path for the words.

He talked about the slow life.

"I've always tried to get by, to make a living. But I get angry when people on the telephone say, 'He's busy.' I'm never busy!

"My friend Hemingway wrote tons of stuff that his wife has to sort through now. I've written five, six hundred pages in seventy years. That's all. About ten pages a year."

He talked about the fast life.

"I've been publicized more this year than ever in my life. It turns me outside in, or inside out. So much pleasant attention. But on the outside, that isn't where you write poetry."

The four-time Pulitzer Prize winner, whose work has brought him the world's honors, put his blunt fingertips together and looked at nothing at all. He wore a faded blue shirt, open at the throat, and an old pair of loose white trousers. In the course of the conversation, he shucked his shoes and wiggled his toes in a pair of gray socks.

His house is simple, utilitarian, and screened from the world by heavy foliage behind the home of his son-in-law and daughter, Mr. and Mrs. Joseph Ballantine, 5240 SW 80th Street. He shipped his cottage by rail from New England years ago, because author Hervey Allen talked him into having a winter home here.

"It's simple," said the poet. "The one thing I mind about Florida is people want to be too Floridan—too much show. This is simple."

Outside, he has plenty of room to putter with his avocados, his mangoes, and the other trees laden with fruit. For Robert Frost is, after all, a farmer. A poet, philosopher, teacher, yes. But also a farmer.[. . .]

"If I have something to do, something to occupy my time," he said, "I'm happy."

Then he talked about people.

"You fly in a plane over the country, and you look down and see all their roof tops. And every man you're looking on the roof of has his pleasures and his pains."

The Frost face softened. The Frost voice deepened. All the warmth of a lifetime of gentle questions radiated from his eyes.

"No government can touch it. No psychologist can touch it. All the jealousy, the emotions that live and die, the little disloyalties—all are in the air. And with that, the great detachment."

A beam of afternoon sunlight stole through the half-closed venetian blinds and found the white, unruly hair, with its stray lock drooping down the forehead.

"Some boys attacked John Glenn, it says in your paper. Who the hell are they? What kind of boys are they? The minute anybody gets to be anybody, somebody else comes along and says, 'Who are you, to get so big?'

"It's everywhere, all the time: friendship and hostility and jealousy and compassion. It's everywhere."

Then he talked of the moon and of people going there some day.

"And where will I be? With my toes turned up, my hands composed.

"There are many who were concerned with the world, now with their toes turned up and their hands composed, thinking of nothing—unless, maybe, they're looking in from another world."

On the Eve of a Birthday

RF returned from Florida in late March of 1962 and imme-diately made preparations to go to Washington to celebrate his eighty-eighth birthday. Milton Bracker visited the poet's Brewster Street home in Cambridge just before he departed for the Capital, and this story based on that interview was published in The New York Times *of March 26th.*

ROBERT FROST went to Washington today, on the eve of his eighty-eighth birthday. With him on the train went old friends and a new book of poems, *In the Clearing*. He will give a copy to President Kennedy, a somewhat more-recent friend with whom he shared an interesting occasion on January 20, 1961.[. . .]

One of the things Mr. Frost wants the President to note is that the preliminary Inaugural poem—the unread one—stayed rest-less until it was trapped finally in print.

"It just grew," he said on Friday, in an interview[. . .]. "I al-most expanded it with the idea of writing a history of the United States in verse."

"The Preface," as the original composition had been titled, ran forty-two lines. They began with "Summoning artists to partici-pate. . ." and ended with "I sometimes think that all we ask is glory."

The poem, now called "For John F. Kennedy His Inaugural," runs seventy-seven lines. It begins the same way but ends with:

A golden age of poetry and power
Of which this noonday's the beginning hour.

"It was in the meaning," Mr. Frost said of the original. "I didn't like it the way it was. I started working on it."

He worked until he had it the way he wanted it. (It was published in *The New York Times Magazine* a year ago tomorrow.) But he still seems surprised that the final revision is more than half again as long as the original.

"Is it?" he asked.

The manuscript left with the President was of the first draft. Mr. Frost leaned forward in his chair. A lock of soft white hair fell over his left brow.

"He'll be seeing it (the ultimate poem) in this book," he said.

A shorter piece in the book is called "Version." Mr. Frost acknowledged that one of his close friends, the poet David McCord, had "asked what it meant."

"There's so many hasty things going on with me these days, and I'm a slow person," he went on.

It seems that he and Mrs. Theodore Morrison, who lives a few blocks away, were preparing the copy for the new book in time for publication on his birthday. One result was an incomplete "Version." But Mr. Frost knew how to exploit the episode.

"What modern editor would ask that a poem should mean anything, anyway?" he said, blandly. "I left it that way in order to be in fashion.

"It's never hard for me to write a poem that doesn't mean anything when I leave part of it out."

The deep-set greenish-blue eyes seemed even deeper beneath the bushy lashes. The light lessened and a clock ticked as he suddenly went serious.

"I've been so interested in meaning," he said.

"A real poem," added the improbable native of San Francisco, who looks as though he was hewn from New England granite, "is a sort of idea caught in dawning: you catch it just as it comes. Think it out beforehand and you won't write it."

And a poet's "first answerability" (like a President's, he said) was "to God and the highest in himself."

"Not to your constituents," he said. "They're your second answerability."

A man has a first book published, he continued.

"You know what that does to him? That delivers him over to the public."

Robert Lee Frost had had no such worry.

"I'd been dammed back for twenty years," he said, referring to his long vain struggle for recognition in his own country. So, finally, by the time a British publisher brought out *A Boy's Will* in 1913, "I had three books written."

"All I had to do was wait a year, then have the second, then the third book published."

Down the years, his descriptive poems showed an uncanny talent for matching the sharpest observation with the exactest word.[. . .]

In the book just published by Holt, Rinehart and Winston there is "Pod of the Milkweed." And it tells of the butterflies clustered on the blossoms so avidly that, "They knock the dyestuff off each other's wings."

He saw these particular butterflies just outside his "voting" home at Ripton, Vermont, "three or four years ago."

"There were a lot of kinds. Some of them were Monarchs."

He added, with humility, "I'm not a specialist in natural history. I don't like to write anything I don't see."

There was one thing he would have liked to see—and would have written about.

"I always wished we had had two moons," he smiled. "To see 'em weaving in the sky, it'd be quite a sky."

It was even darker now, and, again, the ticking of the clock seemed louder. Again, he turned serious.

He kept up with all the news of space; he was dryly amused that Congress was at last listening to informed talk about communication with other worlds.[. . .] But he found it more important that, in a great city in an eastern country, he had heard of thousands of people starving and lying down in the streets to die.

"And I'm not able to do a thing about it," he said. "That concerns me more than the moon. I can't bear it. I can't bear it and I won't."

Mr. Frost brooded a moment. He tapped with the soft blue plaid slipper on his right foot.

"I don't try to be cheerful," he said. "I never tried to be cheerful in my life." And, in a slightly different connection, " 'Know thyself' has never been one of my mottoes. I'm more objective than that."

Then, objectively and not cheerfully, he disclosed that his illness in Florida last month had been more critical than had been known generally. (He was released from Baptist Hospital in Miami, on February sixteenth.)

"When I came near death," he said, "I quoted to the doctor. I said, 'I'm getting pretty old, I'd better go, don't you think?' (I'm half as old as this country—the country's short of two hundred; I'm short of one.)

"The doctor said, 'Pneumonia is the old man's friend. But penicillin is the enemy of pneumonia.' That was quite a triangle: me, pneumonia, penicillin.

"That's what they saved me by. What saved me was a good doctor, penicillin, and my friends. If I died, I'd a been very cross if they hadn't been there.

"I've had three pneumonias and one World War [I] flu. The thought of death never occurred to me. This time it occurred to me. You can say I went up to the edge and I looked over, and instead of going I came back."

In one of his most-quoted earlier poems he had written:

> There may be little or much beyond the grave,
> But the strong are saying nothing until they see.

In "Away!" in the new volume he says:

> And I may return
> If dissatisfied
> With what I learn
> From having died.

"Well," said Robert Frost, willing or not to change the subject, "Those are the little things. You have to think large."

In Washington, where the Library of Congress will fete its Honorary Consultant in the Humanities with an exhibition on his life and works, opening tomorrow, Mr. Frost hoped to see the President. He intended to express concern over the attitude toward the United States of some nations that "don't seem to like us very much."

"I'm going to talk about that—where have we erred, or have we erred."

And he was going to express pleasure at the "Office of Fine Arts" (The White House Fine Arts Committee) the President and Mrs. Kennedy had established "where he and she can look after it."

"There it's very pretty, very pretty," he pursued, "and he doesn't have to go outside and get an appropriation for it. He didn't have to get an appropriation to ask me to say a poem. Just 'Office of Fine Arts'—no 'culture' in it.

"I admire him [the President] so much. I wish I was a better Democrat."[. . .]

Now the room was nearly dark, and, somehow, it seemed filled with the ticking not of one clock but of many.

Mr. Frost rose, a heavy, slightly stooped figure in a gray suit. The lower right edge of the jacket was frayed, almost as if it had been burnt. His white shirt was tieless, open at the throat. He led the way to the door.

Not far from his stoop are sites identified with Henry Wadsworth Longfellow and James Russell Lowell. Just outside the house, a bare tree was somewhat less bare because a bird's nest in it stood out like a black clot against the twilight. Across the street a brown-and-white cat limped along, over the vestiges of snow. The cat's right hind foot shunned the ground, like a creature in space trapped in a low and painful orbit. From up the block a child's voice tinkled. It sounded almost like a bell.

At the head of the seven steps leading to the brick walk and into Brewster Street, the visitor turned and said, "Bless you, Mr. Frost."

The poet snapped it up approvingly, " 'Bless' is a good word— that's what I'm going to tell the President:'Bless your Irish heart.' "

Then he went back inside.

A Medal, a Book, and a Banquet

The celebration in Washington of RF's eighty-eighth birthday was a gala affair. Included in the observances were a White House visit, a formal dinner at the Pan American Union, and the publication of what was to prove his last volume of new poems, In the Clearing.

In advance of the festivities of the day RF met with the press at the Library of Congress. Here given are The New York Times' *story and excerpts from three other papers, reporting (all but one in March 27th editions) on the news conference and alluding, also, to other of the birthday events.*

By Russell Baker, *The New York Times*:

THE fine thing about the nation's poets is their contempt for Washington's political orthodoxy. Today, for example, Robert Frost came to town on a warm spring breeze to join in the observance of his eighty-eighth birthday and announced that he thinks Nikita S. Khrushchev is "a grand man." This sort of talk in Washington is like praising Satan in Paradise. But it is the stuff that the city is coming to expect of a poet.

A few months ago Carl Sandburg dropped in here and said that General Dwight D. Eisenhower had been a pretty poor specimen of a President. In the Washington scheme of values this was like denouncing the flag and blaming mother for juvenile delinquency.

Mr. Frost was not down on General Eisenhower today. Indeed, he was not down on anybody, although there was a hint of a reprimand to Mr. Sandburg for his rough talk on "the old General."

"The Old General," Mr. Frost mused, thinking aloud before a news conference in the Library of Congress. "He's a friend of mine —an admiration of mine, too. I've heard all sorts of cheap things about him."

Mr. Frost's observations on Premier Khrushchev were not directed to the Soviet leader's politics but to his human qualities.

"Oh, what a grand man he is!" he replied when someone asked if he had any thoughts on Mr. Khrushchev. "What a creature! What a creature!"

"With all the fears of us, and fears of what's behind him and round him there, it doesn't seem to touch him at all."

The poet, who was eighty-eight years old today, paused to admire startled expressions of his young audience, which rarely hears such talk in Washington.

"He's my enemy," Mr. Frost resumed with a smile. "But it takes just a little magnanimity to admire him."

The Library of Congress news conference opened an exhibition of Mr. Frost's works, photographs, correspondence, and memorabilia.

Afterward, Mr. Frost went to the White House for bestowal by the President of the Congressional Medal in recognition of his contributions to American letters. In presenting the award President Kennedy said he supposed that the poet was "disappointed that it was not a more controversial decision by Congress, but a unanimous one" by which the medal was voted.

"It was the only thing they've been able to agree on for a long time," the President added.

Mr. Frost presented the President with a copy of his new book of poems, *In the Clearing*. Tonight he was honored at a dinner given at the Pan American Union by Stewart L. Udall, Secretary of the Interior, and Mrs. Udall and his publishers, Holt, Rinehart and Winston.

Through most of the news conference Mr. Frost sat in the library's Woodrow Wilson Room and talked leisurely, answering a few questions, but mostly just ruminating.

By Dan Gottlieb,
Washington Evening Star, March 26, 1962:

[. . .]President Kennedy's name came up in connection with the recent meeting of Mr. Eisenhower and Mr. Kennedy out West.

"It pleases me one can be nice to the other when he is out of office," Mr. Frost said. "I like one to be more patriot than partisan."

He said he was attracted to Mr. Kennedy by what he wrote, when still a Senator, in his book *Profiles in Courage*, about the President having something "higher" than his constituents to answer to.

Asked whether President Kennedy had a "weakness" in his nature for poetry, Mr. Frost replied, "He has a nice Irish weakness for it and his wife a French weakness."

He said he distinguishes between a "conscientious concern" for the arts and a "real weakness."[. . .]

Except for an occasional confusion of names and words, Mr. Frost was still his incisive self today. His most ardent voice was used to state that in all the "play on thoughts and words," even down to wisecracks, "you've got to make a point. . . got to find the phrase."

From the Baltimore *Sun*:

[. . .]At the outset, Frost said no, he didn't object to having a microphone hung around his neck.

"I call it an albatross. The poor old Ancient Mariner had to wear one."

The conference was held in a room housing Woodrow Wilson's books, and Wilson was the one man about whom Frost had reservations today.

"Look around at the books, and you'll see the limitations. Someone said he was so busy he had no time for frills—that's one way of looking at poetry. A noble, conscientious man, but he strained himself. We need somebody who is unstrained, who has time to read poetry and wear flowers," he said.[. . .]

He also said today, "I never get back to where George Washington's monument is without some great feeling. . . . Most of my thoughts have some reference to the U.S.A. I'm a terrible nationalist. Deplorable!"

As for his health at age eighty-eight, he feels a lot better than last month when he lay near death of pneumonia in Miami. But when asked if his new book is intended to be his last, Frost called attention to the last poem in it, a poem about chopping down a maple tree. It concludes:

> I see for Nature no defeat
> In one tree's overthrow
> Or for myself in my retreat
> For yet another blow.

That meant, he said, that he meant to strike many a blow yet.

"Why, I have four books coming. Don't worry about me."

His legs are not what they used to be, he said, but he hopes his wits last longer.

"One of these days," he said, "I may say something foolish."

By Rod Nordell,
The Christian Science Monitor:

[. . .]Some things he said in Washington sounded familiar, more sounded fresh. At any rate, here are some that are now part of Washington Frostlore. They should be read with a shock of white hair in the mind's eye, a finger raised in emphasis, or hands clasped in thought, or a jutting eyebrow wigwagging above a wink.

"The most conservative thing in the world is that like produces like." Human beings give birth to human beings, for example. "The most radical thing is a certain dissatisfaction that that is so."

"Nothing can be more gentle than great strength."

"Getting a sharp pointed meaning into a lot of material. . . , that's what my book is about."[. . .]

"Nearly everything I ever wrote was written at one sitting. . . . I'd think: I'm riding this and it might never be there to ride again."[...]

On extroverts and introverts: "I'm just a plain vert from Vermont."[. . .]

The Russian Adventure

In the summer of 1962, RF was asked by President Kennedy to make a goodwill visit to Russia. The poet flew from Washington on August 28th and his itinerary included both Moscow and Leningrad. The climax of the trip was a September 7th talk with Premier Khrushchev at Gagra on the North Sea.

There follow in this section both Russian and American interview-accounts relating to the journey. The former, containing a few rather uncharacteristic sentiments, have been specially translated for publication here by Prof. Franklin D. Reeve of Wesleyan University, who accompanied RF on the trip as his personal interpreter and who has chronicled this experience in his book Robert Frost in Russia.

By M. Tugusheva,
Literaturnaia Gazeta, September 1, 1962:

THE celebrated American poet Robert Frost is visiting the Soviet Union. Yesterday he received the correspondent of *Literaturnaia Gazeta*, M. Tugusheva. Frost was eighty-[...eight] in March. As a person who knows Frost aptly remarked, a great life is needed to create great poetry.

"Mr. Frost, every American schoolboy reads your poems. Tell me, what do you yourself think about the place of poetry in the life of the people?"

"Everybody needs poetry, for it lives in all people. And therefore it's close to them. And the more natural it is, the more it's understood. Take curly hair. There can be natural curliness, but there's also artificial. You have to be able to tell them apart in poetry too."

"What do you think recognition by the people means for a poet?"

"I didn't call myself a poet until the people did. At first it embarrassed me a lot. The word 'poet' is very great praise. Young people often call me up and introduce themselves: 'I'm a poet.' It seems to me that's immodest. There has to be respectful fear of that word, because, you know, it's just the same as saying about yourself, 'I'm a good man.' "

Robert Frost is not only a remarkable poet, he is also a teacher, an adviser to young poets.

"An adviser, exactly," he emphasized. "You know, I never studied how to write poetry myself. And by the way, in my seminars I never read my own poems and never let them be held up as a model. People often come see me, and we talk about poetry."

"You're a poet of traditional form. You prefer it to free verse?"

"Poetry can also be in free verse, too, but I prefer rhyme and rhythm."

"We know you're not only a hard worker in the field of poetry; you like physical labor too?"

"Yes. Hard work, that's the main thing in life. I've never been a solitary scholar; I've always loved the land. And one time I earned my living working on a farm. My favorite tools are the axe, the scythe, and the pen.

"By the way, I never thought about it before, there's a kind of similarity between them and your emblem, the sickle and hammer. The sickle, that's a little scythe; and the axe, that's a sharpened hammer. On one of my books there's also an emblem: the axe and the scythe.

"I often think about words now: weapon, tool. A tool can turn into a weapon. When the peasants rebelled, they turned their tools of labor into weapons. I often hear that the atom has to become a tool for peace. But you always have to keep in mind that it can be a weapon for war too."

In concluding the conversation, I said that Soviet readers know Frost's poetry in translations printed in anthologies, in *Novyi Mir*, and in *Literaturnaia Gazeta*.

"Unfortunately, we often read poetry in translation, and it's here a good translation is so important. I know your poetry, too, only in translations. But now when I get home," Robert Frost remarked jokingly, "I'll study Russian so I can read your poets in the original."

By M. Khitrov,
Izvestiia, September 3, 1962:

Shortly before the senior American poet, Robert Frost, arrived in the Soviet Union, many people surely had read, in the August issue of *Novyi Mir*, his wonderful poem about two tramps who somehow wandered into the poet's yard and enviously watched him chopping wood. For Frost this work was a delight, a pastime, but for them it was "the way they earned their bread." The poet thinks that in life, work must always be accompanied by inspiration, that hard work must be merged with a sense of calling. Indeed, only the man who well knows the real value both of heavy labor and of creative inspiration can so passionately dream of the harmonious fusion of what might seem contradictory principles.

Soviet readers love Frost's lyric poetry precisely for its harmonious completeness, clarity, and profound human wisdom. I think Eduardas Mezhelaitis, in the poem dedicated to Frost and published recently in *Izvestiia*, very aptly called him "The Blue-eyed Cliff."

Coming to "The Blue-eyed Cliff's" hotel room for an interview, I could not help being struck immediately by the accuracy of Mezhelaitis' words: before me was an old, sturdy, thickset, but at the same time very lively, mobile, and candid man. The time for the interview was short, but I could not help asking whether or not Mr. Frost agreed to being called "The Blue-eyed Cliff."

"For me that's very high praise," said Frost, and added with a smile, "I think I didn't come to your country on a fool's errand. I'd like to get a deeper understanding of socialism. I don't like people talking flippantly about socialism. Communism, democracy, socialism—these are all complex problems of our time. They have to be examined seriously. Right now I have the impression that Soviet society is making the severity of its ideal more and more humane."

I told Frost that the image of a man as a "Blue-eyed Cliff" was, in my opinion, very close to Soviet people; that is how they think of a man whose sense of purpose is unusually clear and who is severe in his ideals, but at the same time deeply human.

"For me that's high appreciation," Frost repeated once again.

Robert Frost aligns himself with that category of poets who seek to be understood by the reader.

I asked him, "That means there's an opposite category of poets —those who don't seek to be understood? How do you feel about such poetry?"

"The hell with them! The hell with it!" Frost exclaimed vivaciously. "I don't like obscure jokes, just as I don't like obscure poems. I don't want to joke in such a way that nobody laughs at my joke. And I don't want to write poems which aren't understood."

"Which of these two categories of poets, in your opinion, best answers the spirit of the times?"

"I'm convinced that the readers themselves will answer that question right. Of course, I seek the readers' friendship, aim toward them. But I never flirt with the readers, don't want to flatter them. Genuine poetry must be understandable, even by children. It doesn't require propaganda."

"What was Frost's first impression of the Soviet Union?"

"I'm delighted," said Frost, "with the freshness and enthusiasm which I felt all around me from meetings with Soviet people. I met some poets too. It seems to me that the spirit of your poetry is youthfulness, freshness."

By David Miller (dateline Moscow),
New York Herald Tribune, September 9, 1962:

The poet confronted the Premier and came away with a spectrum of impressions that perhaps only a poet could sense and voice with chilling simplicity. Said Robert Frost of Nikita Sergeyevich Khrushchev, "He's our enemy, but he's a great man."

The poet told this to a Moscow press conference yesterday. He had had a bedside chat for an hour or more with the Premier Friday in a government-house room near the Black Sea resort of Gagra.

"He's a ruffian. He's ready for a fight. He's not a coward. He's not afraid of us and we're not afraid of him," continued poet Frost.

Mr. Frost came to Russia on a cultural exchange program and was unexpectedly invited to meet Mr. Khrushchev in the Crimea. But when it came time for the interview, the eighty-eight-year-old poet was feeling poorly with an upset stomach. The Premier sent doctors to examine Mr. Frost and then called on the poet in his room.

"I sat on the edge of the bed, and we had a good talk and went at it," Mr. Frost reported. The Premier took a chair nearby.

The poet said his only disappointment was Premier Khrushchev's apparent unwillingness to cut the Gordian Knot of world problems, particularly Berlin.

"I told him he ought to be like Alexander the Great, who didn't believe in fussing with Gordian Knots and untying them. He believed in cutting it. I just hoped a man as mighty as Khrushchev might do something even if we didn't.

"I was like a tramp poet who visits a great monarch. 'I've got just one little request,' the tramp asks the monarch. 'Will you grant it to me before I ask it?' Well, I didn't get that far."

He had hoped to persuade the Russian to compete with America in "strife and magnanimity" and found:

"He agrees with strife and with magnaminity. He's no saphead. No liberal sapheads for me."

The rivalry beween the United States and Russia should rise above "small squabbles," Mr. Frost told Mr. Khrushchev.

He said he discussed the Berlin situation.

"I did say I hate it. I hate it that a small matter like that could decide the fate of the world.

"I told him there might be something we have that he wants, and there might be something they have that we want. We could trade and settle it just like a horse trade."

Answered Mr. Khrushchev, "That is difficult."

Came back the poet, "But with your power you could do it; little things can bring big wars."

But Mr. Khrushchev, reported Mr. Frost, "said he was doing all he could."

The description of the Soviet leader as "a ruffian" was strictly to express admiration. It came after Mr. Frost was asked whether Premier Khrushchev had given him any message to carry to President Kennedy, who is a friend of the poet's.

"Yes, in a way," the poet answered, but his associates stopped him and told him he should tell that to Mr. Kennedy.

Then, Mr. Frost said the Premier told him to tell the President "not to do this, and to do that. . . and quite a few things."

Asked if they had discussed God, Mr. Frost said:

"He didn't. But I did. God wants us to contend. The only progress is in conflict."

But this conflict involves "no blackguarding, no dirty play. That's what I came to say."

He said he and Mr. Khrushchev agreed on this.

"I knew he was that way—a real sport."

"I told Mr. Khrushchev the future of the world for the next hundred years or so lies between the United States and Russia.

"We're laid out for rivalry in sports, science, art, and democracy. By courtesy, we call them both democracies."

Mr. Frost meant by democracy "a more earnest desire than the world has ever had to take care of everybody. To bestow. . . bread and butter, yes; but that's not the top thing. The top thing to bestow is character."

Frost cast his words before Soviet and foreign correspondents crowded into his apartment in Moscow's best hotel, the Sovetskaia. He arrived late from [the] airport, but spry.

When asked whether Russian poets were well known in America, Mr. Frost said, "The chief one seems to be Pasternak."

There was an instant hush. The Russians were shocked and embarrassed. The late Boris Pasternak, one of Russia's foremost poets, is still a name that frightens many Russians. He was hounded by Soviet authorities after his book *Dr. Zhivago* was published in the West. It is highly and sensitively critical of the Communist regime and has not been published in Russia.

When Mr. Frost described Mr. Khrushchev as "a ruffian," a Russian reporter protested, "Maybe you mean rough, but not ruffian."

Mr. Frost, who doesn't hear too well, went right on, totally disregarding her.

Premier Khrushchev revels in his peasant origins, likes to speak rough Russian, and generally tries to make himself a man of the people.

Mr. Frost described Mr. Khrushchev "as just the kind of hero I thought he was."

"He just thinks the Soviet form of government is more natural than ours, and he means it."

"He was a little severe about my country," Mr. Frost said. "He said the dollar was not as strong as it used to be. He said they were beating us in some ways. He mentioned hydroelectric power and said they learned it from us. That just means they're ahead of us now. We will be ahead later."

Their talk, he said, was "very free and congenial." But later, in a visit to the United States Embassy, he commented, "We didn't pretend to like each other."

Mr. Frost is scheduled to return to the United States today.

From *Pravda*, September 9, 1962:

The following is a Russian account of the same news confer-ence detailed in the foregoing dispatch. It will be noted that no mention is made of RF's challenged characterization of Premier Khrushchev as "a ruffian."

The famous American poet Robert Frost, presently in the Soviet Union, held a press conference at the Sovetskaia Hotel.

"I've had a very good time in your country," Robert Frost told correspondents. "The meeting with N. S. Khrushchev made an especially great impression on me."

When the poet arrived in Gagra, he felt unwell. N. S. Khrushchev sent two doctors to him and then came himself to see the sick man.

"N. S. Khrushchev," said the poet, "turned out to be the very hero I had imagined him. He behaves very naturally, talks very subtly, using proverbs and sayings. I gave N. S. Khrushchev my book with the inscription 'From your rival in friendship.' "

R. Frost said that N. S. Khrushchev had asked him to convey his greetings to President Kennedy and the American people.

"I had a splendid time with N. S. Khrushchev," the visitor em-phasized. "It was a wonderful meeting."

Speaking about cultural co-operation between the U.S.A. and the U.S.S.R., R. Frost stated, "It's good when people go both ways." "You met many writers here," one of the correspondents asked. "What, in your opinion, is the climate in the U.S.S.R. for their creative work?"

"I think the climate is excellent," Robert Frost replied. "I was amazed by the size of the editions in which poets' books are distributed."

"I found greatness here, although I knew beforehand that I was going to meet a great nation," said R. Frost.

Associated Press release (dateline New York), *Washington Evening Star*, September 10, 1962:

Poet Robert Frost came back yesterday from a trip to the Soviet Union and impishly told about a secret and a few surprises. The secret, the eighty-eight-year-old poet said, was a message from Soviet Premier Khrushchev to President Kennedy. But when asked to disclose the message, he wagged a finger at newsmen and replied:

"Oh, no; that's up to the President. I couldn't do that."

As for planning to meet with the President, Mr. Frost answered, "I don't plan; I wait for the President."

The white-haired poet then disclosed that Mr. Khrushchev believed the United States would not fight.

"Khrushchev said he feared for us modern liberals," Mr. Frost declared. "He said we were too liberal to fight. I suppose that he thought we'd stand there for the next hundred years saying, 'on the one hand—but on the other hand.'"

Mr. Frost spent ten days touring the Soviet Union, during which he read poetry and met with many Russian leaders.

"I had a great time," he said. "I went over there with preconceptions to confirm or correct, and I didn't have to correct many."

He noted that "the Russians give you the feeling that we have surrounded them with hostility and with camps and things like that. And that's too bad."

Mr. Frost said he told the Russians they were relaxing a bit and "humanizing a little down from the severity of their ideals—easing off toward democracy."

He added, "And they let me get away with it."

The poet also offered a modification of the "grand old ruffian" description he gave of Premier Khrushchev at an interview during his trip.

"I should have modified that and said 'rough and ready,' " Mr. Frost said. " 'Ruffian' is a pretty strong word.' "

Turning to his poetry, Mr. Frost said he had been asked to read his works, especially "Mending Wall" which begins, "Something there is that doesn't love a wall. . . ." However, he said he didn't believe the request for the poem had anything to do with the Berlin Wall.

"Oh, no, no," he added. "Everyone asks me to read that one— 'Mending Wall' and 'Birches' and 'Stopping by Woods on a Snowy Evening.' If I don't read them, I get blamed."

Mr. Frost also summed up his political attitude by saying, "I am not a Communist. No one would think I'm anywhere near it.

"I find it quite hard to strain up to socialism. On the questions of socialism and welfare states I go slow. I drag my feet. I have, however, about decided that socialism is the only way to handle the billions being born.

"I said to the Russians that they're easing down to socialism and we're straining [up] to it. But I'll be dead by that time."

Accompanying Mr. Frost on the return flight was Interior Secretary Stewart Udall. The Secretary had spent ten days in Russia touring power facilities.

"It's hard to get into this world
and hard to get out of it."

Robert Frost came home from Russia tired but triumphant. After his New York interview (which drew special attention because of his report that Premier Khrushchev had declared Americans "too liberal to fight"), he returned immediately to his farm in Vermont. He had been away barely a fortnight.

Soon, as early fall set in, RF left Ripton to begin what was to be his last brief season in the role of "Strolling Bard." The pace the eighty-eight-year-old poet set for himself during those autumn days of 1962 could, however, hardly be described as strolling. It was, rather, a final sprint to the finish line, in a display of spirit and stamina and an exhibition of form.

In the course of less than two months' time, he gave readings and met informally with students at five different colleges in New England (Holy Cross, Trinity, Mount Holyoke, Amherst, and Yale); he traveled both to Washington, D. C. (to participate in the National Poetry Festival), and to Ohio (to help dedicate a new library at Kenyon College); he went to New York (to receive the Edward MacDowell Medal during an evening program at Hunter College); he journeyed to the mid-West a second time, stopping in Detroit (for an honorary degree and to read before an audience of eighty-five hundred) and Chicago (to commemorate the fiftieth anniversary of Poetry Magazine*); and immediately after Thanksgiving he gave a public reading at Greenwich, Connecticut.*

On November 26th and 27th Mr. Frost visited Dartmouth for two appearances in the college's newly dedicated arts center. Although it was hardly evident from his effectiveness or manner on the platform, he confided to friends during the course of his Dartmouth stay that, really, he was not feeling

: 293 :

well. And he ended the second of his two evening readings on what he himself identified as a "dark note": with his poem "The Night Light."

The close of the great race to the finish line was near at hand.

From Hanover RF went to his home in Cambridge and then on to New York to take part in a special closed-circuit television program, staged in the interests of Washington's National Cultural Center. The date was November 29th, and his condition was now such that there was concern over whether he actually should go before the cameras; but with determination he did so.

Three days later in Boston, on the very verge of collapse, he bravely forced himself to fulfill yet another public engagement. This was his final effort. The next morning, December 3, 1962, he entered a Boston hospital; and there eight weeks later, after a serene but heroic struggle for life, Robert Frost died quietly in his sleep.

On December 10th, the very day RF underwent his initial surgery (and before the fact of his hospitalization was generally known) a syndicated news feature by Robert Peterson was released for publication. Ironically, the story, based on an interview done some two weeks before, concluded with a question in which the columnist asked what accounted for the poet's vigorous good health. The query drew from Mr. Frost a reply which built to an unforgettable climax:

I DUNNO," he said with a shrug and a smile. "It can't be my ancestry. My father died at thirty-six and my mother in her fifties. I was sickly as a boy—nobody thought I'd live.

"It's not due to any dietary practices. I eat anything I like that agrees with me. It's my theory that the more you worry about food, the sicker you get.

"I get quite a little exercise: walk a mile or two every day. But I don't worry if I miss a few days.

"Maybe it's my general lack of worry and ambition that has somehow enhanced my longevity. I didn't make any particular effort to win the honors and prestige folks have heaped on me.

"Money and fame don't impress me much. About all that impresses me is human kindness and warm relationships with good friends.

"I guess I don't take life very seriously. It's hard to get into this world and hard to get out of it. And what's in between doesn't make much sense. If that sounds pessimistic, let it stand. There's been too much vaporous optimism voiced about life and age. Maybe this will provide a little balance."